HOW TO MAKE YOUR MONEY DO MORE : :

THE COMPLETE STOCK MARKET ADVISER

HOW TO MAKE YOUR MONEY DO MORE : : :

THE COMPLETE STOCK MARKET ADVISER

by David L. Markstein

Trident Press : : New York

How to Make Your Money Do More **is a compilation of *Practical Ways to Build a Fortune in the Stock Market*, copyright, ©, 1969, and *Six Steps to Successful Investing*, copyright, ©, 1970. Both of the above titles are copyrighted in the name of David L. Markstein.**

SBN: 671-27064-8

Library of Congress Catalog Card Number: 79-121760

Published simultaneously in the United States and Canada by Trident Press, a division of Simon & Schuster, Inc., 630 Fifth Avenue, New York, N.Y. 10020

Printed in the United States of America

ACKNOWLEDGMENTS

Much of the material in this book has been covered by previous copyrights, among them by *Oral Hygiene/Dental Economics* in 1958, 1961, 1962, 1963, 1964, 1965, 1966, 1967, 1968, 1969, and 1970; by *Resident Physician* in 1965; *Investment Sales Monthly* in 1965, 1966, 1967, 1968, and 1969; *Commercial and Financial Chronicle* in 1967; *The Spectator* in 1967, 1968, and 1969; *Business Management* in 1963 and 1968; *Success Unlimited* in 1965; *Elks Magazine* in 1967, 1968, and 1969; *National Future Farmer* in 1965; *Today's Family Digest* in 1968 and 1969; *Long Beach* (Calif.) *Independent Press-Telegram* in 1969; *Drug Topics* in 1969; *Farm and Power Equipment* in 1968; *Automotive Chain Store* in 1968; *Business Products* in 1968; and *Butane-Propane News* in 1968.

To Betty

Contents

Preface

THE SECRET of successful investing can be summed up in a sentence: Invest with probabilities on your side.

That is, invest in companies with the probability of achieving wider, more profitable operations; in companies that offer bargain value in the form of assets worth more than the price of the stock; and in stocks that enjoy such heavy investor demand—or seem about to begin enjoying this demand—that the dollars seeking to crowd into the stock are greater than the desire of existing stockholders to sell, with a hoped-for result of steadily rising price.

Invest when the market is going up so there will be a strong tidal movement to carry you along.

Avoid like the plague markets like those of 1962, 1966, and 1969–1970, when the strong tidal movement carried stock values downward. Don't suffer with the losers, but ride with the winners.

The object of this book is to help you implement the rule of investing with probabilities on your side. Most of the material in *How to Make Your Money Do More* appeared in two paperback books published by Cornerstone Library, Inc. The first was *Practical Ways to Build a Fortune in the Stock Market*, the second, *Six Steps to Successful Investing*. Material in those books, in turn, came from articles, columns, and papers that I have written over the years for magazines like *The Spectator*, *Investment Sales Monthly*, *Oral Hygiene/Dental Economics*, *The Student*, *Business Management*, *Commercial and Financial Chronicle*, *Elks Magazine*, *Physician's Management*, *Optical Journal* and *Review of Optometry, Success Unlimited, Resident Physician, National Future Farmer,* and *Southland Magazine*. Chapters that follow are thus not the result of sudden investing thoughts. They are the considered ideas of a professional, slowly distilled, then brought up-to-date for publication now.

How You Can Use This Book

The first section is titled "Why Buy Stocks?" It begins with an explanation of the stock market rationale in a world of inflation. It tells what stocks are, both common and preferred, and what are the different types of bonds. It explains warrants, goes into how an order is entered and executed, and in it you will meet the brokers, dealers, investment bankers, and investment counselor-advisers who serve you in the stock market. You'll see how to choose a mutual fund among myriad types offered by the fast-growing, fast-moving mutual industry. You'll learn how to start an investment program on as little as ten dollars per month and how the Gifts to Minors Act can enable you to buy and sell stocks for minor children.

Section two is on "How to Choose the Right Stocks." In it are explanations of the many different roads the stock market offers; knowing them is necessary if you are going to pick the best path for you, your needs, your income, and, not least among the considerations, your psychology. (Are you a plunger, plodder, in-betweener? Interested primarily in income? Can you sleep at night if you are exposed to big risks?)

Also in section two are rules for success in choosing and knowing when to sell growth stocks, bargain stocks, income-yielding securities. The section contains a chapter to help you determine when a stock is over- or undervalued at its current market price, and another on a simple ratio for judging the degree of possible reward and risk in any stock at any time.

"Make Psychology Work for You" is the title of the third section. Professional Wall Streeters know that public psychology can sometimes ignore facts and pull the market along paths you might not expect it to take. Intelligent investors do not try to buck these movements. More profit can lie in recognizing and going along with them. Timing becomes of paramount importance. The right stock bought at a wrong time yields only losses. Psychological forces shape stock prices as much as does cold reason.

Tests for spotting breakout points when a zooming advance might ensue are discussed in this section, along with other technical testing methods to give you an idea of how far any advance or decline might be expected to carry. These tests have worked sufficiently in the past—one chapter discusses a research study into the results of chart signals—to warrant using them even though past performance of a method cannot guarantee future results.

Sometimes you will have the itch to take a flier in the market. "If You Want to Speculate" is the title of section four. Its chapters explain leverage that puts others' money to work for you multiplying profits (and also multiplying losses should you prove to be wrong about an investment).

When protracted bear (down) markets come along, they generally erode profits and bring losses in even the best-chosen stocks. How to spot such a market, when to sell out, when to buy back, what to do about investing during the bear period while stocks go down—these are covered in the fifth section, titled "Beware the Bear Years!"

People always have questions to ask about their investments. In the final section of the book, "The Author Answers Questions," I hope that these answers, together with what is contained in the first five sections, will indeed furnish you with a complete guide to success in the stock market.

DAVID L. MARKSTEIN

SECTION I : : Why Buy Stocks?

Chapter 1 : : HOW INFLATION AFFECTS YOUR INVESTMENTS

SOME PEOPLE say it makes the world go round; others say that if you care greatly for it you're a low, crass fellow. People handle it every day and it is the lifeblood of our economy—not to mention the stock market. But few know what is this thing called a dollar.

It certainly is not a measure of value, if by that anyone means a yardstick that stays the same every time something is measured against it. These days the "value" of the dollar wobbles too much—mostly downward—for it to perform that traditional function. And it isn't a storehouse of wealth, that other traditional definition of money, for wealth stored in things of fixed dollar value or in dollars themselves has depleted woefully in recent decades.

It isn't gold; it is not silver. What is it, and why doesn't this dollar of ours stand still long enough for us to get accustomed to some particular buying power?

People believe that "inflation"—defined as steady erosion of the currency unit's worth compared to the things it buys—is some new thing. But inflation is as old as the concept of money, and man has learned over the centuries to live with a certain amount of it.

The U.S. dollar in the beginning was patterned after an old Spanish peso, called a "piece of eight" because it was divided into eight reals or "bits." Thus "two bits" equaled a quarter, four bits a half dollar. And the dollar was silver. Exasperated with worthless Continental money of the Revolution, Americans would tolerate no paper money in their early years.

Metallic money has been around as long as man has been civilized and enjoyed commerce. People today sometimes long for the old days when you couldn't print more bills or inflate the monetary supply by today's ingenious and sophisticated methods. But money was debased then as well as now. The methods were different: by mixing base metals with gold or silver, by sweating bits and pieces off sound money, and by clipping or shaving small slivers away. When an ordinary citizen did these things he was called a clipper or a coiner, and the head of state—usually the king—hanged him in righteous anger. Then the king turned right around and did the same thing. It was his prerogative to do so.

Today we still follow the practice of these ancient kings. Only recently, Congress passed an act providing that silver would no longer comprise our dimes, quarters, halves, and dollars. Gold disappeared decades ago.

But the real erosion of dollars is not accomplished by such means. To understand what your dollar is and how the Federal Reserve protects as well as expands it, it's necessary to look back to money's early days.

The only rightful issuer of money, in those times when if it didn't clink it wasn't cash, was the head of state, our old friend the king. Royal Whoozis VIII had all of the control in his hands. But not for long.

Bankers are nearly as old as money in man's history. At first these folk contented themselves with holding money stored with them by early depositors and occasionally lending out a small portion. Enough had to be held back to meet demands depositors might make for their money.

When minted money was left with bankers, they issued receipts. Without a receipt the depositor usually could not recover his money. Then began a step that in the course of some centuries resulted in swinging control of the money supply away from King Whoozis and into the hands of the private bankers: Customers started paying their debts, not with the gold that had been deposited, but with the receipt that evidenced that deposit. And the bank note was born.

Why hadn't anyone thought of it before, bankers wondered. Here was a Golconda, a way to expand their profits and at the same time furnish needed lubrication to the economy. If people accepted a banker's note, why should he give gold itself to a borrower? Why not hold on to the gold for emergency and lend notes instead? Thus was devised a lending base many times the limited size of that of the older and simpler days.

There have been many "engines of inflation" in man's history. Here was one as potent as anything ever dreamed up by the most unscrupulous kings who melted pots and pans and issued the resulting coinage for money. Under competitive pressure, early bankers sometimes issued a good deal more money than caution would have dictated. And into man's economic vocabulary came a terrible word describing a more terrible event.

Panic!

Men queued up in long lines before banks to convert into sound gold or silver the notes they had suddenly realized were too far inflated. Faced with such runs the bankers dumped securities, real estate, anything of value they possessed to raise real currency quickly. The panic's effects spread until factories ground to a halt, unemployment was rife, and the economy lay prostrate.

This happened at irregular intervals until men realized that, good King Whoozis having been tucked away and no longer available for the protection of his flock, the flock's democratic leaders would have to do something.

They did.

They developed the central bank.

At first the function of central banks such as our Federal Reserve in the United States was to serve as a place where bankers who were faced with panic runs could turn for help. But it was quickly clear that more would have to be done—more even than requiring that a percentage of member banks' deposits be placed with the Fed.

Central banks came to control the money supply of each country and still do today. "Control" in this case does not mean that the Fed or other central bank must keep the money supply rigid, for in a modern economy such a policy would be fatal. It is the Fed's function to expand money where needed and to contract the supply when too many dollars seem to be chasing too few goods and so producing unwanted inflation.

All this sounds complicated and it is. Here is how money "creation" is done today:

The central bank's governors meet regularly. It might be decided at one of these meetings for any of a number of reasons that the country needs additional money. Does the Fed simply print it? It does not. Instead, the governers order their Open Market Committee to buy government securities.

The Fed's purchasers buy these from a dealer in government securities. The central bank then enters these securities on its books and to pay for them credits the commercial bank at which the government bond dealer has an account. This commercial bank, in turn, credits the bond dealer's account just as if he had made a deposit of the same amount in cold hard cash.

Thus new bank reserves have been created.

The commercial bank enters such deposits on its books as an asset. That expands the bank's reserves. It can now make new loans against the assets just created, and when it does make such a loan it hands out no cash; it simply credits the new borrower's checking account, thereby creating new demand deposit money.

This is very sophisticated compared to the clipping tactics of shaving a sliver here and there, or the tactic of mixing in base metals with the precious gold or silver. And the new engine of inflation is a lot more efficient than the older model.

The question a lot of people ask is this: Why would the Federal Reserve inflate our money?

The answer is that in most cases the Fed is not so much doing things to the people as for them.

"Creation" of money is frequently undertaken to provide needed seasonal supplies of dollars—for example, keeping the wheels of Christmas shopping moving easily. But more often it is done to carry out a policy of seeking "easy" or "hard" interest rates.

Money is like beans or boats. Supply (dollars) and demand (pressure of would-be borrowers to obtain funds) determine the rates at which money will be rented. So all the Fed can do, if it agrees to ease money conditions, is to create enough new dollars to see that demand is supplied without borrowers having to bid up the hire price of money (interest).

More often than not, deliberate easing or tightening of money rates is undertaken by the Fed to "lean against the winds" of economic movement. When the economy has been booming along for a while, pressures build up that, if allowed to run their course, might result in a real bust, which might lead us into big economic difficulty. To pull some of the steam out of such forces, the duty of the Fed's bosses is to tighten things a bit. Their problem is always to do just enough to sap pressures that might lead to a bust but not to bring on tough times by making money too hard.

And when we are in tight economic times, the standard recession operating tactic is to ease money conditions, make it simpler (and in terms of interest costs, cheaper) for businesses to expand a bit—perhaps add to inventory—and generally get things rolling at a better speed.

Pressure is always on the Fed. Conservative people say at times that things may get out of hand. "Tighten down on the brakes," they urge the Fed. Others are perennial cheap money advocates; they always want things to be easy.

And complicating those considerations and pressures are such outside factors as the nation's balance of payments difficulties in recent years, the need to provide enough liquidity for world trade to stay on its track (the main motive power is the American dollar), the cold war, the hot war in Vietnam, financing problems of the national debt, the desirability of making a favorable climate for continuing long-term growth of the remarkable American economy.

So our dollar is what the Fed—and you—make it in future.

POINTS TO REMEMBER

1. A rose may be what Gertrude Stein called it—a rose—but a dollar is not a dollar. It is whatever the Federal Reserve Board says it is.

2. To finance the war and a welfare state, the dollar has been tremendously inflated in recent years. Indications are that it will continue to decline in purchasing value despite efforts to stop inflation. This is necessary background knowledge to investment planning.

3. Long ago, money was not money unless it jingled and was made of gold or silver. Now our more sophisticated money consists of credit as well as the paper and small change that circulate.

4. Inflation long ago was accomplished by clipping pieces off the metal money or by mixing base metal with precious metal. Now the central banks (ours in the U.S. is the Federal Reserve) expand or contract money supply by such space age methods as open market buying/selling of bonds.

5. Money is like any other commodity. Supply and demand govern what it is worth in terms of goods, just as supply and demand for the goods themselves govern their worth vis-à-vis money. When the money supply expands, the first result masks as good times. After that, rising prices make inflation visible to everyone.

Chapter 2 : : STOCKS AND THE PEOPLE YOU MEET IN WALL STREET

IN ANY military or naval campaign there are two kinds of planning the generals and admirals must do. The first is strategic. Strategy is the grand overall design whose hoped-for end is victory. The other kind of planning is called tactics. Tactics means all the little grinding, day-by-day actions and maneuvers that are necessary to achieve the big strategic plan.

It is a tactical decision whether to attack an entrenched enemy straight on or to attempt to outflank him. It is a strategic decision whether to attack the spot he holds at all.

Most of the book you are reading is about investment tactics. It tells you how to carry out your financial decisions. The strategy is outlined here.

Before getting into specific steps, let us look at Wall Street. Unless you know its hills and valleys, the people in it, what they do, and the nature of those stocks, bonds, warrants, etc., that you will be buying and selling, then your plans can well go as agley as the best-laid plans of mice and men of which Robert Burns wrote.

When I was a boy in high school, one of my professors made a lasting impression on me, not by force of personality but by force of teaching. He clothed the sometimes dry bones of economics with charts covering three blackboards of his classroom. These charts gave daily quotations from the New York Exchange, and his students learned something about the mechanics of Wall Street by the most practical of methods, "buying" and "selling" securities.

Sometimes I wish that all economics teachers used a method as graphic. Many investors, often men with considerable stakes in the stock market, lack an understanding of what stocks and bonds are, their possibilities and limitations, and how securities are bought and sold. This is understandable, of course, in the case of busy professional men and others whose spare time as well as working time is often crammed with problems and the effort of keeping up with late advances. So here, for what help it can give, is a brief rundown of the big world of Wall Street:

Common Stock: For definition, common stock represents ownership of a corporation. If Corporation A has one million shares of stock outstanding and you own one hundred shares, you own one ten-thousandth of the business. This entitles you to receive dividends if they are paid, and to vote for corporation officers and on corporate matters if your stock carries this privilege. Should that sound like a paradox—common stock ownership without voting privilege—it is nonetheless true. In many cases, when first selling stock to the public, owners reserve a Class A or Class B common for themselves and vest all voting rights in this issue. (Every new issue listed on the New York Stock Exchange, however, must give common stockholders full voting rights. It is mostly among unlisted issues—and we will come to the difference between listed and unlisted markets shortly—that nonvoting common is to be found.)

The common stockholder is entitled to dividends if the company makes money and when the directors see fit to declare a dividend. When directors do not—which seldom happens in leading companies except in the hardest times—this represents no chicanery on their part. They may be conserving cash for expansion that will pay off later, or plowing profits back into research, again aimed at a later and larger payoff.

There is no certainty of how large a dividend will be, or its continuity. But in practice and in well-managed corporations, dividends are pretty steady. If a company grows, so do your dividends; and this is where stockholders differ from holders of fixed income types of securities. If you want your income and capital to grow, the field of common stock is a good bet.

Preferred Stock: A great many investors are confused by preferred stock. Preferred to what? How safe is it? How much equity is given away?

First, preferred stock, like common stock and bonds, is a security. Its issuance calls for the same legal and regulatory steps as does the putting out of common stock. Preferred stock is literally what it's name says it is. It is stock, not a bond or other debt obligation. Unlike common stock, it does not necessarily represent voting rights (although in many cases preferred holders can vote). Sometimes preferred stockholders exercise voting rights only when the company gets into arrears on their payments.

Convertibles: One of the more interesting types of preferred issues is convertible preferreds. (Some debentures also carry this privilege.) This means, quite simply, that the preferred stock or the convertible bond can be changed into common stock at the holder's option and at a predetermined price.

The advantage from the point of view of the owner of a convertible is that if the company grows and the common stock consequently advances in market price, he can cash in on this growth by converting his preferred into common. If things do not work out so well, the holder of a convertible preferred or a convertible bond can play it safe by sitting back with his basically more conservative holding and collecting his more assured income.

That is the whole point of preferred stock. The dividends are more assured than dividends on common stock. Dividends declared on common stock follow the fortunes of the company. They are higher when earnings are up, lower when earnings are down. But preferred stock is given a set dividend rate that must be paid before as much as five cents may be given to the holders of common stock. However, unlike a bondholder, the preferred stockholder does not have protection in the form of collateral to secure his money.

If a company defaults on bond interest and continues to do so, the bondholders may go to court and petition for a sale of assets that secure their bond or even for bankruptcy of the company. In any liquidation, bondholders are paid off first, holders of preferred stock next, and the holders of common stock get what is left.

If a company does not pay its preferred dividends, on the other hand, the preferred stockholder cannot do much except wait, knowing that if the company ever recovers, it must pay him before it can give anything to the common stockholders who own it. Some issues accumulate such arrears; with others there is a limit beyond which arrears cannot go.

Bonds: The investor who holds bonds of a company holds its IOU. Issuance of bonds is nothing but a form of borrowing. A corporation borrows more than it usually could raise from one lender or even a syndicate of lenders, and over a longer period of time.

A bond may be secured by real estate or by the plant and equipment of a firm. If it is unsecured, it is called a debenture. Some bonds, debentures in particular, carry conversion privileges similar to those of a convertible preferred, with the same advantages. Note, however, that conversion into common stock is a privilege worth having only in a company going strongly upward, whose common stock is becoming worth more each year.

Warrants, and Puts and Calls: These instruments are options. The owner of a warrant for XYZ Corporation has paid a set price in order to be able to control a block of common stock using less capital than it would take to buy the stock outright. Warrants generally have fairly long lives and a few are perpetual. That means that the investor-trader employing them can wait things out until, the world having taken a couple of spins, things might —if his original calculations were correct—come his way. Not so with puts and calls. These are options of limited duration. Using them, you can exert great leverage. You can also lose your shirt if you are not careful.

Trading Methods: Stocks and bonds are bought either on an exchange (in which case they are listed securities) or else in a wider but less tangible market known as the over-the-counter market. The latter are unlisted securities.

The best way to illustrate the difference in trading methods between an order to buy or sell on an exchange and one in the unlisted market is to follow two hypothetical orders:

In the first, an investor whom we will call by the new and original name of Doe gives an order to his broker to buy one hundred shares of XYC Corporation. For this order to be executed, the broker must be a member of the exchange in question, or he must turn it over for execution to another broker who is a member. This order is wired to the New York office of the member firm. From there it goes to the company's floor broker, who receives the order and walks to a post where the stock of XYC Corporation is traded. There he finds other brokers interested in buying or selling XYC and another man called a specialist. To the specialist, he asks, "How's XYC?" without indicating whether he will buy or sell. The specialist consults his book of buy-and-sell bids and offers and answers: "20½ offered at three-quarters."

This means that other brokers have placed with him orders to buy at 20½ or sell at ¾. If the floor broker has a "market" order from Doe, he may take the stock at 20¾ unless he can get a better offer from one of the other brokers standing there.

(A "market order" is one to buy or sell "at the market." This means at the best available price at the moment of execution. A "limit order," on the other hand, is one to buy or sell at only a set figure. Doe might have put in the order to buy XYC at 20; in that case his firm's floor broker will have it entered in the specialist's book, and if the stock hits 20, he will buy. Of course it may never hit 20, or it may be weeks getting to that figure. In general, long-term investors do best putting in their orders at the market.)

All of this can take as little as five minutes from the time Doe has put in an order in his hometown. But in the case of an infrequently traded issue or a limited order that is slightly off the market, it may take hours.

To many investors, the over-the-counter market where unlisted securities are bought and sold is a never-never land; to others, it is a trap for the unwary who stray from the safe stocks of the Big Board and other exchanges. But in this market an estimated fifty thousand different stocks are traded. Only around two thousand issues are traded on the New York Stock Exchange and American Stock Exchange combined. It comprises all kinds of issues—speculative stocks, unseasoned equities, penny cats and dogs, right on up to some of the most conservative securities in the country.

Many of today's top growth issues are unlisted, and a great number of those that are listed were traded in the off-board market only a few years ago. So it is not such a dangerous place, if you resist the siren songs of promoters who have some new issues that are "sure" to double or triple in a month.

When Doe gives his broker an over-the-counter order, the broker will get in touch not with the floor of an exchange, but with someone who "makes a market" in that particular unlisted stock. This means that he carries stock in his inventory the same way a menswear shop carries shirts in its inventory. He will buy when Doe wants to sell, or sell when Doe wishes to buy. Doe's own broker may, of course, have a ready buyer or seller for an unlisted stock, in which case this specialist dealer firm will not enter the picture. But most times he goes to the specialist. Some larger brokerage houses make it a rule that the quotes of at least three of those specialists who make markets must be had, and the best deal made out of those three calls.

Doe's quote will come back something like this: "20½ bid, 22 asked." This means the specialist has stock to sell at 22 and orders to buy at 20½. If this seems a pretty wide spread, chances are it is. The purpose of this is to give some leeway for bargaining between you and your own broker-dealer.

Off of this figure you will have to pay commission of course. Some firms charge higher commissions on over-the-counter orders than those obtained on the New York Stock Exchange. Ask your broker whether he is willing to handle over-the-counter transactions at New York Stock Exchange commission. Most will say Yes. Now you have two choices. You can trade "net" without commission or else pay this inside price plus commission. Trading without commission looks inviting, but in most cases you would be well advised not to do it that way. The net price may well contain a markup considerably higher than a commission would have been (although this is not true in every case).

Let's consider the people you meet in the process of investing in those stocks, bonds, etc.:

One is called a "broker." When he acts in that capacity, he is your agent. He does not buy from you or sell to you. He purchases (or sells) for you, charging you the price plus his commission.

When he adds a markup to the price instead of tacking on regular commission, the man with whom you deal ceases to be a broker. He becomes a "dealer." He buys the stock you want to sell and frequently sells direct to you the stock you want to buy. In most cases, he is the same fellow he was when he was acting as a broker, but he wears a different hat. The difference is not entirely academic. It is important to you to judge the degree of bias (if any) in his recommendations or suggestions by whether he "makes a market" in the recommended stock by holding it in inventory as described earlier.

On occasions this versatile broker-dealer wears a third hat. He is then called an "investment banker" or "underwriter." This happens when a new issue of stock comes to market, and, as part of a syndicate, he has "underwritten" the issue by agreeing to sell it to the public. Sometimes he is not part of a syndicate but sole banker. You are seldom charged either commission or markup on an issue being sold through underwriting. The charge has already been paid by the seller. The issue might be stock—convertible or straight preferreds—and debentures, or might consist of both common and preferred with, perhaps, a sweetening of warrants added to give sales appeal to the package.

One who neither sells to or for you is the "investment advisor." In most cases, his sole function is to advise. He does this for a fee. Some adviser-counselors seek only large accounts and won't tell you Hello in a business way unless you are able to bring under their management an account running at least into six figures. Others, equally good, take on smaller accounts—often as small as five thousand dollars—and rely upon high volume to bring in the big amounts to obtain sizable income equal to that which the more exclusive advisers generate by accepting only large accounts.

Some dispense advice individually. A few will undertake complete management of a portfolio for you, even buying and selling in your name, using your limited power of attorney. Still other advisers and advisory firms dispense advice via newsletter, which might be issued weekly, daily, or, occasionally, monthly. Investment advisers are like any other people; their ability is not uniform, and you should look carefully at a firm or an individual adviser.

Sometimes people say, "Why should I pay an adviser? My broker will give me advice for nothing."

Professional adviser-counselors answer that the broker's registered representative is essentially a salesman, not a financial analyst trained to counsel and manage accounts, and that while results from brokerage guidance are sometimes spectacularly good, the results from professional guidance are likely to be better. You pay your money (or don't if you decide to go the broker advice route) and take your choice in this matter.

POINTS TO REMEMBER

1. The basic difference between stocks and bonds is this: Stocks represent ownership, while bonds are debt obligations (I.O.U.'s).

2. There are other securities—preferreds, midway between common ownership and protected debt; warrants and puts and calls, which are options to buy; convertibles, which might be debentures or preferred changeable at your option into common stock.

3. These are traded either on an Exchange (New York Stock Exchange, American Stock Exchange, Midwest Stock Exchange, Toronto Stock Exchange, etc.) or in a bigger, less clearly-defined over-the-counter market.

4. Dealers are people who buy from you or sell to you. Brokers are people who act as your agents. Investment bankers and underwriters bring out new issues. Investment counselors sell professional advice.

Chapter 3 : : THE WINNINGEST STOCKS IN WALL STREET

THE YEAR 1966 was one of black disaster for most investors. The widely followed Dow-Jones Industrial Average peaked during February around 1,000, a level that has not been bettered since. From that peak, the Dow average dropped month by month, bottoming in October below 750. The average losses were as nothing to those that many investors suffered in individual stocks. Some prestigious and popular stocks lost half, three quarters, occasionally more of their value as the market decline deepened month by month.

"The only happy people in Wall Street were those who got out early in the year and held cash, and those who sold stocks short," said one commentator.

However, he was wrong.

Some of the happiest stockholders in that generally unhappy year were people who bought and held a stock that soared from 10 to 25⅝. Howmet Corporation did this while other stocks were halving.

Wall Street has good years and bad. During most years since the end of World War II, the average level of the stock market has gone up. There have been the down years such as 1953, 1958, 1960, 1966, and 1969. But even in those years of sometimes cataclysmic disaster to holders of weak stocks, there were winning stocks in Wall Street. Some stocks "win" by 10 percent to 20 percent. Others are winning-er. They go up 25 percent, 50 percent, even 60 percent in a year. Such gains are enough to make any investor's mouth water. Here, however, we will consider only the winningest stocks of all—those advancing by 100 percent and more. We will look at them with an eye to finding out how they got that way so that, hopefully, the winningest stocks of next year can be in *your* portfolio.

Consider how profitable it might have been for an investor had he chosen such winningest stocks as these during the decade of the sixties:

During 1960 the market, as measured by the Dow-Jones Industrial Average, which most investors follow despite its age and obvious statistical mis-structuring, began on a high, then dropped steadily until midyear, and rallied briefly before settling down to still lower levels. Toward the end of the year, after the Cuban missile crisis had been successfully resolved, the market began a new climb. But the best of that climb was not seen in 1960.

During such years a great many stocks that had earlier been investor favorites fared worse than the market. Just before the heralded "soaring sixties" began their flight with a thud, steel stocks had been in the Street's favor and few of them more so than the doyen of the group, U.S. Steel. At the start of fateful 1960, Big Steel stood at 103. Before the end of the year, it had dropped to 69. "Woe!" cried many analysts and other professionals of the slide rule, divining rod, and hedged statement. "If this can happen to venerable U.S. Steel, what will betide the lesser stocks?"

Chris-Craft Industries, Inc., is one stock considered far "less" in quality than Big Steel, according to the conventional wisdom of Wall Street. A manufacturer of pleasure boats, with a capitalization that–as one observer remarked–could have been hidden in a desk drawer at U.S. Steel and never noticed, Chris-Craft might have been purchased at a modest 10 in the first month of the year. Before the year's last day, it had raced to a high at 52, and a stockholder who bought during January and wanted to close out his position in December could have obtained 23. The gain from high to low was 420 percent. The gain from year's beginning to year's end was still mouth-watering at 130 percent.

Chris-Craft stockholders were not alone in their joy amid general sorrow. Chock Full O' Nuts stock sold on the New York Stock

Exchange during the January market top at 9⅜. It made a subsequent high at 26⅝. A stockholder buying at the start of the year and selling at its end could have realized 26. His profit, above and in addition to original capital, came to 178 percent measured from low point to high point and 173 percent from the January low to December level.

At the same time the common stock of a small, new organization called Coastal States Gas Producing was purchasable during January—when U.S. Steel sold at 103 and the "soaring sixties" was a phrase men expected to come true immediately—at 4⅜. December saw it selling at a high of 9¾. If our theoretical investor in winningest stocks, eschewing venerable U.S. Steel, had bought Coastal States at the January low and sold at the December high, his gain (atop original capital and without counting commissions) would have been 117 percent.

Let's look at what would have happened should such a far-sighted theoretical investor, looking for winningest stocks in 1960, have decided to put one thousand dollars into each of these situations. His modest capital would have purchased approximately 100 shares of Christ-Craft, 107 shares of Chock Full O' Nuts, and 230 shares of Coastal States at the January lows cited above. For the sake of simplifying the computation, we will leave out the cost item of commissions, but to even things up, we will not count dividends accruing.

The year's highest price was not made in December, except in the case of Coastal States Gas Producing. But we will assume that our investor held straight through to the year's last month—for who is gifted with the ability to discern absolute tops on any consistent basis? His opening capital would have been three thousand dollars. Selling his shares in December, he would have realized $2,300 for 100 shares of Chris-Craft, $2,889 on 107 Chock Full O' Nuts, and $2,242 for his 230 shares of Coastal States. Altogether, $7,431, a capital gain (all long-term and taxed as such) of 148 percent.

"Wow!" crowed our happy investor. "How long has this been going on? Me for the winningest stocks again in sixty-one."

And 1961, happily for him and for other players of the Wall

Street game, was a "good" year. Wall Streeters call a period good when stocks go up, bad when they go down. By this definition, 1961 was definitely good. Dividing his stake again into three portions, our investor sought for a position in the winningest investments. He came up with Certain-Teed Products, Crown Cork and Seal, and Food Machinery and Chemical, now known as FMC Corporation.

(The examples cited here, and others, which I am going to cite below, are, of course, compiled by the easy method of hindsight. Later we will isolate the factors involved in winningest stocks with the hope that in the decade to come you will be able—not to duplicate—but at least to come close to the results of our theoretical investor whom we will henceforth call Midas because he indeed has a golden touch.)

Purchasable at around 16 in January, Certain-Teed rose to a year's high of 64, and could have been cashed up in December at 60. The profit from low to high was 300 percent. The profit from January, when Midas will make all of his purchases, until December, when he sold, was still hefty at 274 percent.

Next on his purchase list, Midas noted that Crown Cork, a formerly humble little manufacturer of containers and closings, had a new management that was beginning to work wonders with the earnings statements. January's low for Crown Cork was 10⅜. The high, made in December, was 33½. The percentage gain came to 224 percent.

Food Machinery's common stock was available at a low of 14 in January, from which it zipped to a December high of 43, making 208 percent profit along the way for contented shareowners.

Dividing his $7,431 cash-up of the previous year into three bundles of $2,477 each, Midas instructed his broker to buy 155 shares of Certain-Teed Products common, 233 shares of Crown Cork, and 177 Food Machinery and Chemical.

These shares were sold later in December, following Midas' now-established strategy, for $9,920 in the case of Certain-Teed, $7,805 in the Crown Cork holding, and $7,611 was received for Food Machinery. Joyously, Midas noted that his original theoretical $3,000 had grown to $25,336.

"Winningest stocks are the ticket," he told his wife Dora, a little tipsily, as they opened the third celebratory bottle of champagne. "Let's see what sixty-two will bring us."

But 1962 brought very little, compared to the rapid run-ups of the two earlier years. Yet despite the gloom of the worst post-World War II bear market and the fact that almost no stocks were able to show consistent gaining patterns, Midas fared well.

His $25,336 divided into three packets gave him about $8,445 to place in each of three new commitments. None doubled as a winningest stock should have done. Available at 3⅞ at the year's start, Hayes-Albion Corp.'s stock reached 7 in December, gaining a 75 percent profit. The cosmetic-toiletries firm of Rayette-Fabergé zoomed from 15 in January to a high of 30½ from which it fell to 27 at year-end; profit was 115 percent to the high, but only 80 percent to Midas' established cash-up time of December. American–South African Investment Co. is a closed-end trust, listed on the New York Stock Exchange, which invests in securities of South Africa. Prominent among these are gold mining stocks. To get representation in golds (Midas' reasoning will be shown in a later chapter), our investor chose this vehicle, which was at 10 in January, reached 16 during the year, and could have been sold at about 15 at year-end for a 60 percent profit to the high and a still respectable 50 percent at December closeout.

Putting $8,445 into each of these stocks, Midas' broker bought for him 2,180 shares of Hayes-Albion, 560 shares of Rayette-Fabergé, and 845 shares of American–South African. Cashed up at the end of dolorous 1962, these brought him respectively $15,260, $15,120, and $12,675.

"Only $43,055 this year," Midas moaned to Dora. "We can't buy champagne on that. Would you settle for a couple of beers?"

"Nineteen sixty-three has got to be better," his spouse said. "Let's look for the winningest stocks of next year."

Not one to desert a strategy, Midas again divided money into three packets and found that he could invest $14,352 each in new stocks.

That amount purchased 840 shares of Chrysler Corporation at 17⅛, the best price available during January. It bought 720 shares of Control Data, and 2,870 shares of Syntex Corp. January's price for Control Data was 20 and for Syntex was 5.

Chrysler was a "turnaround" situation in 1963. New management revitalized the company, which had fallen on such evil days that wits in the financial community were cracking that the automobile industry no longer had a Big Three; it had a Big Two-and-a-Half. Chrysler rose to a high of 48 during the year. Midas was able to sell his 840 shares in December for 41, bringing him a gain of 141 percent for the full year.

Control Data rose even more sharply. The holding that had cost twenty dollars per share was sold out in December at seventy-five dollars, bringing Midas a 325 percent profit atop capital he had put in at the year's start.

But the real swinger of sixty-three was Syntex, a pioneer in development of "the pill." It soared to a high of 67 for the year. Our theoretical investor was able to close out his 2,870 shares at 62 in December.

"Yippie!" he said to his wife, counting numbers on his broker's confirmation slips. "We have taken $34,440 out of Chrysler, $54,000 from Control Data, and $180,810 from Syntex. My computer adds it up to $269,250. Quite a way from our starting three thousand dollars. Maybe this year we can afford champagne again."

The year 1964 saw Midas divide his increased stake into bundles of $89,750 each for investment in 6,000 Cerro Corp. at 15, 18,000 shares of Consolidated Freightways at 4⅞, and 16,000 of the common stock of I-T-E Imperial at 5½.

From 15, Cerro Corp. made a 1964 high of 39 and was sold out in December at 33. Midas saw Consolidated Freightways run up to 11⅝ during the year, and closed his position at 11 at the end of the year. I-T-E Imperial made a high of 13, at which figure Midas realized his profit in December.

Next year, Midas divided the total stake—now totaling $604,000—into piles of $201,333 each. One bought 35,700 shares of Chromalloy American Corp. at 5⅝. Another purchased 11,000 Fairchild Camera at 18⅜. The third went into 10,200 of the common of KLM, which Midas purchased during January at 19¾.

Profit in Chromalloy during 1965 was 296 percent as it rose to a December level of 17¼, at which the holding was liquidated. A 510 percent gain was racked up by Fairchild Camera; Midas sold this out at the December high of 110. KLM made him a 310 percent profit; it was closed out at 81⅞.

Midas' capital now totaled $2,660,950.

The year 1966 proved to be almost a repetition of 1962 for most investors, as the general stock market slid sickeningly into its second-worst decline of a quarter century. But things continued rosy for a theoretical investor in winningest stocks, for on Wall Street, something nearly always wins.

With three stakes of $886,983 each, Midas purchased 73,900 shares of E G and G, Inc., a scientific specialty, at 12; 143,500 shares of Fuqua Industries at 6⅛; and 88,600 shares of Howmet at 10. At year-end liquidation time, Midas, who had been away most of the year on a Mediterranean cruise with instructions to his broker not to bother him with calls about price fluctuations, found that E G and G had made a 125 percent gain to 27. At 15⅛, Fuqua had tacked on 150 percent profit. A 162 percent gain was made by Howmet at 25⅝.

"Not bad for a bear market year, Dora old girl," Midas said as he counted up a $6,436,112 stake. "Shall we call it quits here, or shoot for the moon?"

"Shoot for the moon, husband mine," said Dora. "Let's see what sixty-seven will bring us."

And 1967 saw a longer list of winningest stocks than any other year of the decade. It was a period of frenzied speculation. Mutual funds joined in the performance act and were followed, a little gingerly, by formerly staid bank trusts and pension funds. In January, as he divided his capital into neat stacks of 2,145,370 one-dollar bills each, Midas decided to buy 55,000 of a venture capital closed-end fund called American Research and Development at 37¾. He also purchased 65,000 Control Data for 33 per share, and 575,000 shares of Hotel Corp. of America at 3⅝.

When these were sold in December, Midas, now contemplating the purchase of his own Mediterranean island to join Niarchos, Onassis, and other well-heeled habitués of that historic sea, found that American Research had tacked on a whopping 415 percent gain, with Control Data performing well at 354 percent (up from 33 to a year-end sellout price of 150), and that Hotel Corporation was the biggest gainer of all, up 550 percent to 19⅞.

The Midas capital now came to $31,903,125.

"I'll plunk $10,634,375 each into three stocks in sixty-eight," Midas told Dora. "I like Chadbourn-Gotham at 5⅞. Also Dr. Pepper at 18. And I'll take Fedders at 19."

This gave Midas 1,790,000 shares of Chadbourn-Gotham, which rose during the year to 20⅜, and was sold at the December high of 16. He had 590,000 shares of Dr. Pepper; this jumped to the December high of 50 and was closed out there. The final holding came to 560,000 Fedders that, when liquidated at 60 in December, brought in a 216 percent profit.

"Now it's $91,740,000 and I've really got a tax problem," Midas complained to his tax consultant. "Hard to believe that only three years ago, Dora and I were poor folks with only a couple of million dollars to our names. Sometimes I wonder—was there really a year when I began with small change like three grand?"

There was no real George Midas. No one put together the mighty feat of running $3,000 into $91,740,000 in nine years. No one could have done it in real life. There would have been the hefty bite of the tax collector chewing big hunks out of investable capital each year. There would also have been the insuperable problem, in the later years of Midas' speculative spree, of trying to swing such big blocks of stocks without running the price up when buying, or dropping it down with the effort to unload a few hundred thousand shares.

But winningest stocks are there every year. There are certain common denominators these possess. The common denominators can be reduced to recognizable terms so that a future Midas—hopefully, you—will recognize the winningest stocks before their rises begin.

Most of Midas' winningest winners were growth stocks. But other kinds of stocks were also among the winningest.

A frequent sign of a potentially winningest stock is a corporation's interest in new directions humanity may be taking. In the late years of the fifties and the early years of the sixties, the newest direction was scientific. The U.S. was reaching for the moon; we were expanding education; scientific knowledge was enabling us to do our national work with less effort, thus leaving greater leisure time for all Americans to enjoy themselves.

Later on, the new directions changed from technological to sociological; at present, we are expanding our abilities to live the good life and, more important, to bring new millions to participation in that good life. Corporations who set out to satisfy these wants are the current new directions stocks.

Many winningest stocks are what Wall Street calls turnaround situations. They are stocks of companies, formerly wallowing in the doldrums of poor profit and listless investor interest, in which new managements, new products, or new slants are turning things around toward heightened profits. Turnaround situations are always available in the stock market. Where correctly diagnosed and bought before prices have already discounted the happy future, these are nearly always winningest stocks.

Some of the winningest stocks of recent years have been conglomerates, vast and hungry corporations that reach out in all directions like blind and hungry lions searching for food. The conglomerate idea is under fire at present, and objective people in the Street say that there have been abuses in the building of conglomerates and even, sometimes, in the way they have reported profits. Yet, all conglomerates should not be blamed for the faults of some. The conglomerate technique—successfully used—remains a hallmark of some of the winningest stocks in Wall Street.

Conglomerates search for other corporations to be gobbled up. Some of the winningest stocks of all are the gobble-ees, companies whose delighted stockholders are able to view two, even more, conglomerates vying for their shares and beefing up the tender offers in response to each others' increased bids. Shrewd analysts are often able to spot such merger candidates among the sleeping dogs that doze on the bargain shelf of the exchanges.

Since the thirties, the official price of gold has been pegged at thirty-five dollars per ounce. Although a "free" market now operates in Europe for buying and selling gold itself, Americans are not permitted to own the yellow metal. They can, however, own shares of gold mining companies. Periodically, times come around when the economic circumstances are such that an alert George Midas can decide that a rise in gold stocks has to come. During these years, gold stocks, if bought and sold at the right moments, are the winningest of all the stocks on the board.

POINTS TO REMEMBER

1. Wall Street has its bear years and its bull years, but there are winning stocks in every one of these and in most there are winning*est* stocks. Winningest stocks are those with rises of 100 percent or more.

2. Even a small stake, invested in the properly chosen winningest stocks of one year and reinvested each year in a search for the winningest of that year, can lead to a fortune.

3. Winningest stocks usually have the common denominator of growth of earnings (per share earnings, not mere raw profit figures). They achieve this, sometimes, by searching new directions, other times because they are the stocks of turnaround corporations in which new managements, products, or circumstances bring about good times after a period of poor performance. Some ride fads of investor favor, others the tides of human wants. Many are conglomerates, eagerly gobbling new small corporate fish. Some are the fish being gobbled. In times of monetary stress or problem, gold stocks win over almost anything else.

4. You won't achieve performance equal to our theoretical George Midas. But if you diligently search each year for the winningest stocks, you will find some of them—and that is all you'll need to achieve results.

Chapter 4 : : HOW TO CHOOSE A MUTUAL FUND

You HAVE a modest financial stake—not big enough to get up in a class with the Mellons or to swing stocks like a Bet-A-Million Gates—but enough to matter considerably. What do you do with it? Standard advice that self-employed businessmen or such professionals as doctors, lawyers, and dentists often meet is, "Go buy a mutual fund."

This has obvious advantages. It secures for the investor of moderate means the twin blessings of diversification and professional management for his portfolio. But the advice is incomplete, because there is no such thing as "a" mutual fund. Mutual funds are as different as elephants and tomcats.

Some are swift movers, designed to run well ahead of the market pack (but suffering from an inbuilt danger of perhaps breaking an outstretched leg and being left behind the pack instead).

Others plod alongside the market in pedestrian fashion, doing neither better nor worse than the average of all stocks, but planned to avoid some of the pitfalls that the swift movers leap over instead of going around.

A few funds move behind the pack, almost deliberately accumulating less in capital gains than do most funds but paying out greater sums in quarterly dividends instead.

Some are called "closed-ends"; others are known as "open-ends"; and unless an investor knows the bias of each and how it can best serve him, he might make a serious mistake in purchasing a fund not meant for his needs.

A few newer funds have been structured to give a little of

everything to everybody and these, known as "dual funds," have certain plus factors(and other minus ones) of their own.

Finally, a new kind of approach used by a few funds has the paradoxical aim of being conservative by being extra audacious; these are called "hedge funds."

It is hard to choose among such a welter of possibilities. The purpose of this chapter is to examine each approach, concept, and type so that when you next say, "Buy me some shares of a mutual fund," you may hopefully do so with the knowledge of a Wall Street professional.

Mutual funds, by definition, are poolings of capital in which the investment money of thousands, sometimes tens of thousands, of investors is put together for "mutual" management. These holdings might differ vastly in size. Management may be put in the hands of a Wall Street pro; sometimes a committee of portfolio managers makes the decision. The fund then hires financial analysts; it provides the accounting services to credit each investor with his proportional share of gains, losses, and income; and finally, the fund distributes these to its scattered thousands of investors. It holds every security in the fund's own name, and its owners, in turn, receive shares in the fund. Mutual fund shares can be bought and sold like any other stock certificates. The biggest advantages that mutual funds offer are the pooling that permits a small-to-medium investor to hold a sound diversification of stocks and the professional management that presumably makes it possible for him to do better than he would have been able to do on his own.

An investor does not receive any of this for nothing. Like other professionals, the analysts and mangers of a mutual fund serve for money. But in most cases each investor's share in management expenses is small; it averages around one half of 1 percent. Sometimes investors pay a sales commission to buy mutual fund shares; sometimes they do not. But in every case they bear their proportional share of the fund's expenses, and these always include stock exchange and over-the-counter commissions that the fund pays to its brokers for buying and selling the stocks it puts into or removes from its portfolio.

People wonder whether this sort of professional management can really produce results significantly better than the average man might do for himself or better than the celebrated stick-a-pin technique proclaimed by one United States senator. At the end of January, 1968, *Barron's*, a financial weekly, revealed some statistics on the subject which are illuminating.

The funds as a group, reported *Barron's,* did significantly better than the market averages (many financial people believe that the average investor on his own very seldom does as well as these yardsticks of general market progress). Statistics were available for 173 U.S. open-end companies. These, said *Barron's,* scored an average gain in 1967 of 27.7 percent of their net asset values at the start of the year. This was more than twice as high a gain as was racked up by the Dow-Jones Composite 65-Stock Average that comprises the D-J Industrial, Rail, and Utilities indexes.

Moreover, some funds especially dedicated to scoring capital gains did so handsomely. Stacked against the 11.6 percent rise in the D-J composite average was the fact that 33 funds had gains in excess of 40 percent—a whopping yearly profit—and half a dozen funds achieved gains of 79 percent to 114 percent. Altogether, 123 funds (72 percent) outperformed the popular Dow-Jones Industrial Average and 18 more "beat" the composite.

As can be seen from these figures, mutual funds are not all alike. They can differ by their ends, aims, angles, and loads, and an investor should know these differences in order to make a wise choice.

Open-end Funds: When Wall Street people call a fund an open-end or a closed-end, they refer to the fact that it has two ends—the buying operation and the operation whereby shares are redeemed from shareholders at net asset value. When a mutual fund will both buy and sell at all times, it is an open-end fund. Most funds fall into this classification.

To scramble around selling and redeeming every business day, an open-end mutual fund has to have a strange sort of corporate setup. Most corporations—yours if you are a small businessman whose firm uses this business form—must be capitalized at a set number of shares. It is not necessary to always have all of these shares issued. Some can be held in the treasury. But they exist, and to shrink or blow up the number of shares takes a vote of stockholders. The new number they vote then becomes as rigidly set as the one they voted out.

Not so with a mutual fund. It has an infinite number of shares. On any given investment-business day, there might be, for example, ten thousand shares bought and existing stockholders might tender eighty-five hundred of their shares to the fund for redemption. You can't do this sort of thing with any ordinary kind of corporation, and that is why a special name has been coined to refer to the expandable-contractable kind of corporate structure these funds have. They are open-ends.

Closed-end Funds: These are in general, although not in toto, the older funds, formed and sold before the open-end idea took hold. They have certain inbuilt differences, which can sometimes be turned to an investor's advantage, sometimes work against him.

By definition, a closed-end is a normal sort of corporate critter having a capitalization just like everybody else in the world except the open-end funds.

The company doesn't sell its shares to an investor nor does it redeem them from him if he happens to be disenchanted, in need of money, or otherwise minded to turn his certificates into ready coin. How, then, does an investor get into one of the things—or out?

The answer is that he buys (and sells) closed-end investment company shares just as he would sell or buy U.S. Steel and General Motors on the floor of the New York Stock Exchange. Neither of these corporations is engaged in constant issuance of new securities, yet there is a ready market for shares because the trading machinery of the Exchange brings together buyers and sellers. Instead of buying or selling from or to the fund, you deal with another investor who takes the opposite position from yours. (It is always sobering to me, when buying a stock, to realize that someone else, after as much thought as mine, has come to an opposite conclusion, believing that the stock I want to buy should be sold or the stock I deem overvalued is in reality a bargain.)

One advantage closed-end shares offer is that they frequently trade at discounts from asset value. It's nice when buying to know that stock costing $18 per share has $20.50 per share in assets behind it, but when one comes to sell, alas, the same discount usually exists. A few, however, trade at premiums over asset value if the investing public, in its fickle favor, happens at the moment to hold that lucky fund management in high regard.

Balanced Funds: Wall Street uses the term "balance" less to describe distribution of weights than as the construction of a fund "balanced" between bonds and common stocks. Many old-style investors hold that bonds are innately safer than common stocks, and these people are usually more comfortable holding a fund that mixes up its portfolio between ownership certificates (common stock) and instruments of indebtedness (bonds).

Moreover, this school of thought believes, the addition of bonds is likely to slow any downside slip in values during bear market periods such as 1962 and 1966. This reasoning worked for a number of years. It helped arrest losses in capital values for holders of balanced fund shares during the bad 1962 market drop. But when the 1966 market drop came along, some who had accepted the idea of inbuilt "conservative" action of a bond component in the portfolio were astounded to find that tightening money conditions made bonds drop in many cases even more than common stocks.

Nevertheless, the strategy of balancing has worked on sufficient occasions to warrant attention, and, if extreme conservatism is your aim, the balanced mutual funds might be for you.

Common Stock Funds: As the name implies, these are unlike balanced funds. They are for people who believe that the progress of inflation in this country and the world is such that "things" are better possessions in the long run than items of fixed value such as bonds.

Balanced funds are not all alike, but they have marked similarities. Not so common stock funds. There are the plod-along funds run for semi-assured income (no income is assured; it's well to remember that recently even mighty General Motors had to cut its dividend to stockholders). Some are prancing performance funds running to win in the beat-the-averages sweepstakes, and taking commensurate chances in order to hand up a top-flight capital gains record. Common stock funds are of all shades of conservatism or opportunism that might fall between these two extremes.

"Defensive" Funds: These try to guard against loss as a first objective, with the achievement of capital gains only second. The investing philosophy behind many of these funds goes something like this:

If an investor buys into the biggest company in an industry and that industry does not go entirely to pot, he should do at least as well as the economy with a chance of bettering it. In the oil Industry, Standard Oil New Jersey may not grow as fast as Whoozis Petroleums, which is possessed of ten wells and run by a lucky promoter, but when the hard times come, Jersey is set up to weather them a great deal better than Whoozis. Its very size is a safety factor. Oil may dry up for political reasons in one corner of the world and stop Jersey's production there; a war might wreck its refineries in another; a confiscatory tax could hurt it in a third. But these factors are not going to happen all at the same time. And when they do, Jersey's gigantic size and tremendous resources enable it to open the spigot wider in untroubled areas and so its vital lifeblood of hydrocarbons never dries up.

Or take research. A corporation of the size of Standard Oil has the bucks to carry on research and development activity in a wide area. If one project—whose failure might be a financial disaster for a smaller firm—were to go sour, Jersey executives can figuratively shrug their shoulders and direct their scientists to carry on in a new direction. They've got the oil, they've got the ships, they've got the money too.

What's true of Standard Oil is true also of most leading corporations. There may not be the gyrating price possibilities or financial fireworks found in a little firm on the way up, but if we buy stocks of those already "up," then probabilities of success lie on our side.

"Go-go" Funds: The managers of "go-go" funds are generally younger men, and as a group, they have only had experience in up markets. Their elders are quick to point this out. The "go-go" managers counter that, not having been through the wringer of a bear market caused by past conditions, they are free of the fears that inhibit more orthodox money managers, and they answer the defensive argument above by words something like these:

"If one invests in the biggest company in an industry, he has automatically invested in only moderate growth. If a leading big company in any industry grows too big or buys into too many fields, the Department of Justice casts a jaundiced eye and first thing you know it's defending an antitrust suit. Or when it's successful in research, then what? Do its earnings go up appreciably? Not at all. Within such a vast organization, a promising new way to do things has been opened, but its addition to earnings is hardly noticed on the annual statement. The new field which might double earnings of Whoozis Petroleum will make at best only a 2 percent improvement in earnings of Standard Oil New Jersey.

"As for the argument that for bigger gains we take bigger risks—certainly we do. If we're right enough times, we can swallow the losses of the times when we are wrong and still be able to post up on the record board an increase in asset value far better than anything the staid fund approach can bring about."

One of the most successful of this breed of "go-go" managers was Fred Carr, once manager of a fund that in one year beat the averages by 114 percent. Here's Mr. Carr on the performance approach:

"I think the companies that are enjoying rapid growth have 'good guy' management," he said. "You can count on their records. This type of management is going to make you right because sooner or later its record hopefully will be reflected in the market place."

On the same subject of "go-go" money management, another

well-known manager, George Chestnutt, Jr., had this to say: "I don't care whether the company makes women's sweaters or atom bombs, just if it's going up. *Why* is for others to figure out."

Regarding the propensity of "go-go" managers to discount diversification and take larger positions in fewer stocks, William Brokaw, a third follower of the performance cult, said: "The traditional weakness of money managers has been that they have wanted to own a slice of the whole market. But the economy is maturing and many areas aren't growing fast. We're not looking for gains of 10 percent or 20 percent over two years. We want 50 percent to 100 percent. I don't think there are ever twenty-five such major opportunities at any given time."

Dual Funds: These are the effort of some thoughtful Wall Street people to put together a mutual fund package that will give everybody what he wants. For the income investor, the dual fund offers income. For his capital gains-minded brother, the fund offers hope of a swinging "go-go" performance. The dual funds are relatively new and the idea has had little "seasoning" through diverse markets. Their setup should be understood before an investor decides to plunk his capital into one.

The basic gimmick is that a dual fund is divided into two parts. An investor who wants high yield on his capital can buy the fund's income (sometimes called preferred) shares. These entitle him to all dividends and interest received by both halves of the fund. Or if he's an aggressive investor aiming at the accumulation of an estate, he can opt for the growth (or capital) shares. These entitle him to all of the capital gains racked up by both divisions of the fund's portfolio.

An income-oriented investor shouldn't be hurt in a bad year that drops the growth component. For his income is semi-guaranteed. Most dual funds assure income investors of a minimum return over the life of the contract. That return might not be earned in certain years. But if unearned it accumulates in arrears. The income portions have maturity dates. Any income that has been guaranteed but not paid will come out of the growth investors' asset values at that time. After the income portions mature the capital shares thereafter own 100 percent of the fund. Dual funds are generally closed-ends.

Hedge Funds: Hedge funds are one of the hotter ideas going around Wall Street these days. An approach to investing rather than a specific investment, a hedge fund, say enthusiasts, is at one time the most audacious and the most conservative way to put money to work.

The objectives of the new concept are: (1) to attempt to make money on both sides of the market by holding long positions (stocks the fund owns) and at the same time selling other stocks short. The fund depends upon these for "hedge" against sudden short-range shifts in the market since the counter-trend positions will, hopefully, make profits even if the main positions stand still. (2) To vary the percentage of long and short positions in accordance with the stage of the market so that a typical hedge fund might at one time consist of 80 percent long positions and 20 percent shorts, at another time be 40 percent long and 60 percent short, perhaps at unsettled periods hold 50-50 positions, and at bearish periods be 80 percent short and 20 percent long.

Industry Funds: The industry funds are a less popular idea today than they were a few years back. Such a fund invests in only one area of the economy. This may be a profitable slant until the day comes—as it generally does in the history of American business—when that industry ceases to prosper or runs into unexpected snags. Sometimes an industry's prosperity goes on, but the fickle folk of Wall Street tire of the group and it is no longer "in." When this happens, the results for an investor can be hurtful.

Because this drying up of interest or falling upon evil economic times has happened often enough to drive a lesson home, many former industry funds have broadened their areas of investment. Nevertheless, some industry funds still operate and have successful records of performance.

"Load" and "No-load" Funds: On a closed-end fund, an investor pays normal stock exchange commissions to buy and sell fund

shares. But open-ends can be either "load" funds or "no-loads."

The load in question is a commission, nearly always higher than the New York Stock Exchange commission, that is charged for buying or selling closed-end shares, but with one difference. The load goes on the "front end" only. It is charged when an investor buys a fund. With some few exceptions, the open-end mutual funds make no charge for redeeming investors' shares at the net asset value of the moment.

The commission (or load) is added to the asset value. Thus if a share of ABCDEF Fund has a per share asset value of $10 on Tuesday morning, that morning an investor will pay, probably, $1,085 to buy one hundred shares. Loads go on a sliding scale and they become proportionally smaller on larger purchases.

Some funds are called no-loads because they skip this charge and sell direct to investors. Many of them have brilliant records for performance. But an investor should not make the existence or absence of a load the only factor in his decision; it is better to shop among the wide offerings of this big financial field for a fund whose approach, tactics, and strategy suit his objectives.

POINTS TO REMEMBER

1. Mutual funds have shown mighty growth in size. They are perhaps the greatest financial phenomenon of our time since they allow small investors—and many large investors as well—to institutionalize their capital.

2. Funds pool all kinds of money from all kinds of investors. They offer diversification many of us could not achieve alone, plus the advantage of professional management of money.

3. But mutual funds are not alike. They come in all sizes and serve all kinds of purposes. It is a mistake to buy funds without being certain of the objective you want to achieve. For most investor objectives, a selection of mutuals can be found to accomplish what is wanted.

4. In addition to serving different ends, mutual funds are sold in different ways, most over-the-counter, some on exchanges.

Some are closed-ends, some open-ends. Among the latter group, some assess commissions, others do not.

5. A fund should be chosen on its record and the expectation of accomplishing what you want to bring about, not merely because it is (or is not) a load fund.

Chapter 5 : : YOU CAN START AN INVESTMENT PROGRAM ON $10 A MONTH

AN UNUSUAL meeting was held in Chicago around the end of 1967. More than thirty thousand investors, some neophytes and some quite otherwise, attended a "How to Invest Show." It was sponsored by the National Association of Investment Clubs, which pointed out proudly that attendance was sharply up from the eighteen thousand who had gone to see a similar show in Detroit a year earlier.

The investment club idea has certainly come of age. It is an approach worth knowing about because it offers people a chance to learn about the wiles and ways of investing at moderate cost —many clubs' dues are as low as ten dollars per month—while at the same time accumulating a stake in stocks. Membership in an investment club is one of the ways to put periodic payments to work that will be discussed in this chapter.

Investment clubs are educational, sometimes profitable; you can enjoy one for its social aspects and at the same time get some sound economic training that probably wasn't included in your school curriculum. Club membership permits the investor to get his feet wet in financial waters at small cost—a form of "learning while doing" along with others in your situation. Investing through a club has the important advantage of diversification without having to pay mutual fund loading charges or management fees.

Let's consider the case of John Doe, twenty-eight years old, a graduate of a midwestern university, who is now in a third-echelon management rank of a national corporation. Doe is a man on the way up. Recently he met some friends for lunch, and conversation over coffee veered to the stock market.

"You know," said George Jones, a thirtyish physician just starting out in practice, "I have a few dollars in savings and I'm beginning to earn a little more than I need to live on. After putting aside some money for emergencies, buying insurance, and all the things my kids seem to need, I can put about twenty dollars a month into stocks.

"Now if I buy one stock on the New York Stock Exchange's Monthly Investment Plan, all my eggs are in a single basket. Moreover, unless I choose a low-priced stock—and the price of a share is certainly no criterion of whether it should be bought—I'll probably be able to buy only one full share every two or three months. But I would like to get started on some sort of investing program."

"My neighbor who is a building contractor," Doe replied, "a couple of weeks ago told me about an investment group he and some of his associates had formed. He said it gave him the chance to diversify, obtain group thinking, be guided by a broker or a professional financial counselor, and learn something about investing at the same time. Maybe we should consider such a setup."

Out of this and subsequent meetings grew the Professional and Executive Investment Club. Its rules were simple.

Each member paid in ten dollars a month. (It could have been fifteen dollars or twenty dollars or thirty dollars.) In any month, a member could put up more if he chose, but only in multiples of ten dollars. These would buy him equivalent equity in the club's investment portfolio.

A member could withdraw upon reasonable notice, and a cash backlog was set up to buy out his interest. (Establishing such a cash reserve is not absolutely necessary. In some clubs, members are given the option of buying the withdrawing person's shares. If no members exercise their option to buy, the club sells sufficient securities to raise the necessary money. The cost of selling these securities is charged to the account being liquidated. People often have to drop out of an investment club for one reason or another, and setting up machinery for buying out their shares in a financially orderly way can be worthwhile.)

The club was formed as a partnership. It could have incorporated or, as some other clubs have done, set up as an informal group with no regular business organization.

The membership was limited to fifteen, on the basis that more members would make it unwieldy and difficult to arrive at decisions. (Some clubs set higher, some lower ceilings.)

Members met once a month. It is almost obligatory that each be at the meeting. Otherwise, as Doe told his colleagues, there would soon be only a small steering oligarchy making all the decisions; nonattending members would become disgruntled, and the club would fall apart.

A three-man committee was set up to study investing opportunities and report back. Committee members serve three-month terms, which are staggered so that a new member must be elected by the club at each monthly meeting. The investment committee goes over investment ideas, consults with the club's adviser, and reports three suggestions to the whole group. Out of these three, the entire club membership votes on one as the investment of the month. (Sometimes previous investments are repeated; they are simply included as part of the three recommendations.)

The club also decided to secure professional assistance. A local investment counselor, registered with the Securities and Exchange Commission, was retained to consult with the committee and at times address the whole membership. (Some clubs utilize the services of the broker who handles the club account. Such advisory service is provided free of charge.)

Thus the Professional and Executive Investment Club was formed. Such a group can be organized anywhere. Sometimes professional or business colleagues get together. Sometimes it is a church group, a number of friends, a neighborhood association, even fishing or golf companions. There are thousands of these clubs in the United States with overall membership in the hundreds of thousands.

Help for any new organization can be secured from the National Association of Investment Clubs at 1300 Washington Blvd. Building, Detroit, Michigan 48231.

However, you don't have to be an investment club member to invest on a periodic setup. New York Stock Exchange members offer their Monthly Investment Plan. Here is how one leading Exchange member (Merrill Lynch, Pierce, Fenner and Smith) explains the MIP:

"Let's say that you find you have seventy-five dollars a month that you can invest in stock through the Monthly Investment Plan. Your first step is to select a common stock that seems to suit your needs. . . . Suppose the stock you want to buy is one that costs thirty dollars a share. There was a time when you could buy only full shares of stock. Then if you had seventy-five dollars to invest and wanted to buy shares of a thirty dollar stock, you had to decide whether to buy two shares, pay the commission, and put the balance back into your pocket, or buy three shares by adding to the seventy-five dollars you originally intended to invest. Under the Monthly Investment Plan, you can buy stock by the dollar's worth instead of by the share.

"The next step is to fill out a Monthly Investment Plan purchase order and mail it with your check. Your stock is then purchased for you. . . . The only requirements are that you must be at least twenty-one years of age and that you declare your intention of investing with any amount of money from a minimum of forty dollars every three months."

Mutual funds also offer accumulative plans in many sizes and shapes. While an investor can withdraw from the MIP without penalty, some of the mutual fund plans are contractual and a few are "loaded" so that if an investor withdraws in the first year or two he will find that a sizable portion of what he believed to be invested has gone instead into salesmen's commissions. It is well to read a contract carefully although most mutual fund plans are not bear-trapped in any way.

POINTS TO REMEMBER

1. Investment clubs have grown into a sizable movement in the U.S. and Canada.

2. A club allows you to enter the market at moderate expense, sometimes as little as ten dollars per month. It further offers education-through-doing, and most club members say it offers a lot of sociable fun as well.

3. A typical club might meet once a month. It usually consists of people with something in common, although it need not. That something could be living in the same neighborhood, working for the same corporation, membership in the same profession, or just a penchant for being on the first tee of the golf course at 11:02 every Sunday morning.

4. You can also invest on the forty dollar (or any other amount) per month plan through purchase of stocks under the New York Stock Exchange's Monthly Investment Plan, or through purchase of mutual funds on what is called an accumulative plan.

Chapter 6 : : BENEFIT FROM THE GIFTS TO MINORS ACT

Once you had to tie your money and yourself in a welter of red tape in order to pass along things of value to minor children. Now it is as easy as giving an order to your broker—although irrevocable—and thanks to Gifts to Minors acts in the fifty states, it is simple for any investor to handle youngsters' securities and to minimize taxes through gifts.

What is this magic Gifts to Minors setup, and how does it work? What benefits does it offer directly, and where lie the fringe benefits such as tax savings?

Serious investment people had long been concerned about investors' difficulties in giving things to children below the legal age of adulthood. In most cases the benefits were not worth the legal involvement. Then in the early 1950's the Association of Stock Market Firms proposed a model law to make things simpler, and fourteen states quickly enacted it. This sliced away the red tape, made it easy to give capital to a youngster and to shift it about in the inevitable switching that a knowledgeable investor has to do to meet changing conditions. Later a shorter, better version of the model law was proposed. It was called the Uniform Gifts to Minors Act, and today all but two states have enacted the uniform law. In those two, Alaska and Georgia, the older model law applies.

The questions and answers that follow are meant to be helpful, but not to take the place of a lawyer's advice in specific cases.

Q. What do these laws provide?

A. Despite the use of "uniform," the state acts are not exactly the same, but they differ in details only. In all states you can give securities to youngsters. In all but Alaska you can donate cash, and in some (California, District of Columbia, Illinois, Kentucky, Massachusetts, Michigan, Missouri, Nebraska, New Hampshire, New Jersey, North Carolina, Ohio, Tennessee, and Wisconsin) you can give insurance.

But once you give away money, securities, or insurance, it is given irrevocably. You cannot get it back. It belongs to the minor. However, the custodian whom you as the donor choose (most givers pick themselves as custodians) can sell one security and buy another, hold cash for a time awaiting better investment opportunities, or otherwise behave as a prudent and intelligent investor would. Note that provision about prudence and intelligence in the seeking of income and preservation of capital. You can be held accountable for your stewardship if you fail to exercise both.

In general, however, you are almost as free to manage a youngster's capital as to handle your own; except that it remains his, must be registered in his name, and cash items must be carefully segregated from the donor's own.

Q. Must the minor live in the same state as the donor?

A. Not necessarily. If he does not, the donor can give under the laws of either state.

Q. If I give some stock, may I continue to hold it?

A. Not unless you are also the custodian, and then only after it has been transferred into the name of "John H. Doe, Custodian for John H. Doe, Jr., a minor under the (name of state) Gifts to Minors Act." The wording formula changes slightly in some states, but the sense is the same. Gifts must be put in the physical grasp of the custodian and be registered more or less as stated here. The gift is not legally complete until actual delivery.

Q. How about a gift of money?

A. Here, too, the money must change hands and should be put into a separate account with a bank or broker in the name of the custodian for the benefit of the minor. (No money gifts in Alaska, however, under this law.)

Q. Then what of insurance gifts?

A. It is best to find out from your lawyer or insurance counselor the exact procedure in your state, provided you are in one of fourteen that allow this.

Q. May I give as large a gift as I wish?

A. Of course. But you will encounter tax troubles unless you bear in mind the federal tax laws limiting the size of gift capital transfers. Sometimes there are advantages in creating a trust to handle a substantial gift. It might pay to talk to your lawyer and the trust officer of your bank if you have this in mind.

Q. Do mutual fund shares qualify under these laws?

A. Yes. You can give any security except one of which you (the donor) are the issuer. In many states, savings and loan certificates qualify, as well as stocks and bonds.

Q. When does custodianship end?

A. When the minor reaches twenty one, all that has been held for his benefit becomes his with the full right to hold or sell. The custodianship is therefore at an end.

Should the custodian resign, die, or be disabled, the guardian of the minor usually becomes custodian, or the courts may appoint one.

Q. Suppose the minor dies? Does the property revert to the donor?

A. No, it goes into the minor's estate.

Q. Can I give margined securities for which I have not paid the broker in full?

A. Only what is owned outright. Donated securities may not remain in "street name" either (that is, in the name of a brokerage house which holds securities for investors in their own names, crediting the securities to their accounts). They must be registered as indicated earlier.

Q. Then donated securities cannot be used for collateral for a bank loan?

A. Again, no.

Q. We cannot sell them to pay for my son's education later on?

A. Custodial property can—indeed should, if needed—be used for support, maintenance, and education, without court order and without considering other property that might belong to the minor.

Q. Suppose the custodian and the guardian are not the same person and that they disagree. Has the guardian power over custodial property?

A. He does not, although in New York a special guardian may be appointed by the court during a proceeding for the protection of the minor.

Q. Must the custodian make an accounting when he turns over property?

A. California requires that he do so when the minor reaches twenty-one, and in Massachusetts the custodian must deliver an account within six months of the ending of his custodianship. Louisiana permits a minor, parents, or guardian to petition for an accounting if none is given after a written request (this right to request an accounting exists for four years after the minor reaches twenty-one or dies). In Oregon an accounting can be demanded during two years after the minor becomes twenty-one, or after his death. (In this, as in everything connected with law, check your attorney.)

Q. What are tax consequences and advantages of giving to a minor under this law?

A. One of the prime benefits of making a gift of securities is to shift the income from a higher tax bracket (the donor's) to a lower one (the recipient's).

Parents of a minor receiving income, even if it goes over the yearly personal exemption, may still get the exemption provided they contribute more than half the child's support *and* he is under statutory age or still a student.

But in any tax matter, it is wise to secure the exact-to-the-occasion advice of a tax specialist.

POINTS TO REMEMBER

1. Under state laws (check your attorney for exact provisions in your state), you can put securities in a minor's name and still retain ability to switch them for him. The stocks or other securities are bought under Gifts to Minors acts. Usually, you remain custodian and as such can take the same steps you would with your own funds, keeping in mind, however, that you can be held accountable when the minor reaches majority.
2. "Custodian" stock like this cannot be registered in your name. It must be put into the minor's name. Phrasing of the registration varies from state to state. Most brokers will automatically see that proper phrasing for your state goes on the certificate if you explain that a purchase is a gift to a minor.
3. Custodian property can be used to pay for the minor's education, support, etc. Check your attorney for provisions in your state.

SECTION II : : How to Choose the Right Stocks

Chapter 7 : : THE ROADS TO SUCCESS

ANCIENTLY THERE was a saying: "All roads lead to Rome." Today many roads lead to the hoped-for land of investing success, and, like the diverse roads that led Romeward in the days when Rome's word shook the world, all of these can carry you to Wall Street success provided they are chosen with intelligence and followed with diligence and care.

The trick, say veteran Wall Streeters, is to go on a road and at a pace that suits you as an individual investor. Some investors are like swift chariots that barrel at top speed toward Rome, risking the loss of a wheel here or a horse there if speed can be achieved. Others prefer to go more slowly in the hope of doing so with greater safety and less wear and tear on the nervous system. Thus, while many avenues lead to success, it is well to understand the pace and the methods of each.

Numerous investors take the "performance" road via individual stocks or mutual funds attuned to trading for profits. Others believe in buying "good" stocks and holding them for a long pull, which, with some investors, means for a lifetime. Another group is completely sold on the "new directions" approach of seeking small firms, firms that do new things or put new twists to old tasks, and relying on a diversity of these firms to hit it big, risking losses on those that do not. Some investors rely on the balance sheet for guidance; others ignore it and put all of their attention into analyzing the earnings statement in a search for corporations—regardless of the industries into which they might fall—which seem able to generate consistent growth of profits from year to year.

There also are devotees of an approach that calls, of all things, for seeking *un*popularity in the marketplace, provided it is accompanied by what appears to be a sound earnings potential. Another school of financial thought looks only at the supply-demand balances and imbalances within the stock market itself, ignoring the corporation affairs and hoping to buy in when there is an apparent imbalance of demand from seekers of stock over supply in the form of stock tendered by sellers, so that the greater pressure of buying will force prices up and produce a profit. And a final group follows the hallowed path of searching for high current income.

The performance seekers have often had things their own way of late, and even institutional investors such as mutual funds and insurance companies are presently choosing this path.

The performance cultists, whom some scoffers dismiss as "go-go boys," hold that in a time of inflation nothing less than rapid capital gains will possibly bring about success. Performance followers tend to be short-term, in-and-out investors who abandon a commitment the instant it stops performing. Statistics showed that mutual funds, once conservative professional investors, turned over their portfolios 38 percent during a recent year. Considering the continuing conservatism of some older (and larger) mutuals, this would appear to indicate a turnover of sizable proportions on the part of the "go-go boys." Some of these fast-moving funds never report a holding to their stockholders at all—it is sometimes bought after a quarterly report period and sold before the beginning of the next period.

Wild as it may sound, the "go-go" approach works. To follow it calls for good information and a fine sense of timing. But the average housewife or business and professional man, engrossed throughout most of the day's working time with the affairs of his own field, scarcely finds time to obtain or apply this kind of fine touch. So increasing numbers of mutual funds have sprung up to take the job off his hands (for a management fee), and a number of stock-market letters concentrate upon timing advice applied to fast-moving stocks—even to timing the purchases and sales of "go-go" mutual funds.

And now even the dark-suited, conservative advisers to individual accounts are coming out in bright sport coats and with trading programs geared to "go-go" management of at least a part of their clients' funds.

Some non-Wall Streeters find it easier to apply the older, more staid approach of buying good stocks for the long haul. While results have not been as spectacular in late years as those racked up by the "go-go" managers, some of the profits from long-pull holding of first-rate corporate stocks are impressive:

A hundred shares of General Motors bought ten years ago might have cost about $4,250. In a decade they would be worth around $8,150.

If in the fast-moving electrical-electronics field an investor had bought Westinghouse rather than volatile Whoozis Hot Road, he would have paid on average $3,200 for stock worth $7,350 by 1968's end.

Some younger drug companies have scored spectacular results with new products and their stockholders have benefited in proportion. But all of the drug profits have not accrued to the far-out companies. Consider the purchase a decade back of one hundred shares of American Home Products, which would have cost an investor $1,700 on average then and would bring $5,900 on the New York Stock Exchange in 1969.

Other examples of the technique can be pointed out, and, while all have not been profitable, the added safety makes this approach desirable to many investors not temperamentally suited to "go-go" gyrations. Even an investor unschooled in Wall Street ways can practice this approach on his own. Does he feel that a certain industry should prosper over the next decade? Picking the biggest and financially strongest company in it will not assure him the greatest possible profit, but if he is correct in his thoughts, his stock should participate in expected growth.

A road that appears to branch out through uncharted woods has led some of its travelers straight to tremendous profits in the Street (and has led others up the wooded path to nowhere). This is the road taken by searchers for "new directions" stocks.

These are the stocks of companies, often small and nearly

always technology-oriented, where one big product success can zoom the value of the stock to many times its cost. There is a danger to this approach, of course. If the research doesn't work, an investor frequently takes a roller-coaster ride. One such company in recent years zoomed from 23 to 800, and then dropped right back again when the new product on which its stockholders' hopes were pinned failed to find a market big enough to pay for the research. Investors who bought at 23 and watched their hopes and their finances boom—then collapse—were not to be envied. Worse were those who bought at 800 and then stared disaster in the face when price quotations reached 23 again.

The example cited above was abnormal; few stocks in any category experience such skyrocket rises and falls. The new directions investor reasons that he can afford some failures of judgment in a field where being right can be richly rewarded as Wall Street rewards the people who correctly pick a new technology early.

But new directions companies are not all technology corporations. Some operate in prosaic service fields in which they have divined a new human need and set out to supply it. Americans dine out more often than ever before. Much of this eating is done by persons newly able to afford moderate-priced meals, and by teen-agers who are more affluent than their parents of the Depression era. Noticing these facts, McDonald's Corp. designed a nationwide chain of franchised short-order establishments, which have prospered so well that McDonald's stock, purchasable at 3 in 1965, sold at 33 in 1969.

Thinking totally different from that of the new directions seeker is done by the follower of the classic balance sheet approach to stocks. This is the approach taken by the fathers and grandfathers of today's "go-go boys." Yet it continues to work and the reason is rooted deep in human nature. Everybody likes a bargain.

A typical bargain to the balance sheet man might be a company meeting this description: sales falling or stable, little growth, profits sometimes nonexistent, a great deal of plant and machinery not being used profitably, high cash holdings or holdings of things that financial people consider akin to cash (for example, short- or medium-term government bonds, a portfolio of marketable securities or accounts receivable on which payment is not in doubt).

Often such a company sells for less than its balance sheet would indicate to be its true value, and sometimes for less than the amount of its cash and cash equivalent items.

Although sometimes such a company has no earning power and might specialize in buggy whips or locomotive cowcatchers, shrewd investors do a double take when their eyes light on the statistics. They know that, in this age of acquisition-minded conglomerate corporations and of entrepreneurs interested in any situation that is worth more dead than alive, sooner or later someone will be attracted by the sweet smell of a turnaround possibility. Searching out such balance sheet bargains has been the basis on which many considerable fortunes have been made.

Undervalued securities can include: defaulted bonds, if there is sound reason to believe that arrears of interest will be paid off; bonds that are selling well below their real worth because investors incorrectly believe the interest to be in danger (note the key word, "incorrectly"); and special situations where specific information indicates an imminent merger or new product that will lift the real worth of the security. Unless an investor is actually in the inside group, however, it is not wise to take rumors or tips about corporate developments as a signal for the existence of an undervalued special situation. These situations are uncovered the same way buried treasure is found—by digging in corporate statistics.

Warns one analyst, "Even genuine undervaluation does not mean that the undervalued security is about to move back up to book value. There are a host of corporate developments that must be under way first. You cannot always be certain about these developments, but you can determine when an inside changeover is likely to be under way. Watch the accumulation of the stock and study the technical market action of the security to detect early buying that is likely to lift the undervalued and unwanted security into profitable investor favor."

While an older school studies the balance sheet, today's financial analysts are more prone to look at earning power, and most investors, led by such an earnings-minded philosophy, do the same.

The earnings approach calls for less emphasis on the areas in which a corporation operates or the state of its "bricks-and-mortar" account (as irreverent analysts call book value) than on its ability to generate ever-higher earnings.

"I don't care whether a company runs buses to the moon or shuttles to Joe's Diner," one such investor told me. "What matters is that it makes money. It matters even more that its per share earnings are able to increase every year at a steady pace—above 10 percent to keep ahead of inflation."

As this investor points out, profits can be a misleading term. Professional financial analysts do not look so much at the overall profit figure as they do at a statistic they call "per share earnings." Per share earnings is a figure derived by dividing net profits —left over after service of debts and preferreds—by the number of shares outstanding. Happily, no investor has to perform this division. The standard statistical sources of investment information always furnish a breakdown of per share earnings, and it is growth in this department that marks a truly growing situation.

One group in the investment community seeks something few humans want: unpopularity. The "unpopularity portfolio" approach is taken by Wall Streeters who know that while the Street's favor can lift value by hundreds of percent, that same favor is fickle. The electronics stocks had a day in the sun, followed by a day in the shade, and reemergence into sunlight again. Utility stocks were the darlings of the Board, then they sold off badly; one investor quipped, "They're giving two sticks of bubble gum today with every share of utilities." The tale can be told and retold for every group of stocks.

A point remembered by followers of the "unpopularity portfolio" idea is that those stocks up today might go down next year while those down may very well go up. "I buy my straw hats in December," Thomas Fortune Ryan, an old-timer of the

Wall Street scene, is reported to have told one questioner who wanted to know how Ryan made money in the market.

Straw hats still sell cheaper in December for an investor with the patience, courage, and plain bullheadedness to wait around until summer's heat lifts their value.

However, there are the followers of still another approach who say that they don't care who lifts the value of a stock or why, so long as they can tell by their trend-following methods that it is indeed going up. These investors and analysts deal in supply and demand, but not the supply or demand for a corporation's services or products. They are interested in balance or imbalance between bulls and bears trading in stock certificates. In the jargon of Wall Street, these people are called "technicians."

The technicians reason like this: "Everything everybody knows —the ignorant and the well-informed, the smart and the dull-witted, the rich, poor, and in-between—finds its way to Wall Street and is reflected in the price movement and volume of trading through the buying of these people. It does not matter whether the ill-informed predominate over the smart ones; as long as they have the most money, their opinions have to prevail and the price will therefore go their way. By researching supply and demand within the market, it's possible to determine the direction of a trend and the balance between buyers and sellers, and on that basis build a profitable investing strategy."

The oldest Romeward road of all is that taken by the investors whose primary object is not appreciation but high yield. They set out to build capital through compounding the yield from dividends and interest. This method often is slower than the other methods of estate building, but advocates claim that compounding is surer. This approach, however, is subject to the risk of capital loss just as are the other two approaches, although in many ways the risks are smaller. Special factors—some advantageous and some detrimental—come into play in times of high yields and borrowing costs.

So there are eight roads that can, with proper planning of where to start and where to get off, and with an eye to the hazards of the highway, lead investors to perhaps not a pot of gold but to a portfolio of stock certificates worth more tomorrow than today.

POINTS TO REMEMBER

1. Just as all kinds of roads once led to Rome, crossing different deserts and mountains and going by straight or twisting ways, always toward one objective, so an investor has a choice of many approaches.

2. One road is by way of "performance," usually through in-and-out trading of what the investor expects to be fast-moving hot stocks.

3. Another approach, which is aimed at combining the profit approach with added safety, is to single out for investment the oldest, most staid, strongest blue chip stocks in an industry.

4. "New directions" investors seek the opposite of blue chip stocks—stocks of companies striking out into new areas of scientific or sociological growth.

5. The classic bargain approach is through companies that have underlying corporate value greater than the price of the stocks in aggregate.

6. Analysts and investors who take the earnings approach ignore those balance sheet items that intrigue the bargain seeker, but look instead to a company's capacity to generate growing profits.

Chapter 8 : : THREE APPROACHES TO FORTUNE BUILDING— *THE GROWTH STOCK*

ONCE UPON a time there were three little pigs named Growth, Undervalued, and Compound, and in the classic manner of little pigs they each set out to build a house—only they called these "estates."

The first little pig built his estate out of earning power.

The second little pig built his out of compounded cash throw-off.

And the third little pig naturally built his out of brick and mortar.

Now the usual little pig stories show that the pig who built out of brick and mortar was the smart one. But such was not necessarily so in the case of this fable, for these three little pigs were actually investors, each of whom wanted to build an estate and each of whom took a different way of doing it. In Wall Street, things sometimes work out differently than in Disneyland and, as events turned out, all three investors were right.

The important thing about building an estate is to know your building approach (in this case investing technique) and to practice it consistently and intelligently. There are, as the three little Wall Street pigs demonstrated, a trio of methods available. Each one is good, provided it is followed consistently.

Method one is to build by investing in growth stocks; this is the method followed by the pig named Growth. The second is to seek undervalued situations; this is called the brick-and-mortar approach because, while growth investing leans on earning power as the prime determinant, investors who seek undervalued situations often count the company's assets (brick, mortar, machinery, and cash) in relation to the stock's price. And the investor who builds with cash throw-off, as did the pig named Compound, looks at the amount of income (dividends, interest, rentals) and relies upon compounding to make his estate grow.

Each approach can be effective. In this chapter we will look at the growth approach. Subsequent chapters will assess the other two.

Growth companies grow in diverse ways. There is almost no common single factor you can say applies to every growth company.

Some companies, such as some of the aerospace, drug, and electronic companies, grow by vigorous and active research in dynamic fields. Others grow by equally vigorous and dynamic research in what seems to be staid and steady fields; examples are some of the progressive food companies, which have applied the same techniques the drug and science companies use to discover everyday things such as a new Jell-O or an instant ice cream—and with the same tremendous results. Some companies grow by diversifying widely into a number of fields. Other companies grow through expanding their stakes in one or two fields. Some concentrate on a single product or service that itself has tremendous growth possibilities.

So there is really no one single way in which growth companies grow. In exploiting the methods referred to here, they can act in either of two ways, both of which are good even though they are seemingly contradictory. The two are growth internally and growth externally.

A company that grows internally depends upon its own inside-the-organization generation of cash through depreciation and through the portion of earnings that are not paid out in dividends but are reinvested in the corporation, and sometimes through judicious borrowing. This money is put into the company. It goes for research for new products, new plants, new distribution channels, new ways of getting the product to the consumer. Sometimes it goes into new foreign manufacturing operations. But the company stays on its same internal track. It minds the business it knows best. Many of the big growth companies have become great from small beginnings by steadily and wisely following this policy of internal growth.

And some companies grow with equal and sometimes greater success *externally;* that is, they go out and acquire other companies. They find that it is cheaper to buy a company that is making the new product they wish to market than it is to build a factory, teach their personnel, and go through all the aches and pains of start-up expenses and development. Instead, they buy an already going proposition. Some companies carry this to great extreme. They move out in all directions externally, buying companies in this field and in that field, and depend upon their own overall ability to keep all of these baskets full of increasingly profitable eggs. They are called conglomerates or multi-industry corporations.

Many investment analysts make the mistake of looking at this type of external growth in which sales are booming tremendously and saying, "Brother, look at Whoozis Corporation. What a growth company this is!" when in plain fact it sometimes happens that Whoozis has so watered its stockholders' equity through the constant issuance of new stock to buy these companies that, considering profits, it is not really going anywhere.

The foregoing sentence is certainly not meant as an indictment of external growth by acquisition, no matter how widespread. Many excellent growth companies have done this, done it wisely, and been able to buy firms they wanted without watering down the earnings base by paying out more in stock than they are receiving in equivalent profits. But a great many companies have most unfortunately put on tremendous corporate pyrotechnics and ended up nowhere. The investor should be warned to look not merely at sales growth but also at the *earnings* growth. Has the growth of sales been accompanied by an equal (and preferably a greater) growth in earnings?

Thus your problem becomes one of choosing a true growth company, not one whose growth is merely seeming. Some firms have elaborate, comprehensive, well-staffed research laboratories that unfortunately never develop anything with a profit potential. Some companies put only rather small amounts of money into research, but spend it wisely on profitable new products. So it becomes important to search for companies whose growth is real and not merely seeming.

You can see that it is a tricky—but rewarding—business, this investing in growth stocks, and the first rule of the business is for an investor to realize that growth goes in *phases.*

Companies have phases during which they grow fat and fast; then things often slow down, and occasionally stop.

And *price* growth, of greatest importance to investors, also goes in phases. There are phases during which investors love electronics stocks, others when the dirtiest word in Wall Street is electronics. Some segments of industry are always "in" with investors, others "out."

Smart investors try to ride with the phase during which a company is growing rapidly and also the phase when the fickle stock market holds its industry in highest regard. Those who master the trick of riding such phases do indeed grow rich on growth stocks.

They are aware that there is no such thing as a typical growth company, but there is one thing all such companies have if they are to qualify as real growth investments. Their *per-share* earnings must steadily increase and do so at a clip faster than the economy as a whole, faster than the erosion of inflation.

That's the touchstone an investor can safely apply: earnings growth. If he is knowledgeable in analytical ways, he will not look closely into the sales of a company, nor even at its overall profits. It's the *per-share* earnings that matter. (These are computed by statistical services, who take the total net profit after service of debt or preferred and divide it by the number of shares outstanding to determine the equity each share has in a company's profit.)

It helps if there is simultaneous growth in sales and dividends as well as earnings. But what counts is growth of earnings from year to year. The company may pay no dividends, but if it is plowing the money back and producing a crop of increased earnings figures, that's all to the good. Sales may actually decrease, yet increased earnings may result because a growth-oriented management has lopped off an unprofitable division to concentrate its capital where the growth action is.

The patient holder of growth stocks should minimize taxes by selling only when he is convinced that a trend has ended. But then he should sell without fail.

And that applies, say knowledgeable analysts, as much to the phase of market favor as to growth of the corporation.

What is in the minds of people determines what they will do with their money, and facts won't dissuade them. If they believe that Whoozis, Inc., is going to grow, they will buy it. If they believe that something is changing Whoozis' growth trend, they will sell. They may be wrong, but it will little profit you to have been right about the company while the stock goes down and stays there.

But how does an investor know when a stock group is coming into favor or dropping out of it? One way is to study the most active stocks each day. The financial pages of most daily newspapers publish these tables, and from them you can tell which groups seem to be in the favor of the fickle buyers who can make Whoozis, Inc., a favorite today and an unwanted dog tomorrow.

In addition, an investor who is aware that growth is an inconstant, if profitable, thing, watches for certain other signs of when to sell:

He will sell if the earnings of Whoozis, Inc., drop for two successive quarters.

He will sell when the stock trades in a tired range for a lengthy period, then plunges downward out of it. He knows that this is a sign of decreased market favor.

He will sell when governmental, tax, or competitive factors seem to be inhibiting the growth of the industry of which Whoozis is a part.

If he is smart about picking the stocks of companies with good growth records and that seem to be continuing that growth, *if* he makes sure from examination of the most active tables that he is socking capital into an industry that the market views currently with favor, and *if* he is nimble and quick about bidding good-bye to yesterday's stock friend when these advantages vanish, our investor can be one of those who does, indeed, grow rich in growth stocks.

POINTS TO REMEMBER

1. There is no pattern for how growth companies grow. They can become bigger and more profitable through acquisition-merger, through hewing to a single path but hewing effectively to that path, by generous doses of outside financing, by financing only from internally generated funds.
2. But one thing a stock must have if it is to be considered a growth stock: The per share earnings must be growing and, more important, give promise of continuing to grow in months and years ahead.
3. Growth companies, like people, plants, and most things on this earth, grow old and some of them eventually die. It becomes important for the growth stock investor to be alert to signs of possible slowing of growth and to the other signals of age and possible corporate decrepitude.

Chapter 9 : : THREE APPROACHES TO FORTUNE BUILDING – *BRICKS AND MORTAR*

THE LITTLE Wall Street pig named Undervalued looked up from a corporate report that he had been studying to find his brothers, Compound and Growth, engaged respectively in reading a banker's table of compound interest and the latest reports of quarterly earnings in the financial section.

"Hey, fellas," he piped. "Have I got a bargain! Here's a company–Small Business Investment Company, no less–that has over $17.20 in assets for each share of stock, mostly good, green cash in the bank, and it's selling for 10¼ per share. A chance to buy $17.50 for $10.25 doesn't come every day!"

Finding such bargains, and hoping that investor attention, the scrutiny and buying power of a merger-minded bigger company, or just plain fortuitous circumstances will soon lift the undervalued bargain off the low-priced shelf where it has so long lain, is the strategy pursued by one school of investors typified by the little Wall Street pig named Undervalued. Many such investors drive Cadillacs and not a few are chauffeured about in their big cars. Some are rumored to possess Caddies of the solid gold variety.

Finding undervalued bargain stocks and then riding them up their true worth can be a fascinating sport and a rewarding way to make a living. It can also be a frustrating method of tying up capital, sometimes for weary years, and in the hands of some not overly smart practitioners of the art, a quick channel down the Wall Street drain. In this chapter we'll look into the technique with ways to (hopefully) maximize the profit potential and lessen the dangers to nerves and/or capital that are inherent in this as in every other approach to investing success.

According to my desk dictionary, a bargain is "an agreement to exchange, sell or buy goods; the terms of such an agreement; such an agreement considered in relation to one of the parties as, 'he made a good bargain'; any mutual agreement or contract; something offered, bought, or sold at a price favorable to the buyer." The last meaning of the word contains the sense in which Wall Street bargains are sought by such investors as our little pig Undervalued.

These bargains are by no means hard to find. *Forbes*, a leading financial publication, annually publishes a list of what it calls "Loaded Laggards" in the market, and a bargain-sniffing investor can find others almost any day. Among the bargains on a recent date were these:

A corporation having $16.41 in total assets per share, $11.64 of which were working capital, priced at 12⅜.

Another whose working capital alone was $15.13 per share, with $24.40 per share overall net assets, priced in the market at 16½, slightly more than working capital alone.

A third whose price of 17⅜ hid the fact that the working capital, without regard to fixed assets, amounted to $20.22. Total assets of this bargain stock came to $24.80 per share.

Another with working capital that by itself was in excess of the stock's price. It was valued at 8 in the market and had $10.13 in working capital. The figure of $17.51 total assets was more than double the cost of the whole package to a bargain-minded investor in undervalued situations.

Statistically, these are bargains indeed. And for astute investors who follow the classic undervalued asset approach and are wise in timing, such bargains are frequently true roads to riches. But other investors often see undervalued companies stay undervalued year after year, and sometimes become even more undervalued as time passes.

Why should this be so? Why should such bargain stocks sometimes spurt up to and beyond their asset values and in other cases lag further behind? How can the investor who takes this approach pick the right undervalued securities?

Let us first define terms and see what is meant by the phrase, "undervalued securities." If a corporation has assets of one million dollars in plant and equipment (fixed assets) plus another five hundred thousand dollars in cash and investments such as short-term government bonds that are equivalent to cash—and if this corporation has one hundred thousand shares of stock outstanding with no prior debt—we can say that the assets behind each share of stock are fifteen dollars per share. This is called the book value. We would break it down this way: Corporation A has a book value of fifteen dollars per share, of which five dollars per share represents quick assets. Should the stock be selling, say, for $4.50 per share, it would certainly fit the definition of an undervalued security. (Note that nowhere have we said such an undervalued security must go up to its book value. It may or may not do this. Later, we will give suggestions for determining whether and when such a climb to asset value might be under way.)

It should be noted that undervalued securities can also include defaulted bonds where there is sound reason to believe that arrears of interest will be paid off, or bonds that are selling well below their real worth because investors incorrectly believe the interest to be in danger (note the key word, "incorrectly"), as well as special situations where we are specifically informed about a merger or a new product shortly upcoming that will lift the real worth of the security. It should be stressed that unless you are *really* in the inside group you should not take rumors or tips about such corporate developments as signaling the existence of an undervalued special situation.

Such situations are uncovered in the same way buried treasures are found—by digging. That is, by carefully checking into corporate statistics and data. Most public libraries have *Standard & Poor's Corporation Records* or *Moody's Industrials* where such data may be found; they should be supplemented by study of annual reports.

But as noted before, even genuine undervaluation does not

mean that the undervalued security is about to move back up to its book value. There are a host of corporate developments that must be under way first. You cannot always know about these, but you can determine when such an inside changeover is likely to be under way by watching accumulation of the stock and by studying the technical market action of the security to detect early buying likely to lift the undervalued and unwanted security into profitable investor favor.

POINTS TO REMEMBER

1. Some investors have made fortunes seeking Wall Street's bargains. These are stocks with bricks and mortar (book value) worth more than the market price. Sometimes they are stocks undervalued on an earnings basis.

2. Bargain stocks do not always go up immediately. Occasionally there are wearying months, even years, to wait before the crowd sees what you have seen. But with patience, if you are correct in appraising a stock as a bargain, you are likely to make profits over the longer term on undervalued securities.

3. It takes digging to find these. Once found, they can be an avenue to affluence.

Chapter 10 : : THREE APPROACHES TO FORTUNE BUILDING – *INCOME*

MANY INVESTORS have heard what is sometimes called the "Medici bit." This is a calculation that if the Medici family of Florence, Italy, had, in the days of its wealth during the Renaissance, invested one hundred thousand dollars at 5 percent compound interest, the sum would be greatly in excess of five hundred quadrillion dollars in the twentieth century.

The "Medici bit" (which is, by the way, an accurate mathematical calculation) is cited to show the advantages of the approach many investors take to the building of an estate—the compounding of yield (interest, dividends, etc.) to build up capital itself.

It is often slower than the other two methods of estate building (seeking of undervalued situations, and investing for corporate growth) discussed in these three chapters, but its advocates claim that it is surer. It should be noted, in regard to the claim of being surer, that this approach is subject to risks of capital loss just as are the other two approaches, although in many ways the risks are smaller. Moreover, there are special factors—some advantages and some drawbacks—which come into play in times of high yields and expensive borrowing costs.

Today's estate builder who seeks to compound income faces a hazard not known to the Medici—the U.S. Treasury Department's tax collectors who take a larger chunk out of ordinary income—resulting from most (but not all) interest, dividends, or rentals—than they do from long-term capital gains. There are exceptions and later we will consider the ways an investor can legally have his yield and eat it too—all of it.

Whether the times are characterized by "tight" and expensive money, or by "easy" money and low yields, bonds can fluctuate as do stocks, although not to the same degree. For example, during the year 1969 these fluctuations happened in bonds of impeccable quality:

American Telephone and Telegraph Co. 3⅞'s of 1990 had a high of 72½ and a low of 59 (consider how an investor felt who bought them at par of 100).

Cessna convertible 3⅞'s brought a price as high as 108 during 1969, and sold as low as 87¼ during that hectic year.

Detroit Edison 6.4's of 1998 ranged between a high of 96¼ and a low of 79½.

General Motors Acceptance Corp. 7⅛'s of 1990 brought as little as 86, yet sold up to 103 during 1969.

I've cited these figures to indicate that it is not a foolproof approach and to alert you to the advantages of good timing in bond purchases and other purchases of yield securities. Compounding does work, and if you are interested in how long it will take to double money at any given rate of return, you can get a rule-of-thumb answer by dividing the percentage of yield into the number 72. If you have a 6 percent return, for example, capital will double with compounding in approximately twelve years. Just for information, a table is appended that illustrates what compounding of different yields will produce in a few short years.

Where should an investor who wants to follow this approach to estate building begin? What sort of return can he expect?

Yields from different sources vary, and to some degree where you invest will depend upon how much risk you want to accept. A bigger return (say 9 percent) entails a substantially greater degree of risk than an average return (of something above 6 or 7 percent as this is written in early 1970).

It should be mentioned that, since interest compounding is a conservative approach to estate building, it is foolish, in my opinion, for anyone to desert caution by going after a big yield

5-YEAR COMPOUND INTEREST TABLE

PERCENTAGE	AMOUNT	PERCENTAGE	AMOUNT
1	1.05	24	2.93
1½	1.08	25	3.06
2	1.10	26	3.17
2½	1.13	27	3.30
3	1.16	28	3.44
3½	1.18	29	3.57
4	1.22	30	3.71
4½	1.25	31	3.86
5	1.28	32	4.00
6	1.34	33	4.16
7	1.40	34	4.32
8	1.47	35	4.49
9	1.54	36	4.66
10	1.61	37	4.82
11	1.68	38	5.00
12	1.76	39	5.28
13	1.84	40	5.37
14	1.95	41	5.55
15	2.01	42	5.75
16	2.11	43	5.97
17	2.20	44	6.19
18	2.29	45	6.41
19	2.39	46	6.64
20	2.50	47	6.87
21	2.60	48	7.10
22	2.70	49	7.33
23	2.81	50	7.59

at what is sometimes enormous risk. If risk is desirable then you will be well-advised to take a growth or undervalued security approach to investing, or you might frankly speculate in bonds.

From good grade corporate bonds, the investor can obtain an average yield of around 7½ percent today with small risk.

And it is in bonds that the investor can save himself from some of the tax bite, for the bonds of states, counties, municipalities, and other non-federal public bodies (referred to in a group as municipal bonds) are exempt from federal taxes as all investment people, but not all of the public, know. These are usually exempt from state income tax as well, in the state of issuance. They sometimes pay rates above 5 percent today.

By assuming only a small added risk, the interest-compounding estate builder can obtain yields up to 10 percent out of corporate bonds that are only slightly less gilt-edged. Even the rates today on Treasury bills are historically high. The bills are as liquid as anything except cash and have great attraction as a haven for funds temporarily out of the market.

The principles of diversification apply to yield-conscious investment just as to any other and the wise investor seeks a package—bonds of different types, some municipals, some common stocks.

The important thing about this whole concept is to stay with it. There can be no withdrawals of income for current use, or all the magic effects of compounding are lost. The investor must make up his mind that growth through compounding is his objective. Therefore, all yield must be reinvested instead of being used for current purchases.

POINTS TO REMEMBER

1. In these days of rapid inflation the fortune-building potential of plowback (compounding) income tends to be forgotten. It exists nevertheless. Income of 7 percent compounded yearly will double in roughly ten years.

2. Yet, there are dangers as well as opportunities in income securities. Any investor holding bonds and stocks of impeccable character through the tight money of recent years has incurred serious losses.

3. It therefore pays to couple income investing with study of market phases and study of the state of monetary affairs. There will be more about this in chapters to come.

Chapter 11 : : TOMORROW'S STOCKS TODAY

A FELLOW analyst said to me recently, "I don't trust this market. The quality stocks aren't moving." When I asked him to to define quality stocks he mentioned blue chips of the kind found on the Dow-Jones Industrial Average.

In the eyes of an older generation of investors, any question about the quality of these D-J blue chip stocks is akin to a manifesto against American motherhood. Not to be done. Economic heresy. Preposterous. Despite such bluff thoughts as those, a number of younger analysts today seriously question whether the big, old companies are the quality stocks any longer.

Once, long ago, a true investor bought only bonds because those were the investments of quality. Then around the 1920's an investor got to be defined as a fellow who bought good railroad stocks; all other stocks were considered speculative junk. Now an investor, some people say, is a man who buys the so-called blue chips and those who seek the leaders of tomorrow aren't buying "quality."

But the fact is that wise investors never invest in today. They try to invest in tomorrow. And quality comprises something that it is hoped will grow to be bigger tomorrow, just as the rails—speculative trash in the last century—prospered into quality by 1920, and as the industrials, once considered junk, grew into the blue chips of now.

The future will be found in endeavors that are currently far-out. But I don't believe this to the extent of considering all far-out activity promising, for some companies are so oriented to science that they can't seem to turn a buck in the world of business.

Furthermore, new processes in old areas are likely to make those who develop them the leaders tomorrow that the current big corporate names are today. Most of all, management that is oriented toward finding future human needs and planning now to satisfy them is the sort of management that tomorrow's investors will look on with the adulation that business students of today have bestowed on the builders of the present corporate giants.

Among some it's fashionable to scoff at the trend to conglomerates. "How can management be expert in so many fields?" these analysts ask. The answer is that the managements that have built successful conglomerates are experts at just that—management—and rely upon lower echelons to provide needed expertise in their varied fields. (I refer here to conglomerates that make profits by operating businesses, not to some of the far-out firms that make it only by accounting.)

Following the breakout from October's market bottom in 1966, Texaco gave a buy signal at 67½. Around the same time, Textron—a conglomerate—also gave a buy signal; Textron's was at 22 (adjusted for split). According to older analytical ideas, there could be no comparison between the two. Texaco, blessed with depth of good management and operating all over the globe, having decade after decade of operational history, was a quality stock. Blue chip was an accolade few bestowed on Textron.

Yet the full extent of Texaco's move from the up signal was only 11 points or 16½ percent and much of that was later retraced. Bursting up from the bear market bottom, however, Textron soared to 46 in less than a year. The signal in the stock of seemingly lower quality preceded a 109 percent increase, while the "quality" stock went up only 16 percent (and soon lost most of that).

Three quarters of a century ago, most of the prosperous manufacturers of buggies and buggy whips regarded themselves as being in the buggy business. When the horseless carriage came in, they laughed; when it made initial inroads into the market for horse-drawn vehicles, they shrugged it off as a passing fad.

Those manufacturers long ago passed from the American economic scene because they were product-minded.

But a few more alert firms saw themselves not as being in the buggy business, but the transportation field. As the new means of transportation by internal combustion engine rather than oat-burner began to catch on more and more, these alert transportation-minded manufacturers switched to where the action was—and prospered.

The range of new human wants, needs, and trends is vast today, and yet there are manufacturers who regard themselves as being in the field of making specific products rather than meeting human needs and solving human problems. They are not long for the economic scene, and their products not long for the marketplace. But the businesses that spot and move to meet people's new needs are the ones whose stocks are likely to be worth more tomorrow than today, and more the day after tomorrow than they will be tomorrow.

A computation was made late in 1967; it showed that if during that bouncy year an investor had bought every stock with a name ending in "ics," he would have fared well financially. The year 1967 was indeed one for science stocks. Yet there are years when the "ics" stocks—those equities of tomorrow-oriented corporations—languish on the Wall Street shelf and the action, for the time, is in older blue chips. So although the market is increasingly "ics"-stock conscious, it pays to know when it is not so that money can be put where the moment's action happens to be.

Investors were disillusioned with numerous aspects of Wall Street when stock prices began to move up feebly, then faster, from the shattering bottom of the big 1962 bear market. Not the least of their disenchantment was with the frenzied speculation that had preceded the 1962 drop. Following the big drop, as prices appreciated with gathering momentum in one of the big, sustained trends of market history, the market was clearly a market of blue chip stocks.

This emphasis on blue chips continued into 1965. A short but hurtful decline occurred during May and June when prices dropped alarmingly to bottom in a clear selling climax at the end of June. After that decline, things in the market were different. The blue chip stocks of staid, heart-of-the-economy companies in turn went begging; while the performance issues climbed steeply, the stocks of a blue hue sank steadily.

POINTS TO REMEMBER

1. Blue chip is an indefinite term. Older investors and financial analysts apply it only to stocks of the biggest and seemingly (but not necessarily truly) most staid, safest corporations.
2. But a true quality stock is one on the way up.
3. Such stocks are generally tuned to tomorrow, while blue chips tend as a group to live in today's or even under yesterday's conditions.
4. Tomorrow's stocks are likely to be those riding the latest emerging trends. They can be (and in the past have been) stocks of research-oriented scientific companies. Often today they are stocks of companies attuned to new social directions and movements.
5. One way to find such areas is to ask yourself, Where is government spending tending to grow? In such areas, the profits of tomorrow are often made.

Chapter 12 : : WHEN DOES A STOCK COST TOO MUCH?

Over the years since they first began analyzing stocks, Wall Street's pros have developed a simple and seemingly effective yardstick for deciding when any stock is a bargain or when it costs too much. This yardstick is called the price-earnings ratio and is very easy to compute. Say the price of Whistle Missile is 40 and the earnings per share are $2.50. Dividing the price by the earnings, an analyst is able to announce triumphantly to his clients, "Aha! Whistle Missile sells for fifteen times earnings."

Very simple and neat. But how high should such a ratio go? When analyzing stocks, every student of the market must eventually answer that question, "How high is too high?"

Take a stock—call it XYZ, Inc.—which is valued in the market at thirty-five times earnings. Over priced? Perhaps. Yet two years later XYZ has doubled in price. Then take another called Whoozis, Inc., which is valued at a modest ten times earnings and would therefore appear at quick glance to be much more of a bargain than XYZ and possess greater room for appreciation. Yet after the same two years have passed, there is good old Whoozis, stuck in the same price rut.

It is easy to say that XYZ, Inc., was probably a growth stock and that growth stocks should of right command higher price-earnings ratios. Few investment people would argue the proposition. But that brings up a question analysts have to solve constantly: How much higher? For how much growth? And again —how high is too high?

Wall Street's pros have many formulas for working out this

problem. Answers range all the way from intuition and feel—"I can tell when something is too high, just by feel," say some old hands—to complicated equations that call for the use of a computer to solve. But all of these are structured around that simple statistic called a price-earnings ratio, which isn't so simple at all.

To replace the bald, unadjusted PER figure arrived at by dividing earnings into market price, we have developed a plan for determining the *relative* price-earnings ratio. Most things in life are relative. An elephant of average size is "heavy" only if he is stacked against a man, a cat, or a horse. The Percheron horse is "big" only in relation to horse breeds of smaller size. And so it goes with most of the things we say, do, have, or decide in this world. They are relative.

Thus a price-earnings ratio can't be considered "high" at thirty-five unless an analyst or investor wants to establish an arbitrary norm. Once long ago people set that norm at ten times earnings and anything over ten was considered too high.

When an investor paid over that magic figure for a stock, his colleagues in high collars swiveled around at their rolltop desks and clicked their tongues. "Poor Jones," they said. "Paid too much for that stock. Bound to lose money. What will his wife and children do?"

But if Jones succeeded at some fortunate spot in buying the stock at a price-earnings ratio of seven, the same high-collared colleagues slapped him on the back in congratulations and perhaps stood him a drink at the old Waldorf bar after the market closed. It was a simpler world then and a simpler market, and, by golly, men knew what was what.

No one uses ten any longer as the magically "right" price multiple—which brings up a problem. If ten can't be defended as the arbitrary norm, then it becomes difficult to defend the use of any arbitrary number.

Relative price-earnings valuations don't use arbitrary numbers at all. They take into account a company's rate of earnings growth, compare that with the growth of average earnings in the marketplace, then see what the market at any moment, in its collective wisdom, believes to be a right price for average earnings. It next stacks exceptional (or slow, or plod-with-the-pack) earnings against this.

The computation sounds more difficult than it is; anyone with a slide rule can work it in a moment. The result is a relative figure, which informs the investor or analyst whether XYZ, Inc., enjoying earnings growth at a compounded annual rate of 24 percent, is indeed high or low by comparison with a norm that calls for earnings growth of 8.2 percent and a PER of 15.5.

(Analysts' tasks in determining what are *true* earnings in a company with large potential dilution have now been simplified. The accounting profession has adopted a rule that calls for annual statements to express earnings at both stated and after-dilution figures. If XYZ, Inc., earns one dollar per share but has potential dilution of 10 percent from conversion of preferred stock, earnings will be additionally stated as ninety cents per share after allowance for the convertible feature of the preferred stock.)

The first step in establishing a relative price-earnings ratio is to discover what investors collectively believe average earnings should be worth. The simple way to do this, since its figures are readily available, is to employ the Dow-Jones Industrial Average data.

Each Monday morning the *Wall Street Journal* publishes latest earnings figures and a price-earnings ratio for the D-J. In addition, its earnings history is available. From this data it became simple to establish that on a recent Monday morning, the Dow-Jones Industrial Average, collectively, had a compounded average earnings growth of 8.2 percent and was selling at 15.5 times latest earnings. (Compounded average earnings, in turn, are readily available from bankers' tables of compound interest such as that illustrated earlier.)

The next step is to relate this PER to the amount of compounded growth in corporate earnings. Dividing the 8.2 average compounded growth figure into the PER of 15.5 gave a *relative* ratio for the market on average. This figure was 1.9.

With such a computation we have something indicating investors' idea of the value of *average* growth against which to stack our stocks of exceptional growth. We want to determine whether, at the time of valuation, they are truly under, fairly, or overvalued. This is done by repeating the process for the stock under study. If our hypothetical XYZ, Inc., is selling at thirty-five times earnings and has a compounded average earnings growth of 24 percent (as determined by referring overall growth to a compound interest tabulation) then it has a *relative* PER of 1.46, which, for easy use, we will round off to the nearest single decimal as 1.5.

Since the number 1.5, representing the earnings valuation relative to the earnings growth, is obviously smaller than the figure of 1.9, which is the current average relative price-earnings ratio, stock of XYZ, Inc., would appear to still be undervalued in relation to what people pay for the overall market's earnings growth.

A danger in all of this, of course, is the fact that we deal with the past, and there is demonstrably no guarantee that a company that has been able to pile up average compounded growth of 24 percent over five past years will be able to do it in the next five years—or even over one year ahead.

But unless there are clouds on the corporate sky to lend doubt to XYZ management's ability to bring about continued growth, then an old dictum must be followed. "I know of no lamp to guide my steps into the future but that of the past," said a sage—and he was right.

POINTS TO REMEMBER

1. The finest stock can be a bad investment if bought at the wrong time—as when it is selling too high on a basis of price to earnings.
2. There are no precise rules to tell you how high is too high. Some stocks sell at eight times earnings and deserve no higher multiple. Some sell at twenty-five times earnings and are fairly valued at that level.
3. The difference is growth. Investors rightly put a higher price-earnings tag on a stock whose earnings are likely to be

greater in future than at present. But even these stocks can sell at multiples that are too high.

4. The relative price-earnings ratio, worked out by steps detailed in this chapter, can help to answer that vital question, "How high is too high?"

Chapter 13 : : THE RISK-REWARD RATIO

SAY YOU are in a poker game. The pot has heated up. You sit with a straight, but across the table, looming ominously, is a four-card flush. Should you call? Throw in? Part of your decision will be built on your ideas of whether the fellow with the four-flush over there is given to bluffing. Part should consist of risk-reward analysis. Without using the words, every good poker player makes these analyses many times during every night he plays.

He weighs what it may cost him to stay in the pot (risk) against the size of the pot he might eventually win (reward) should his friend with the four-flush not have a fifth heart. He takes into account the known or guessed proclivity of the other player for betting four hearts heavily when his hole card is a spade. On his analysis of risk versus reward, he calls, kicks, or folds his cards.

Investors need to weigh the potential risks against the possible rewards, too. They have to do this every time they buy a stock. They also have to do it every time they continue to hold a stock for, as one wise man said, "Don't hold a stock you wouldn't buy because if you do, you're buying it again every day it stays in your portfolio." But investors have the advantage over poker players of being able to take time out for computations.

This chapter will describe a simple system for risk-reward computation.

It would be pleasant in this uncertain and chancy world of Wall Street, where things don't have to wait for overnight to change, but frequently do so while you are looking at them, to present a plan for removing all risk and concentrating upon the more pleasant aspect of reward. The plan proposed in this chapter won't do that. However, it may increase the number of times you are rewarded and, hopefully, decrease the chances of risks becoming eventualities. If an investor chooses situations where reward potential seriously outweighs risk, he should have a better chance of compiling numbers in the profit column at year's end than if he were to buy only into fifty-fifty deals where he might lose as much as he could win.

The computation will not get you away from the hard homework of digging out facts about a company and the technical market action of its stock. But the computation should assist you to put things in perspective.

You need to answer these questions:

What is the present price of the stock?

How far might it go in a year?

What basis is there for expecting such appreciation?

What is the dollar gain that could come about?

What percentage of invested capital does this represent?

What factors would make me sell the stock?

At what price should I sell out if cutting a loss?

What is the possible dollar loss if I have to make this sale?

What percentage of invested capital is this?

The resulting gain-loss (risk-reward) ratio is a direct result of computations of the above information.

Let's take an example:

Swingeroo, Inc., is in a field that is currently very much in investor favor. It is, therefore, riding a fashion tide. As a company it is enjoying excellent earnings growth. Study of the fundamentals has convinced you that Swingeroo's best growth years may be just beginning. Yet, at the present price it is selling at a price-earnings multiple of expected earnings for the current year that makes it seem one of the market's rare bargains.

Moreover, technical study shows that it has just broken out of an important and lengthy congestion range (a wobbling back-and-forth price pattern going nowhere; congestions and how you

Stock: ____________________________

Date: ____________________

Present price: ________________

How far might it go in a year? ______

Basis for expectation ____________

____

____

Dollar gain expected: $__________

Percentage gain expected: ______ percent

Count in commissions

What would make me sell the stock?

____

____

____

At what price should I sell? ______

Possible dollar loss: $__________

Possible percentage loss: ______ percent

Gain-risk ratio: ________________

can use them profitably are discussed in the next section). Good upside potential exists. The chart says Go!

So we write down:

Stock: Swingeroo, Inc.

Date: The present. (Reason for dating such a study is that in Wall Street, as in the rest of the world, expectations as to earnings, market action, or investor favor do not always work out as infallibly as we would order them in a perfect world. You are sometimes wrong. If new and less favorable factors rear their ugly heads, you can't go on clinging to an outmoded risk-reward computation any more than you can afford to use outdated data of any other kind.)

Present price: 47.

How far might it go in a year? 71½.

Basis for expectation: Rise in earnings to $5.50, an increase that appears achievable, with price-earnings ratio of 13, a conservative multiple.

Dollar gain expected? $23.50 (in computing this, allow for commissions since these will be assessed in any event).

Percentage gain expected? 50 percent.

What would make me sell the stock? Drop in earnings and/or poor chart action indicating that, whatever the fundamentals might be, the stock did not appear a winner.

At what price should I sell to cut loss? 42.

Possible dollar loss: 6 (this allows for estimated commission cost).

Possible percentage loss: 12¾ percent.

Gain-risk ratio: 50–12¾.

A ratio like that for risk versus possible reward should tempt any investor's money. It is dependent, of course, upon careful advance homework to determine the likelihood of expected action really taking place.

Any ratio that is two to one or better is a good one. A risk-reward ratio lower than that does not allow sufficiently for the times when we poor humans err. Since, presumably, the poor humans involved in finding good stocks want to come out big winners, they have to seek big odds in their favor.

POINTS TO REMEMBER

1. It is useful to be able to measure, using numbers, the probabilities of gaining against those of losing in any proposed investment.
2. Such things as these must be weighed: expected appreciation, probable technical action, projected profit, point at which a loss would be accepted, comparison of possible loss with hoped-for profit.
3. No risk-reward ratio weighted less than two to one in favor of reward is worth accepting.
4. Computations are based upon subjective data and get out of date quickly. They must be constantly reevaluated.

SECTION III : : Make Psychology Work for You

Chapter 14 : : HOW "CROWDISM" AFFECTS YOUR INVESTMENTS

NOT LONG ago an investor asked me, "Where are the Wall Street favorites of a few years back? I remember when duPont was the hottest thing in growth stocks, when investors clamored for Gerber, when Grace was the model of a modern conglomerate, when the food stocks shared high status with the utilities. Almost without exception the companies have continued to do well. So have the industries, but where are the stocks? Where are the high price-earnings multiples of a few years ago?"

There is one answer: crowdism. These stocks were favorites but, in the fickle favor of the financial district, are now "out." Tomorrow they may be "in" once more.

Fads, whether in hula hoops or common stocks, exist because of the behavior of the crowd. It pays to know how crowds operate and how crowdism can be used to further investing success, because when the crowd begins to sell en masse, disaster can result. On the opposite side, when crowds take the bit in their teeth, they can carry a market to unreasonable heights.

We all are, for investing purposes, part of the crowd. This is true even if one is sitting in the privacy of his apartment reading the afternoon paper or is watching television at home surrounded only by his immediate family. This is true for the lonely diner in a restaurant, for the bus or subway passenger catching up on his reading on the way home, or for the salesman listening to radio news while traveling to a distant city. It is true of everyone.

Individual opinions of public figures tend to be crowd opinions that differ, generally, only insofar as the makeup of the crowds may differ. This is true for investing ideas as well. Psychologists have established certain principles about crowd thinking. A crowd has characteristics quite apart from the individual characteristics of the people who make it up. Gustave Le Bon, a turn-of-the-century French observer, was possibly the first person to apply scientific methods to the analysis of crowd behavior and his book *The Crowd* is still considered a classic by many behavioral scholars.

There are two kinds of crowds, noted Le Bon, and the kind that is of interest to investors he called a psychological crowd. This type is not always or necessarily a large group gathered together; scattered dozens of investors who have never seen or heard of each other might well constitute a psychological crowd.

Crowd behavior, said Le Bon, is never shaped by reason, and pressures that a crowd can exert will force the denial not only of logic and reason but, sometimes, the clear evidence of an individual's own eyes and ears. A British observer, reporting nearly three quarters of a century after Le Bon, told of experiment after experiment both in the United States and Britain in which people "saw" or "heard" that which group pressure told them they should have seen or heard rather than the actual evidence. In these experiments, a subject usually was brought into a room where a number of people were seated. Unknown to the subject, all the others were in on the experiment. A pair of cards was produced and each person was asked whether the lines on one card were longer than those on another. Unhesitatingly, the crowd would pick the wrong card—and the subject, faced with crowd unanimity, usually denied the plain evidence of his senses.

Le Bon noted that "a crowd scarcely distinguishes between subjective and objective. It accepts as real the images evoked in the mind, though they most often have only a distant relation with the observed fact."

In his treatise, Le Bon stated what he called the "law of crowds." A crowd has a "collective mentality which makes them think, feel and act in a manner quite different from that in which each individual would think, feel and act were he in a state of isolation," this observant Frenchman noted. He went on to describe how the crowd becomes a "provisional being formed of heterogeneous elements which for a moment are combined, exactly as the cells which constitute a living body form by their reunion a new being which displays characteristics very different from those possessed by each of the cells singly."

In crowds (even when widely scattered) the intellectual aptitude of the individual becomes weakened. "The heterogeneous is swamped by the homogeneous and the unconscious qualities obtain the upper hand." All this becomes a fact because "the individual forming part of a crowd acquires, solely from numerical considerations, a sentiment of invincible power."

Contagion and suggestibility, concluded Le Bon, play a large role in the leaping of ideas from mind to mind in a crowd. He told how "images evoked by words vary from age to age and from people to people, the formulas remaining identical. Certain transitory images are attached to certain words; the word is merely, as it were, the button of an electric bell that calls them up."

Writing a half-century after Le Bon, an American behavioral scientist described an experiment in which subjects were given a paper identified as a scientific report. The paper read by half of the group reported that subjects with high intelligence responded to *details* on Rorschach inkblot tests. The other half of the group was informed that people with high intelligence ignored details and concentrated upon the overall *form* of the blots. Both groups then were given the Rorschach inkblot test and the first group "saw" only the trivia of the blots, the second only the broad outlines.

Suggestion and contagion, in a similar manner, are powerful psychological forces in the stock market. If you say "chemical" at a moment when chemical stocks are in favor, the average investor's emotions will take over his reason. If you say "utility stock" when utilities are out of favor, the average investor will view the suggestion with disdain.

The action of group pressure to enforce group norms was revealed in another recent test. Discussion groups were set up that included persons who disagreed on questions and problems of the moment. The groups were instructed to reach an agreement if they could. Interestingly, each group reacted in the same way. At first the middle-of-the-roaders directed all discussion toward those who held extremist views. If this failed to produce a consensus, however, the crowds soon ostracized these individuals; all communication with the nonconformists was cut off.

Individuals often reach conclusions by the association of ideas, and so do the people who make up investing crowds. Has the Jones Company been accused of contributing to air pollution? Investors as a crowd tend to assume that Jones is a bad company, and Jones stock a poor investment.

Throughout the investing process, it is important to know what the crowd ideas of the moment are, for these ideas are the key to the fads that sway Wall Street values—fads that may make a group of stocks sell during one year at an average of forty-five times earnings, and during another year at twelve times earnings, even when there has been no real change in values or prospects. Utility stocks sold at very high price-earnings ratios in the early years of the Sixties when investors seemed assured of a year-to-year growth of profits stretching far into the future. These investors were right; what they foresaw did indeed come about—but woe to the utility investors of 1961 who held their utilities through later years when the darling of the crowd became a neglected outcast.

There are instances of stocks that sold for high multiples in expectation of growth that did in fact come about—stocks that today sell for half the earnings multiples of five years ago despite enhanced actual prospects. Stocks the investing crowd once regarded as worthless trash stayed on the bargain shelves at the market at six and seven times earnings until they caught the eye of the financial crowd; now these stocks sometimes sell at forty times earnings. It is important for every investor to remember that crowd psychology, more than hard facts, can make the prices of securities move.

POINTS TO REMEMBER

1. A crowd, it has been determined, is a sort of provisional person—not, usually, a very bright person and one almost completely subject to suggestion and to contagion of ideas.

2. Investors often tend to form such a crowd, even though they may be located far distant from each other. Their crowd actions then affect the trends of stock prices. It becomes necessary to understand crowd psychology to invest with success.

3. Tracing the patterns of idea contagion and susceptibility can key you in to important future price movements of stocks.

Chapter 15 : : TRAPS YOU SET FOR YOURSELF

NOT ALL of the pitfalls into which investors fall are laid for them by the workings of the market and the chances and mischances of corporate fortune. Some of the deadliest traps are those that people lay for themselves. These spring from causes deep in human psychology.

If you're going to be successful, you must avoid the following:

The Hot-tip Trap: No one thinks that he is influenced by tips. But when the brother-in-law of a director lets drop the word that Swingeroo, Inc., is going to merge with American Whatzat—that surely isn't a tip. Or is it? Think back: How many of these have you heard in boardrooms, over luncheon tables, in your office, or across a desk—and what percentage came true?

I know about rumors of a big oil find that were started by a smooth operator who knew there was nothing behind them but found occasion to pile up some personal profits that way. He always picked a small oil firm where a rumor, supposedly from inside, would generate enough buying to move the stock several points. By the time the rumor died down and the price sagged back, this fellow had picked up some nice change. Yet it surely looked like no ordinary tip at the time some cautious men, who normally would have made no move without careful investigation, bought heavily.

Sit around the boardroom of any brokerage office for a few days, even a few hours, with your ears open. You will hear rumors and tips by the dozen. These are hardest to ignore when they come from a person you know to be intelligent and thoroughly honest. Just remember that someone less intelligent or honest may have roped him in.

And ask yourself, "Why is this fellow doing me the big favor of letting me in on the news? Is it so I can make a profit—or so he can? Or did he learn it honestly but inaccurately himself?"

The Ride-off-in-all-directions-at-once Trap: There are many accounts whose owners are seeking long-term growth—and who hold for that purpose such staid and steady breadwinners as American Telephone and Telegraph. This is meant as no back-hand slap at any of the gilt-edge securities. If you seek steady, dependable income with minimum risk of capital, they are for you. They are known in the investment business as widows' and orphans' securities. They are not for the investor who seeks capital gains.

Neither are uranium, volatile electronics, or fast-moving (and risky) young firms recommended for the conservative investor who wants solid dividends without risk or worry.

The important thing is to determine where you want to go, then pick investments for carrying you there. Have an objective clearly in mind every time you make a purchase.

The Conventional-wisdom Trap: Wall Street is full of "wisdom" that is plausible and persuasive. Many sayings we learned at our fathers' financial knees and they seem true with the dignity of age: "If you buy stocks only to sell them you're a speculator." "Get a sound, steady income and pay no attention to market fluctuations." "Never touch principal." And others.

The cold, calculating mind that is usually successful along Wall Street does not reject or accept any of these blindly. It applies (or rejects) each in the light of the particular situation. Sometimes it pays you to hold a stock for years; other times, the maximum result is achieved in months and holding it for years produces only losses. Each case should be considered separately.

The Hog Trap: I know one man who considers himself an investor. But he is known around the brokerage offices he frequents as a lunch-hour trader. "He comes in promptly at noon," one broker told me, "buys something and sits down to watch the board. If the stock is not up by one o'clock, he sells. He seldom makes enough on even his best deals to pay our commissions."

Of course a lunch-hour trader is a rarity. But trying for the fast buck can wreck an investment program. It is an adage with some Wall Street people that patience is worth more than brains. Another Wall Street adage that applies here is, "A bull can make money, a bear can make money—but not a hog."

The I-won't-take-a-loss Trap: One of the toughest things for any of us—investor or baseball player, executive, doctor, lawyer, or Indian chief—is to stand up in public and confess, "I was wrong. I goofed it." That's what you have to do when you sell a stock at a loss. Before selling it, you have the comforting but fallacious thought that no loss exists unless it is "realized" by a sale. That is balderdash, of course, but it comforts the ego. When you sell, you have to step from behind that flimsy shield and admit you were wrong.

I've heard it put this way by many investors, "I can't sell that stock as you advise. I'd have a loss. Let's wait until it comes back to what I paid for it."

Often, of course, the stock never comes back to that point. The plain fact is that a loss exists whether you realize it by converting the loss into cash or whether you continue to hold the stock. All you have is the market value of the stock right now. The question then becomes, Will you recoup this loss best by holding the same stock or by taking the loss (and obtaining a tax deduction) and reinvesting in something else that is on the way up?

The Loyalty Trap: It seems foolish to give loyalty to a piece of paper, but people do this. "I have to hang on to Amalgamated Nowhere," one investor told me. "My father bought it back in 1920 and he thought a lot of the company and its prospects. 'Twouldn't be right to sell the stock."

While this investor's father perhaps had sound reason to be impressed by Amalgamated Nowhere fifty years ago, in 1970 there remains nothing for an investor to like about it. Keeping the certificate amounts to being loyal to a piece of paper. Doing so certainly inhibits investment results.

As soon as the times turn against an industry or an individual company, a smart investor or trader quickly sells those stocks. He stays with an investment only as long as it is good and wastes no emotion on a security that has fallen upon sour times. As a result few pros ever ride an investment up, then ride it right back down again. They look for and recognize the cloud no bigger than a man's hand when it first appears on the horizon, scudding for shelter long before the storm is apparent to everyone.

The Committed-capital Trap: Most successful Wall Streeters are restless men. They like to keep moving, to stay where the action is, and if you're going to be as successful on your scale as they are on theirs, you will have to do this also.

Keeping capital in motion doesn't call for aimless, continual switching about. It does call for a weather eye out for stagnation after an upward movement in a stock. Sometimes these stagnant, sidewise movements last for months, even years. It makes sound sense to switch capital out of a stock that is floundering in such a sidewise congestion and invest it instead in the next strong upward mover.

The High-yield Trap: You can always find investments that pay bigger dividends or yield greater interest than the going rates that equivalent securities bring in the market at the time. You court serious trouble if you buy these.

Usually that yield is high because, in the opinions of professional money managers, there is danger to the situation. Earnings may not be covering the yield and it may later be reduced. There could be other factors you haven't seen on the surface that make the pros shy away. It seldom pays to rush in where they fear to tread.

(However, sometimes there is merit to such a situation and the pros have muffed it. If careful analysis convinces you that what is frightening them has already been corrected, you can often make a minor killing by purchasing what the pros don't want.

But investigate carefully. They didn't become professionals by being wrong too much of the time.)

The Over-diversification Trap: Sometimes four or five stocks, carefully chosen, give good diversification, and if they are "in" stocks currently moving upward, an investor is better off with this seemingly limited list than with an over-diversified group that gives only average results or less.

The Averaging-down Trap: An amateur and a professional both purchase one hundred shares of Swingeroo, Inc., at 20. It subsequently declines to 17. At or before this point, the pro is likely to cut his loss by selling, but the amateur feels that he has been presented a bargain opportunity and buys more. He has "averaged down" by bringing the average cost of his shares below his original purchase. But his average cost is still below the market and, worse, he has assumed the risk of buying into a declining situation.

Should events go the other way, with Swingeroo rising to 23, probabilities are that the professional may buy more to "average up."

True, he has paid more for his second purchase, but he has an average cost below the market and is buying into an improving situation.

It is not the mere mechanics of this that distinguishes amateur and professional—for pros will occasionally, for good reason, break the rule and also average down—but the hard-headed thinking of the professional who waits for evidence of improvement before adding to a commitment and generally avoids increasing his investment in a worsening area.

POINTS TO REMEMBER

1. Your biggest enemy in the search for investing success may be yourself. Certain psychological traps people lay for themselves spring from causes deep in human psychology.

2. One group of such traps begins with greed. Another is built

upon fear. A man's greeds and fears can whipsaw him back and forth, in and out of stocks, preventing normal success.

3. Awareness of the personal psychological traps—particularly the ten enumerated here—is the first step in keeping the greeds and fears from taking over. Wall Street has a saying: "A bull can make money, a bear can make money. But not a hog." Nor a timorous mouse.

Chapter 16 : : TRAPS THE MARKET LAYS

CAMPAIGNING FOR success in the conquest of Wall Street means constant awareness of the booby traps and pitfalls that lie in wait for unwary would-be capitalists. Some of these traps are laid by the functioning of the market mechanism itself. Others are laid by your own unconscious and conscious yearnings, fears, and greed. In this chapter, we will look at ways to avoid the traps that the market lays.

The Panic Trap: Black panic hit the stock market back on a day in 1955 when news broke that the then President of the United States, Dwight Eisenhower, had suffered a heart attack. Prices on the New York Stock Exchange tumbled and volume on the downside was at a record high. All over the country, men stood in sober small groups watching the tape in brokers' boardrooms and watching their investment values dwindle away in minutes.

"My friend," I heard one man tell a broker, "when I go back to my office, have the porter mop up here. I've been bleeding all over your place."

Following the crowd in selling cost untold hundreds of millions of dollars to investors that day. But countering the crowd, a small group of much wiser investors bought, and mopped up sizable profits before many months had passed by going counter to the trend and recognizing the limits of crowd psychology.

The Crowd Psychology Trap: In an earlier chapter, I discussed some of the findings of psychologists and behavioral scientists about crowd psychology. These indicated that a crowd becomes a sort of provisional single person, endowed with the brains of its lowest members and subject to being led about by any who choose to steer its paths. The findings show that all of us are parts of crowds and subject to being swayed by what we read, see, and are told.

It seldom fails that the soothsayers of Wall Street foresee the sunniest kinds of future skies just when the skies are about to cloud over and storms start to build. They see nothing but gloom ahead just when the sun is starting to come through the clouds. During a recent bear market, I wrote:

> On the economic front, things could not look gloomier. However, that is the way they always look when the market is around its worst in the same way that things look economically cheeriest at a top. I don't believe the market is ready to turn up on a long-term basis—yet. But I don't see things as hopeless and, in fact, have been laying strategy plans for what to do when the bull trend appears to have returned.

The Hidden Poor-earnings Trap: Recently, I was looking over the earnings statement of a leading company. "Best earnings yet," crowed the president's report to stockholders. And he was indeed right on the basis of a full year's figures, for the company's earnings were more than 10 percent higher than in the previous year. However, the third and fourth quarters were down from year-earlier figures and the fourth quarter was particularly dismal because earnings had slid off to practically nothing.

When a company ceases to grow, the halt may be only momentary, or it may be the first sign of sickness setting in. A wise investor thinks hard about a holding whose per share earnings have dropped for more than two consecutive quarters, and does not let soothing sayings of Wall Street pundits and corporation officials deter him from applying further tests—particularly technical ones—with an eye to possibly bidding good-bye to what had once been a good friend.

Careful observance of this rule helped investors to avoid later grief in many one-time growth stocks, such as airlines in 1966.

The Trap of Idiotic Buying: A Wall Street old-timer of my acquaintance is fond of saying, "When idiots are buying a stock, it is time to let them have mine." It is this financial analyst's way of warning against buying, or even continuing to hold, stocks with astronomical price-earnings ratios.

A few such blue chip growth stocks as Internationl Business Machines and Avon Products have held up in price or even advanced when they were selling at fifty, sixty, and seventy times earnings. But in general, any price-earnings ratio above twenty is fully valued for new buying. Above thirty is a definite danger sign that the buying is becoming idiotic, for such discounting of growth too far into the future does not allow for unexpected earnings stumbles.

To avoid the idiotic buying trap, check the technical tests and be ready if necessary to bail out in a hurry.

The Ease-of-accessibility Trap: When anybody can get into an act, then a company's products or services stand in danger of becoming price footballs. Still, people are fooled every day in Wall Street into paying to buy stock participation in "growing" industries that any firm with a few thousands as a stake is able to enter.

An investment is safer—and the accessibility trap avoided—when the cost to compete gets into tens of millions and the technical expertise is so complicated that few will want to try hard competition.

The Milk-it-for-everything-it's-got Trap: Bernard Baruch once said he had observed that consistent buying at bottoms and selling at tops could only be done by liars. The smart investor or trader is willing to buy a little too late and sell a little too soon because he knows that in such a policy lies safety.

The Ride-it-down-because-it-will-come-back Trap: Wall Streeters have a saying: It doesn't pay to fight the tape. (The tape is the movement of prices.) A group of very wealthy men didn't have enough money in 1929 to fight it successfully. An average amateur investor isn't likely to have enough money either.

When the tape and your charts say that the market is having a serious sinking spell—sell. You can always buy back tomorrow if you prove wrong, and if you should be right you will probably be able to buy a lot more stock for the same money after a bottom has been made.

While there is a constant ebb and flow of investment favor in even the strongest of upward bull movements, a downward market crash such as those of 1962, 1966, or 1969 may carry everything away with it as a tidal wave would engulf the good and the bad in its path.

The Catapult Trap: When a stock catapults in the reverse of the direction you're playing it for—catapulting downward from congestion when you are holding it long and betting it will reach the top edge of the chart, or catapulting upward when you have sold it short—then the signal to bid a swift farewell to old Swingeroo has been flashed in your face.

But not all investors spot such signals or do so quickly enough. Even technically oriented investors sometimes goof such a get-out message.

It pays, therefore, to keep up with the charts and always to be aware of the spots at which a move would become a catapult.

The Unnoticed-change Trap: Every change affects the climate of your investments. It may denote a turning down for one area in which you are interested. Or it may give a peep through a door opening into new opportunity. Life is full of changes. Keeping a lookout for them and analyzing to determine whether they should be acted upon is a way of life for the calculating, cold, successful investor whose object is avoidance of the Street's traps and pitfalls.

POINTS TO REMEMBER

1. Certain traps and dangers are inherent in the workings of the market itself, and as long as stock markets mirror the hopes, alarms, knowledge and ignorance of a wide cross-section of America, this will continue to be so.
2. The panic trap, the crowd-psychology trap, the hidden poor-

earnings trap, the trap of idiotic buying, the ease of accessibility trap, the milk-it-for-everythings-it's-got trap, the ride-it-down-because-it-will-come-back trap, the catapult trap, and the trap of unnoticed change can each or collectively cause you to stumble on the road to investing success.

3. As with the traps an investor lays for himself, awareness of these pitfalls puts the alert investor or trader ahead of the game.

Chapter 17 : : THE KINDS OF STOCKS IN FAVOR

MILLIONS OF us were taught in school that the shortest distance between two points is a straight line. But the fastest time is not always the same thing. The fastest time to make big gains may be a hot industry, provided the two points you wish to connect are your present financial state and a state of increased net worth.

In other words, from here to success may be, as for many in Wall Street it has been in the past, stocks in an industry traveling faster than the rest of the stocks on the Board.

There are two kinds of industry action you will need to study to find such stocks. The first is whether the new little stocks of the far-out firms are in favor, or whether investor tastes are running to blue-chip stocks. Second, you must discover the kind of stocks—automotive, or hamburger, or research and development—which basks most warmly in the moving sunshine of Wall Street.

Blue Chips or Speculative Stocks? When stock prices began to move up, feebly at first, then faster, from the shattering bottom of the big 1962 bear market, investors were disillusioned with many things about Wall Street. Not least were they disenchanted with the frenzied speculation in growth issues that had preceded the 1962 drop. As prices appreciated with gathering momentum in one of the big, sustained trends of market history, it was clearly a market of blue chip stocks at Broad and Wall. Growth issues, hot issues, performers, and swingers of all kinds now went begging.

This condition continued into 1965. Then there was a short but hurtful decline during May and June when prices dropped alarmingly to bottom at June's end. After that the market was different. The blue chip stocks of staid, heart-of-the-economy companies in their turn went begging.

Throughout stock market history one of the two types of investments receives the attention and regard of both public and professionals. Either it is a market of blue chips, as it was from the end of 1962 until mid-1965, or it is a market of growth stocks as it was after mid-1965.

Knowing which it is at any given moment can make a whopping difference in investment results. But how can you tell?

What is needed is a simple, single yardstick. This has been developed by constructing an index to measure the ratio of relative interest. Two scales are required to construct this yardstick, since the analyst must know what is going on in both growth stocks and blue chips in order to express relative action as a ratio.

Start with the Dow-Jones Industrial Average as a representative measuring scale of stock market blue chips. Components of this old, widely quoted average are the upper-crust corporations of American industry. The average comprises Allied Chemical; Aluminum Company of America; American Can; American Telephone and Telegraph; American Tobacco; Anaconda; Bethlehem Steel; Chrysler; duPont; Eastman Kodak; the three Generals, Electric, Foods, and Motors; Goodyear; International Harvester; International Nickel; International Paper; Johns-Manville; Owens-Illinois; Procter and Gamble; Sears Roebuck; Standard Oil of California; Standard Oil (New Jersey); Swift; Texaco; Union Carbide; United Aircraft; U.S. Steel; Westinghouse Electric; and Woolworth.

A growth stock index provides the other side of the ratio. Ours is an index (not an average) of thirty performers in which the advances and declines of each week are balanced off and the plus or minus differential is put into a cumulative differential line in the same way that other indexes employing this technique are computed. It is easy to maintain such an index without resort to chart paper. All the investor requires is a weekly comparison of gains and losses among any thirty (the number could be twenty or forty if he chose) growth stocks. Such a price comparison can be made in minutes from the weekly market statistics that newspapers carry.

The level of the growth stock index is divided each week by the closing price of the Dow-Jones Industrial Average. The result is the growth stock-blue chip index.

When this index rises, it indicates that investors are bidding with greater fervor for growth stocks than for staid blue chips. When it declines, you know that money is reaching for the bluer stocks rather than the corporate performers.

The weekly changes have little significance. It pays to look at this index over a broader, longer period of time.

Which Industries Are in Favor? Watching an industry in investor favor is like watching a runaway team of horses drag a stagecoach on a TV western. That coach, previously lumbering along, goes at a mighty clip. Sometimes the enthusiasm of the horses carries too far, and they pull the coach and its occupants over a cliff—with unhappy results for all except the few passengers nimble enough to hop off in time.

If you read "public" for horses, and "industry" for stagecoach, you have a good simile to what happens in the stock market when investing enthusiasm drags a group of stocks along at a rapid clip.

Whether the public turns out to have been right or wrong matters as little as the judgment of the horses in a sagebrush saga. The result is a fast ride. And sometimes a crash at the end.

However, if you can get aboard the industry coach when it begins its breakneck ride and nimbly hop off before the cliff edge looms, then the result is likely to be riches.

This is a neat trick, if you can do it. The answer might be provided by momentum studies. When he compiled the dictionary that sits on my desk, Webster defined momentum as "the impetus of a moving object; the quantity of impetus of a moving object, equal to the product of its mass and its velocity." But in Wall Street, momentum is something quite different.

Momentum shows relative action of a group of stocks compared to the average of the whole market. Your objective should be to invest in stock groups that can compile gains 10 percent, 20 percent, maybe even 50 percent or 100 percent better than the whole market is doing.

Two things are required. The first is a small library of charts, which show the price action of a number of industry groups such as the steel stocks, auto stocks, television stocks, copper stocks, etc. Many subscribe to a technical service that offers them. Or, you can keep them yourself from figures on group averages offered in financial publications.

These charts tell if an industry group is in a basically bullish or bearish path. The trend is bullish if there is a pattern of ever-higher tops and ever-higher bottoms. Similarly, a trend is bearish if each top is lower than the one that precedes it, and if the bottoms are made at ever-dropping levels.

Where there is no pattern at all—if the chart makes only small, generally sidewise ups and downs—the trend of that industry group average is neutral.

Observation of these things can tell even one who is unfamiliar with chart reading whether an industry group is moving satisfactorily upward, whether it's declining, or whether it's in one of those drawn-out frustrating sidewise movements that lead nowhere. But it won't measure momentum. To do that, an investor needs a second kind of chart. With practice, momentum charts are surprisingly simple to maintain.

First note the percentage of appreciation or loss on the New York Stock Exchange Index, or any other standard market measuring stick you may choose. Note closing price for the week under study, and compare it with the closing price of a week earlier.

If your market average went up, the price increase is divided by the preceding week's level and the result is a percentage of gain. If it went down, the same procedure is followed to obtain the percentage of loss on the market as a whole. The computation takes thirty seconds, if you use a slide rule.

Percentage of gain or loss for the group under study is computed in the same manner.

Did the industry average do better than the market as a whole? Worse? Or was its performance the same? If your market average dropped 2 percent and the electrical industry average, for example, went down 1 percent, that industry average did better than the market, even though it went down during the period.

If the industry average did better than the market, it is rated plus, if worse—minus, and an even-stephen performance receives a neutral rating. No attention is paid to the degree by which the industry average performed better or worse. The plus or minus is then put into a cumulative differential line.

While the momentum chart continues to ascend, an investor knows that he is looking at an industry group that enjoys market favor. Buyers are bidding more forcefully to get stocks in this field. The stocks are "in." Later, as the momentum curve rounds over and drops, it depicts a drying up of investor favor.

While an industry remains in favor, that favor is likely to make almost everything in the industry move. Often, in a hot industry, the buying momentum will eventually drag along just about every stock in the field.

POINTS TO REMEMBER

1. A quick way to profits is to go along with industries that are in favor. Usually some in the group will be better than others. But in most cases, all stocks of the group will benefit from the trend.

2. First decide whether it is a market of blue chip stocks or a market of more speculative growth-type issues. A growth stock–blue chip index, studied week by week, can clue you in so that you won't find yourself seeking the growth stocks when blue chips

occupy market attention, or buying blue chip stocks when all the action is in swingers and performers.

3. Within that context, study industry group charts. Discard any which are not in clear bullish patterns.

4. Carry this on another step. Study *momentum* to discover whether a group appears to be advancing at a steadily faster clip than the market as a whole is moving. It is in the stocks of such a group that bigger, better profits are often to be found.

Chapter 18 : : THE OPPORTUNITIES THAT PANIC OFFERS

Panic happens when a crowd's mass fears are carried to their ultimate extreme. Wild *enthusiasm* occurs when the same investing crowd is so carried away by its liking for a stock, a group, or the enjoyable idea of owning all stock certificates, that caution becomes utterly lost.

The effects of panic and wild enthusiasm are visible through timing studies and furnish unusual long-term opportunities to buy (when everybody has panicked to such an extreme that cool heads step in to pick up the bargains) or sell (when the enthusiasm has reached a peak so hectic that the same cool heads are disposing of their stocks because they believe unbridled collapse will follow unbridled boom).

Market gloom was at its worst for the year in the last week of June, 1965, and some investors were dumping stocks in panic when a few astute technical students spotted what proved to be the bargain of the year for stocks of high quality. Investors who bought General Motors around 91 saw their stock at 112 seventeen short weeks later. The occurrence that had so excited technicians and indicated a bottom for General Motors was classic "spin-on-a-dime" action. Some analysts call this action a climax. The semantics of the situation are less important to a technical student than the ability to analyze it correctly, for correct analysis of spin-on-a-dime action can lead to profits that are both quick and sizable. Climactic action able to make a market spin on a dime comes as a result of panic at a bottom, or unfettered, frenzied enthusiasm at a top.

The ability to spot a topping formation of this type helps investors pin down accumulated gains close to an absolute high. Such a spin-on-a-dime top occurred in American-South African Investment, a closed-end trust listed on the New York Stock Exchange. This occurred shortly after the bottoming action in General Motors. An upside sensation of 1965, ASA increased in value from around 40 to a lofty top at 76 toward the end of 1965, rising most spectacularly while the general market dropped in the early summer of 1965. At the end of July, ASA put on a booming fireworks display. The price zoomed straight upward from 60 to 74 in two weeks. Volume was enormous. Over a four-week period, with large volume lending interest to its gyrations, American-South African darted up and down around its top. After the climax, it dropped to 65. There it encountered minor support for four weeks, but the support level was broken, and with a thud the stock fell to 58, to 56, and finally to 52.

Technical analysts who were able to recognize the four-week action, with a churning range and high volume, as a somewhat drawn-out spin-on-a-dime (or climax) pattern were able to sell for maximum gains.

These technical formations are indeed profit-makers and profit-preservers, yet they are as difficult to diagnose as anything an investor will encounter. Here are some of the signs by which analysts know them:

1. A climax top must be explosive. The price should literally jump upward.

2. Volume should be similar to the price action—explosive. It should increase as suddenly as the price and, of course, simultaneously.

3. A climactic bottom is built in the same way. The price drops suddenly and sickeningly. It is as if the earth had opened up and a heavy object was hurtling down the resulting chasm. An observer might conclude that there was no bottom at all.

4. Spin-on-a-dime bottoms have volume similar to that at a top. It is generally greater than any volume along the preceding down movement.

5. Sometimes the run-up—or decline in the case of a downside

spin-on-a-dime—lasts only a single day. It might last a week; the bottoming climax action for General Motors showed as a single neat line on a weekly chart. It might even last two weeks, occasionally three or four, as happened with the top action for American-South African in 1965.

6. The crucial turning week usually has the greatest volume of all. During this week the price moves relentlessly upward—if we are watching a buying climax—with apparently no ceiling. With volume very high, the price then "churns," moving around in a restricted range but with abnormal, inflated volume. In a typical action the price might close in the middle of its range although such a close is by no means necessary to prove a genuine spin-on-a-dime formation.

During a climax the same type of action is occurring as that found at reversal formations and other turning points. Instead of being spread out over weary months, the struggle—between bulls eager to exchange their dollars for stock and bears with stock certificates they want to sell—takes place in a short space of time. The volume that might otherwise have been extended over a long period occurs with a sudden splash.

Analysts look for quick, explosive movement that continues an existing upward or downward trend but is entirely out of proportion to the size of previous movements in the trend, volume that dwarfs anything seen during the trend, and a churning around and a change of direction. Experts in timing study look, moreover, for all these signs to occur within one, two, or three weeks. The signs occasionally occur within a single climax day.

The spin-on-a-dime is the hardest of all technical actions to spot when it is happening and is the most potentially profitable to an investor who is knowledgeable enough to recognize it. Not all concentrated moves are genuine climaxes. Not all increased volume will bring a turn in direction. Mistakes in calling a climax correctly often come from impatience; an amateur sees things happening and, in eagerness, makes a decision before all of the facts are in. Climax action is not rare, but it is not usual either, and it must have churning, rather than continuing, price action to have meaning.

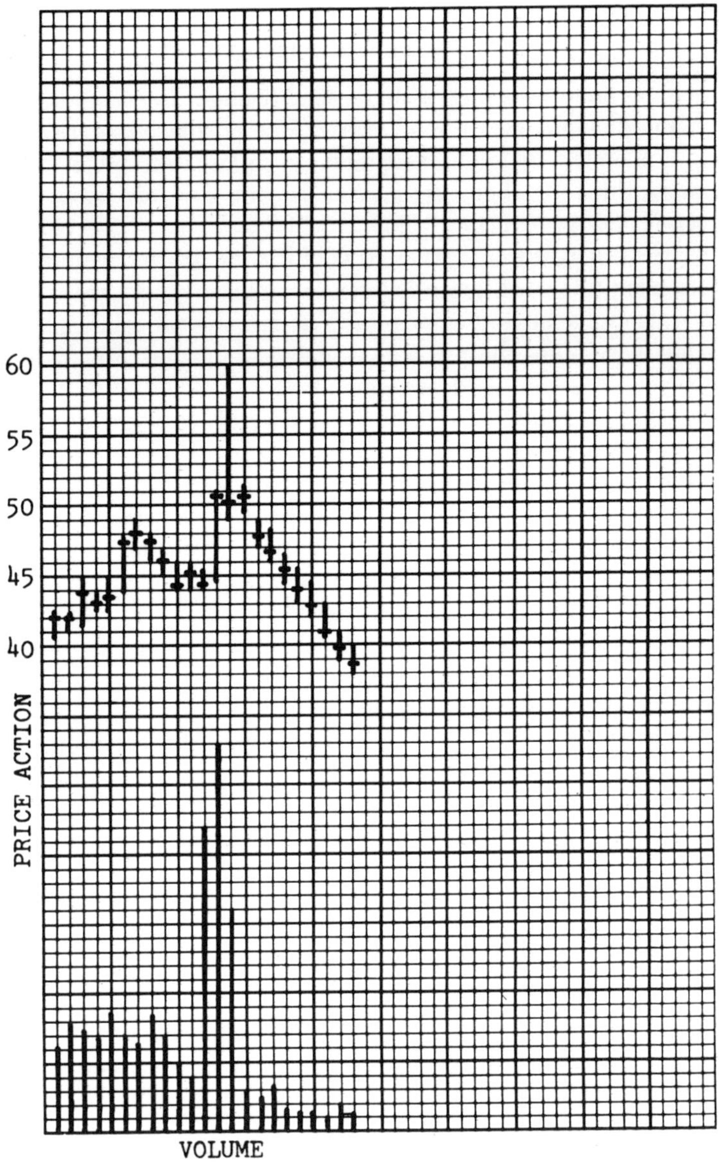

A climax top like this (there are also climax bottoms) packs all of the action that might have been spread out over months of slower trading into one or two weeks—sometimes only a day. Here, volume shot up on the sudden, climactic increase in price. But in the key week, prices churned about, made no further headway, closed far below the top after hectic trading had subsided. After that, prices sank tiredly.

An astute analyst is often able to call a climax at the top or bottom. If an investor waits for a consolidation to follow the churning turn, however, he can be surer of the signal. Such consolidation often takes place. Should it occur, a technician would mark his chart with the resistance level of the consolidation if it is a bottom that he believes will turn up, or the lower support of the consolidation if he suspects that spin-on-a-dime action has ended an upward movement. When, and if, these levels are broken, he can then move with probabilities on his side. His best evidence, however, will be the climax itself.

POINTS TO REMEMBER

1. When public psychology goes too far in one direction, panic results. Too far in the other direction often brings about *unbridled enthusiasm.*
2. Both can be clues to profit by determining what is going on in the market itself, or in the price action of an individual stock.
3. Stocks bought at times of panic tend to show future profits. At times of wild enthusiasm, wise investing heads often sell stocks. "When fools are bidding for stocks, they can have mine," said such an old hand.
4. Typical signs of a panic turnaround at a bottom or a wild enthusiasm turnaround at a top include "churning" action of the price after a big drop (or rise) in a short period of time.

Chapter 19 : : IS THE PUBLIC EVER RIGHT?

A STORY has been knocking around Wall Street for decades to the effect that the public is always wrong. Anyone who has been in the Street for very long knows that 'tain't so—not always, at any rate. The public will generally prove to be spectacularly right during a long market rise. But it tends to be wrong at crucial turning points by letting its enthusiasm cloud its judgment when judgment should be saying "Beware!" And it sometimes lets its pessimism cloud that same judgment at the spots where stock prices bottom and the buying would be best.

That is why it pays an investor to know about "odd lot" study and the study of speculative fever. Both can be followed from statistics that are available in most city newspapers.

By tracking the public with these two tools, it is possible to know something of its thinking and to appraise the point at which public emotions have reached an excess stage, indicating that a crucial turn—when the public will be wrong—is building.

Basic to each field of study is an assumption that holds that the odd-lotter is likely to be a public rather than a professional investor and, furthermore, that the buyer of low-priced "cats-and-dogs" is also more likely to be a member of the public than a professional.

Odd-lotters behave in a generally predictable way. They boil with enthusiasm at bull market tops. They walk and talk with gloom at bear market bottoms. When a market tops, this occurrence does not immediately spell odd-lotter enthusiasm. The odd-lotters continue buying on what they believe to be temporary dips as prices slide off. Only later do these investors turn bearish and dump stocks. After this point, the odd-lotters are right throughout the bear leg—but they are not right at its turn.

When the new bull market begins, it is some time before the odd-lotter is convinced that the sun is indeed shining once more on the financial scene. Thus, the odd-lotter is right all during the long legs of up-and-down swings but tends to be enthusiastically wrong when the market presents him with a long-term opportunity to realize profits (at a bull market top) or initiate new positions (at a bear market bottom).

Analysts have worked out many ways to handle the raw statistics of odd lot activity. Most employ them in a ratio. The construction of such a ratio, like the rationale behind odd lot study and, indeed, the interpretation of odd lot data in general, calls for an assumption. The assumption this time is that the odd-lotter normally buys approximately 10 percent more stock than he sells. This is not because he is tenacious; rather, it is based upon the idea that stocks, accumulated as odd lots, are usually sold later in round lots and do not show up as sales on the odd lot statistics.

Most analysts compute an odd lot ratio in this manner: they utilize the number of shares *sold* during the period under study. This period might be a week or a day, although generally a weekly computation of market statistics tends less to random whipsaws. The figure is then divided by shares *bought.* It is important to work with shares, not dollars, in each case because to do otherwise would be like comparing apples with oranges. Dividing the number of shares sold by the number of shares bought gives a ratio. Since the assumption is that the odd-lotter normally buys about 10 percent more shares than he sells, the ratio, when it stands at .91, is "even."

As long as the index remains above this median you know that participation of the odd lot public in a bull market is not excessive. Most students of odd lot behavior ignore as random a drop below median that lasts only a few weeks. But when the index stays consistently below median, public participation in an up movement is becoming very hot.

Odd lot study is a long-range indicator. The professionals of the trade know that, after a danger signal, it can be long months before a top is reached. The index is thus a long-range tool for spotting regions where danger or opportunity exists.

Another form of odd lot study embraces short-selling activities. The assumption is the same as with other odd lot research: that the public buyer of odd lots is not always wrong, but will be when it is most important to be right. One of the earliest signs of the October recovery from the long 1966 decline was a spurt in odd lot short selling. "There just isn't enough room in the market for that many uninformed people to be right," one old pro commented at the time of the turn.

A speculative fever index is similar to the odd lot index in being based upon an empirical assumption. This assumption is that the public is likely to dabble in low-priced stocks, often called cats and dogs, to a greater extent than do the cool, hardheaded professionals. The public does this, according to the assumption, because they like the feeling of owning many shares and because there is apt to be more action in cats and dogs.

Unusually large public activity in low-priced stocks of dubious quality is likely to occur at a crucial turning point. As in the case of the odd-lotter who is right all through a movement but likely to be wrong at its culmination, speculative fever in low-priced stocks reaches a frenzied pitch when a top-heavy bull market is at its weakest point.

Activity in the low-priced stocks can be measured with the help of a number of indexes of low-priced stocks published by news media and statistical services. These can be used in their "raw" state to measure public activity in the cheaper stocks. As soon as an investor does this, however, he finds that certain complications arise. If the market is on a strong uptrend, the cat and dog index should normally also rise. What, then, would constitute a degree of rise indicating heightened speculative fever in low-priced stocks?

The speculative fever index is constructed by taking any index of low-priced stocks and dividing it each week by the closing price of the Dow-Jones Industrial Average. The Industrials represent, by and large, a segment of blue chip stocks of the type that attract many institutional buyers. If the ratio rises from one week to another, this will indicate that the rise in participation in low-priced stocks has exceeded the rise in participation in blue chips.

One week, or even two or three weeks of this type of action, indicates nothing. But when the level of this ratio continues to climb it becomes clear that activity in low-priced stocks is consistently greater than that in the solid blue chips that are the backbone of the economy.

Continued upward movement of this ratio shows that the public is strongly involved in the market. The speculative fever index, however, does more than merely corroborate the verdict of the odd lot index: it indicates how frenzied the public activity has become.

Like odd lot study and unlike some other forms of chart analysis, the speculative fever index does not clang a signal that says a bear market is here or that the market has turned to the bullish side after a protracted downturn. It is a long-range indicator. Markets often remain strong for months, sometimes even a year or more, after developing dangerous speculative fever. During this time, the index permits an analysis of public activity and indicates the degree of public buying and selling. Most important, the index will give a feel for the type of areas in which important tops occur.

POINTS TO REMEMBER

1. A Wall Street saying holds that the public is always wrong. This saying is itself wrong. But the public is frequently wrong at vital turning points, and if you can spot such times, you can make profits by going counter to the public's actions.
2. Odd lots are purchases and sales of stocks in less than round lot (generally one hundred-share) size. Premise of odd lot study is that it is usually the public, not professionals, who deal in odd lots.
3. Whenever, therefore, odd lot behavior becomes excessive in buying or selling, a turning point may be at hand.
4. Such turning points do not as a usual thing come immediately. Odd lot study is a long-range proposition.

Chapter 20 : : CAN STOCK CHARTS REALLY HELP?

THERE IS a considerable body of analytical opinion among pundits who form the national Financial Analysts' Federation—the pros of the trade in picking stocks—which holds that the stock price outlook cannot be determined by chart analysis. The more academically inclined have conducted tests with computers that prove that stock prices are a "random walk" and thus any movements must be trendless.

But among the young Turks of the slide rule and stock chart, a different opinion is held. These aggressive, often younger, analysts hold that the thing that makes price movements happen is less a balance of supply-demand factors for a company's products than the balance between supply (shares for sale) and demand (dollars seeking investments) at Broad and Wall streets. These analysts are not lacking in computer time of their own and their computerized research has tended to prove that stock prices are not a random walk.

Each side to the argument has said, in gentlemanly fashion of course, that its opponents have researched the question less to find facts than to prove a point. So is the whole matter up in the air? Not necessarily.

We have gone back over five years of extensive chart records to pull out every important signal on charts of the thirty big corporations that comprise the Dow-Jones Industrial Average.

Only upside signals and positions were considered because short selling is seldom done by the general public and almost never by the institutional investor.

Only completed movements, those culminating in recognizable "sell" signals, were considered. This rules out many that were still under way at the time of compilation.

Although the "trend line" is a basic tool of chartists, trend-line breaks were not considered as primary buy signals since so many of these result in sidewise consolidation movements rather than reversal moves. An exception was the breaking of "fan lines"—three ever-flatter trend lines—which are a recognized change-of-direction signal.

Altogether, seventy-four major-trend bar chart buy signals occurred in the thirty D-J stocks during the five-year study period. Taking these to the culmination of each move, they resulted in a total profit of 1,034.00 points with a loss, to the end of the move, of 8 points. Average profit from the bar chart signals was $13.97, with an offsetting average loss of $0.11 per transaction.

Profits, of course, seldom run to the very top of any movement and not even the most eager of technicians would claim consistent ability to sense long-term tops. So the seventy-four trades were considered a second way, more realistic than measuring to a top. From buy signal to sell signal the seventy-four D-J transactions would have produced an overall profit of 545.75 points. Loss on the unprofitable trades would have totaled 47.50 points for our theoretical trader buying the industrials on bar chart signals. On this more reasonable basis profits averaged $7.37, losses $0.64, for a net average profit of $6.73.

The bar chart signals considered were breaking of an intermediate resistance level; the head and shoulders bottom; the rounding bottom; rectangle breakouts; breakouts from a bar chart triangle; fan line signals.

A word about these "signals":

The bar chartist uses a piece of paper ruled both horizontally and vertically. He scales the paper vertically for prices, horizontally for periods of time. The period of time can be a day, a week, a month. Sometimes daily charts are too sensitive and they always take more trouble to maintain. Monthly charts are downright insensitive. Therefore, weekly charts were used in this study.

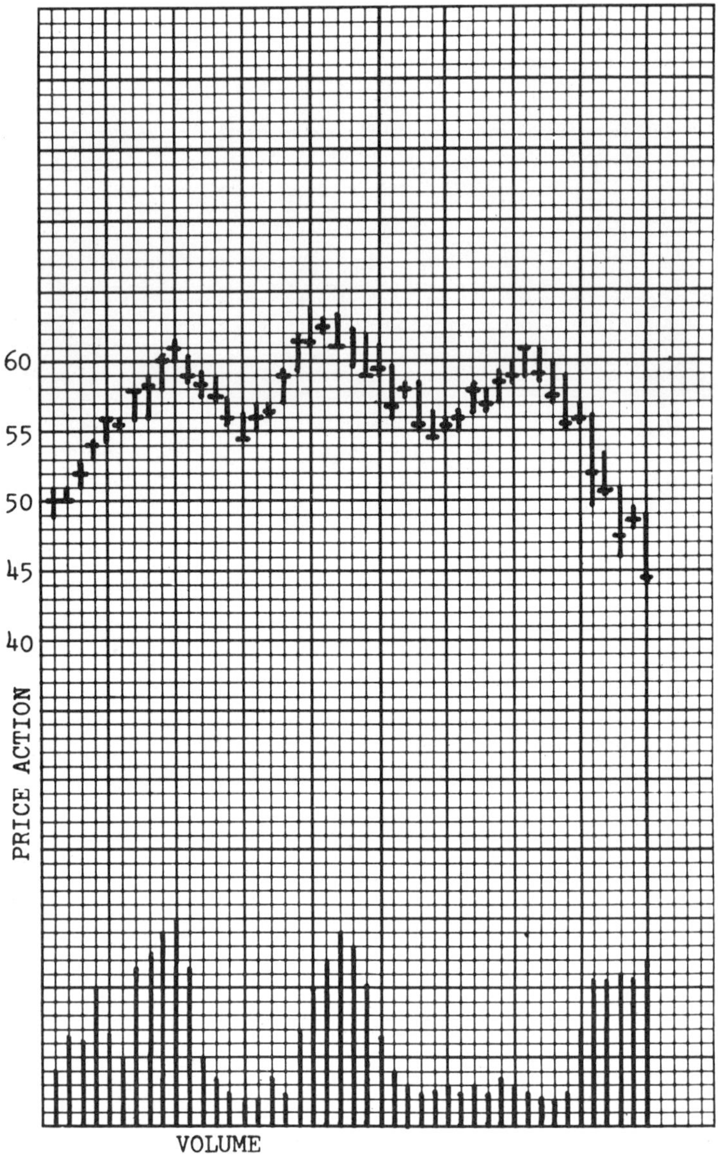

During typical head and shoulders reversal, volume picks up on the first rise (left shoulder), drops during the decline, picks up again on the middle rise (head), usually not to as great an extent as on the left shoulder, although head volume sometimes exceeds left shoulder volume. Then volume again drops on the decline, remains flat during the third rise (right shoulder), tends to pick up when the "neckline" connecting two bottoms has been penetrated.

TABLE OF RESULTS FROM 5-YEAR TEST OF CHART SIGNALS IN 30 STOCKS COMPRISING THE DOW JONES INDUSTRIAL AVERAGE

TECHNICAL SIGNAL TYPE	TOTAL TRADES	PROFITS TO END OF MOVE	LOSSES TO END OF MOVE	PROFITS TO SELL SIGNAL	LOSSES TO SELL SIGNAL	PERCENT OF TRADES PROFITABLE
Support-Resistance Break	50	708.75 (Aver. 14.15)	8.00 (Aver. 0.16)	401.25 (Aver. 8.025)	36.00 (Aver. 0.72)	80%
Head and Shoulders Bottom	1	22.50	—	13.50	—	100†
Rectangles	6	93.75 (Aver. 15.13)	—	45.50 (Aver. 7.58)	—	100‡
Triangles	12	147.50 (Aver. 12.60)	—	53.50 (Aver. 4.45)	8.50 (Aver. 0.708)	66
Rounding Bottom	1	30	—	18.50	—	100†
Fan Lines	4	31.50	—	13.50 (Aver. 4.50)	3.00 (Aver. 3.00)	75
AVERAGE, all bar chart trades	74	1034.00 (Aver. 13.97)	8.00 (Aver. 0.108)	545.75 (Aver. 0.737)	47.50 (Aver. 0.64)	79.5

† (On one only). ‡ (On six).

In preparing a bar chart, if the stock being charted traded for the latest week at a 44 high, 40 low, and closed 43, the chartist would draw a vertical line from 40 to 44 and put a cross mark, denoting the close at 43. Then on the bottom of the page he would mark another line for the volume.

Can an investor predict stock prices from all of this? The more sober among the analytical brethren of the slide rule and chart paper are quick to answer "No." But, they quickly add, while neither charts nor crystal balls predict the future, charts enable an investor to spot trends, and if he is adept at his trade, they say, he can spot them sufficiently early to make worthwhile profits even in such nonswinging stocks as the blue chips of the Dow-Jones Industrial Average.

POINTS TO REMEMBER

1. Stock charts are often derided. But a study of effectiveness of the classic chart signals, applied to the slow-moving, prestigious thirty stocks of the Dow Jones Industrial Average, shows them still workable.
2. Since the question of when to buy a stock is fully as important as what stock to buy—the right stock at the wrong time can only bring losses—charting techniques can pay an investor.
3. Charts do not predict the future. Nothing does. They do, say chartists, show developing trend changes. While they are not infallible, the rewards for knowing when such a change has appeared on stock charts in the past—even though the past performance does not guarantee future results in any way—can be very worthwhile.

Chapter 21 : : SUPPORT AND RESISTANCE — IMPORTANT KEYS TO STOCK TIMING

A "TECHNICIAN" is an analyst who studies timing as applied to stock purchases and sales. His dogma is that the market knows more than anyone. Price movements, according to the technicians, reflect the actions, not the words, of everybody who invests. Whenever insiders begin to buy securities, their purchases will force certain things to happen. As these things occur, the technical student of the market will know as surely as any insider that the price is about to move up. Conversely, big investors cannot sell in quantity without revealing that something is afoot, say technical analysts.

Technicians further believe that it is not necessary to know who is buying or selling—only to know that something large enough to affect the supply-demand balance of the stock is under way. Fundamental analysts ask, Why? The technician wants to know, What? Where? When?

The first tool of every technician, whether he works with the familiar bar chart or point and figure, is support and resistance study. Support and resistance study underlies even the Dow Theory, and is required for an understanding of patterns such as head and shoulders, double top, rectangle, triangle, and the like.

If a stock, moving upward, stops at 45, churns a day or so, and then declines over a period of two or three weeks to the level of 40, a technician would predict that the stock should meet "resistance" at 45 on the next up move. A technician's reason for this prediction is rational: He knows that two things happened previously at the price level of 45. The demand from bulls dried up and the resistance of bears, evidenced by selling activity, increased. It is logical, the technician states, to expect that some of the bears who wanted to unload at 45 will not have succeeded the last time; these investors will be waiting, stock certificates in hand, at the barricade of 45 for another opportunity to unload at what they consider an advantageous price.

If prices do push above the level of resistance, this is also significant for a technician. He then knows that the entrenched bears have been overwhelmed by the bulls as bulls' dollars clear the way for a further advance, at least for a time. If prices in this hypothetical situation move up to the 45 level, fail to penetrate it and retreat, and further assault mounted by buyers at last hurdles the 45 level with increased volume, the chartist would become excited. From his lines on ruled paper, he would deduce that a large block of overhanging stock had been bought by bulls, thus increasing the likelihood of a sizable advance.

A "support level" is a resistance level in reverse. If, in a bottom area, sufficient buying to stem a decline is introduced into the market, a technician would use the same type of reasoning as he did on the appearance of resistance to an up move, but in reverse.

One of the more spectacular blue chip performers of a few years ago was General Electric. Dropping to a low of 91 in the summer sell-off of 1965, GE rose on high volume to 120 by October. From there the stock slid off in a normal reaction to 112, then rose again—but with smaller volume—until it reached the area of previous resistance at 120. Prices bumped against the barrier at 120 for three weeks but could not penetrate the selling resistance of bears. The stock then dropped again, and technicians watching GE wondered if the support level at 112 would hold, now that resistance had stopped a rise at 120.

It did not.

The buying that had once appeared at 112 was absent. When General Electric went through the support level, chart-minded analysts knew that the rise was over. Although GE produced one more flurry, which did not quite reach the old resistance level at 120, the stock declined precipitately thereafter and was soon down to 80.

Radio Corporation of America had enjoyed five straight years of rising per-share earnings in 1965. The price of RCA stock during ten patience-trying months, however, remained within a trading range with a closing high of 37½ and a low of 30. The company was prospering, but RCA stockholders did not leap for joy when they watched other television stocks go up daily while theirs remained comparatively static.

Each time RCA reached 37½ it was as though a ceiling existed through which it could not pass until suddenly, in early September, 1965, the price pushed through the upside ceiling and took off with a roar. Investment men who had recommended RCA at the old top, nearly a year before, could at last face their customers without apology. But the technically oriented investors, who delayed making a recommendation until the "resistance breakout," were heroes.

What placed them in that enviable position? They knew that the company is one thing, and the stock is quite another, and they were able to predict when the stock—not the company—was going to move. In this chapter we will examine one method by which you can tell when a stock is likely to rise in such situations. This method is not infallible, but it works a good percentage of the time:

1. A resistance level is an area where more than one advance has been stopped; the more tops there are along a horizontal resistance line on the chart, the more valid it is and the greater the significance a technical analyst can assign to its being broken.

2. A resistance breakout has little validity if it is only nudged through and the stock then goes no further. Some technicians apply a rule calling for 3 percent penetration if the resistance breakout is to be taken as a good buy signal. As a practical matter, looking for a closing price at least one full point above the resistance line works well in avoiding the whipsaws of tiny, random movements.

3. If the breakout is to carry any distance, it usually is marked by an increase in trading volume at the time of the breakout. This brings up the question: How big is big? What constitutes an increase? The answer is that volume is a relative thing. Anything

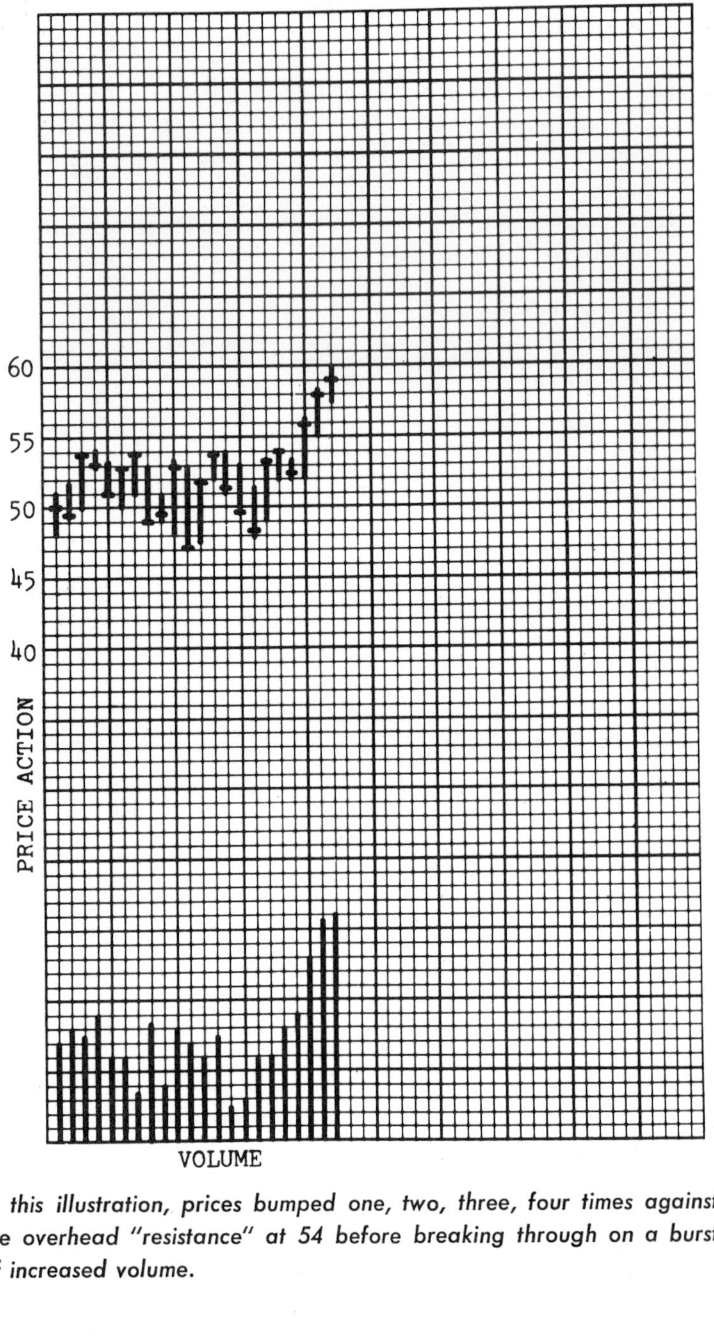

In this illustration, prices bumped one, two, three, four times against the overhead "resistance" at 54 before breaking through on a burst of increased volume.

markedly greater than the usual trading volume of the past many weeks or months constitutes a valid volume confirmation of the breakout signal. Beware of breakouts that are not accompanied by increased volume. Occasionally these go on and build into worthwhile moves, but the odds on any breakout without volume are slim. Chances are that such a breakout will prove false, and that prices will retreat back below the resistance level.

4. Technical analysts are careful to attach significance only to the breaking of truly major resistance levels. The mere bettering of an old top has none of the movement-about-to-begin importance of a true resistance break, where several tops along a horizontal row have finally been passed. Similarly, the breaking of a short-term top, where resistance was met on two or three scattered days, has little long-term importance. A major resistance line is one where up movements, each lasting many weeks, were stopped. Minor resistance areas are constantly cropping up; disregard them if you are looking for a stock that is likely to show a worthwhile profit during the months ahead.

The charting of resistance lines, like all technical analytical methods, is not an exact science. Sometimes a move begins with all the signs flying and then fizzles out. When that happens, your best bet is to ride it out. The chances are that the eventual breakout of a trading range will be in the same direction as a first, false move. Or, should the decline carry below the resistance line by a significant amount, you can sell with a small loss.

The suggestions given here apply—but in reverse—to the spotting of support level breaks, which clang out signals to sell a stock in which a major past bottom has failed to hold.

POINTS TO REMEMBER

1. Stocks often meet resistance in the form of sell orders that stem a further advance at points where such resistance was met before. This is particularly true if the same resistance level stopped not one advance but two, three, even four or five.

2. Similarly, stocks' declines often tend to stop at the same support levels that halted earlier declines, because the buyers who

believed the stock was a bargain at that price frequently come out again to buy stocks, and their buying again stops the reaction. As with support study, this is especially true of levels that halted several earlier declines.

3. Support-resistance areas that stopped rallies or reactions of only a few days have less significance than levels at which mighty, tidal moves halted.

4. When a tested, longer-term overhead resistance level has been decisively penetrated, an investor can be justified in assuming that the buying demand has probably proved greater than selling pressure, and sellers being sold out of stock, the buyers will have to bid prices higher to bring out fresh stock for sale. Prognosis: higher prices. (None of this is certain, nor can past actions guarantee future results.)

5. In the same way, when persistent selling has driven prices under a tested, longer-term support area, the assumption exists that the buyers who were mopping up stock offerings at that point no longer have buying power to do so and sellers will therefore have to drop their asking prices in order to find fresh money for buying. Prognosis under such conditions is for a further decline.

Chapter 22 : : THE "ICS" STOCKS

"ALL A guy had to do to make money in sixty-seven," said one comedian, "was to buy anything on the board that had a name ending in 'ics'."

He was right. In 1967 you just couldn't lose money with these little science (and pseudo-science) companies. Wall Street was on one of its periodic madnesses, and the yen this time was for research and development, the farther out the better. The harder it was to understand a company's work and products, the more desperately investors clamored for its stock.

Suddenly—whoosh! The science stocks folded back like one of their own rockets gone out of control and crashing back on its startled crew. Whatever 1968 was for people able to catch the big swing that began after former President Johnson's peace-and-no-nomination speech in the spring, it was hardly a bull year for science stock investors.

The "ics" stocks lagged the market badly.

Why? Whatever happened to them? Is it that American investors at that time ceased to believe in the future of research and development?

As I see it, a number of factors underlay the unpopularity of "ics" stocks at that time and the losses sustained by investors attuned to an atmosphere that no longer existed.

Investors were looking harder at profits. Once, if an "ics" company had enough Ph.D's in science on its staff, investors considered profits assured. They assumed that something new and startling would have to result in profitable entries on the books. In later years, there had been a growing awareness among the analytical brethren and among investors who follow their advice, that while a nuclear scientist may be admirably fitted to perform at his specialty, it becomes necessary to have someone more prosaic and less exotic at the financial helm.

I asked a specialist on science-oriented stocks to explain the disappearance from new high price listings of stocks slanted to research and development. His answer was, "People began to be aware that profits matter more than glamour in business, and that not all 'ics'-oriented companies were showing up as well on the profit ledger as they did in the Patent Office listings of new products. Happily, I can report that this awareness is not confined to investors. Lots of 'ics' companies are putting business administration men in charge of the front office, while the science men man the labs."

A second factor in the popularity decline of "ics" stocks was that the technological time grew shorter. Once, when a company patented a hot new scientific product or process it could count on a period of years of exclusivity before competition caught up to it. The technological time lag is still lessening. It now runs months rather than years. Some experts say it may even shorten to weeks before too much time has passed. "There is just too much scientific brainpower working in the same direction for anyone to have an exclusive for long," commented a professor of engineering.

The result of this shrinking technological time lag was that profits based upon an exclusive could not be stretched out, and a hot new product degenerated into a price football almost before anyone in the labs could begin working on the next brilliant discovery.

A third factor is that science was no longer a new direction. A decade ago, and even as little as a few years back, America's frontiers lay out on the fringes of space and all of its new directions were technological.

In 1968, new directions were people-oriented and aimed at improving society. The hot stocks became those of companies that rode this newest wave of the future. Hamburger merchants were more glamorous than electronics engineers, and while Boy Scouts still queued up to see a brilliant innovator of spaceware, the people who spent money on stock watched the queues at the fried chicken palaces, and observed the markets that might exist when our national energies turn to renovation of our inner cities, and did their queuing before the executive offices of seemingly prosaic companies whose futures appeared more exciting than science, research or development.

Electronics and other science-oriented activities just got out of favor. This happens—and it's what makes working the Street such an interesting, if sometimes demoralizing, way to earn a living.

Research and development stocks were in; then they were out. By the time you read this, they may once more be the hottest of investor favorites. Ask a fashion expert to tell you why hemlines go up some years, down others. Change is the nature of life, and another change back to investing favor must hit the "ics" stocks one day.

When I was a young boy (a time so far back that my children sometimes ask what George Washington had to say the last time I talked to him over an evening Scotch and water), every good story was supposed to have a moral. This story about the "ics" stocks is no exception.

The moral is: You need good technical analysis to go with technology.

At this point we are going to study a very sophisticated set of analytical tools called "point and figure." The purpose of doing so will be to help you spot when to buy a stock and when to sell it so that you may be able to ride the up currents in "ics" stocks or in any other favorites, and be able to abandon them when the down currents begin to blow.

Why should you study point and figure for individual stocks instead of orthodox bar charting? Is it not true that point and figure charts often give the same signals, sometimes at the same places? Support and resistance, head and shoulders, and other patterns found on bar charts are found also on point and figure charts. Bar chart analysis will tell when a move probably is beginning, and through trend line study, will keep its practitioner appraised of the health of an existing uptrend or downtrend. It would be helpful to know in addition how far a trend might carry. Certainly an investor would be in a better position if he knew where the eventual end of a movement might be. Point and figure study frequently will provide this information.

A bar chartist carefully marks the range of every week to judge where support and resistance might be met and, most of all, to determine whether there is a strong trend and which way it heads. Bar charting tells when a stock is in a sidewise movement that exhausts the patience of watchers but out of which numerous profitable trends grow. Point and figure analysis explores the same things in a different way. Point and figure has a methodology and a mystique of its own. Instead of marking a high, a low, and a close for a period in one column, the analyst might need five columns for the same period of time—or no columns. Point and figure study is not built around periods of time. The point and figure chart is one-dimensional, indicating neither the passage of days and weeks (except indirectly) nor the volume of trading. Point and figure analysis is built upon reversals.

The typical financial page might report activity for Swingeroo, Inc., on a typical day in this way: opened 42—high 44—low 40—closed 42. Making a bar chart, an analyst would draw a vertical line from 40 to 44, with a cross mark to indicate the close at 42. If he set out to make a point and figure chart, he would need to know how many times the price reversed itself and how far each little move carried. If the analyst had the tape to study instead of a newspaper, he might learn that Swingeroo, after opening at 42, traded at 43, at 44, back at 43, down to 42, and 41, and 40. After that the price rallied to 41 and closed there. The illustration shows what this action would look like on a point and figure chart. Note how different the trading for the day appears on this chart than it does on familiar bar chart lines. The point and figure chart indicates the track of price reversals. Each time the price changed direction—from up to down, and back to up once more—the point and figure technician used a different column for his X marks.

(Price change information is available from commercial sources. You can also buy books of point and figure charts.)

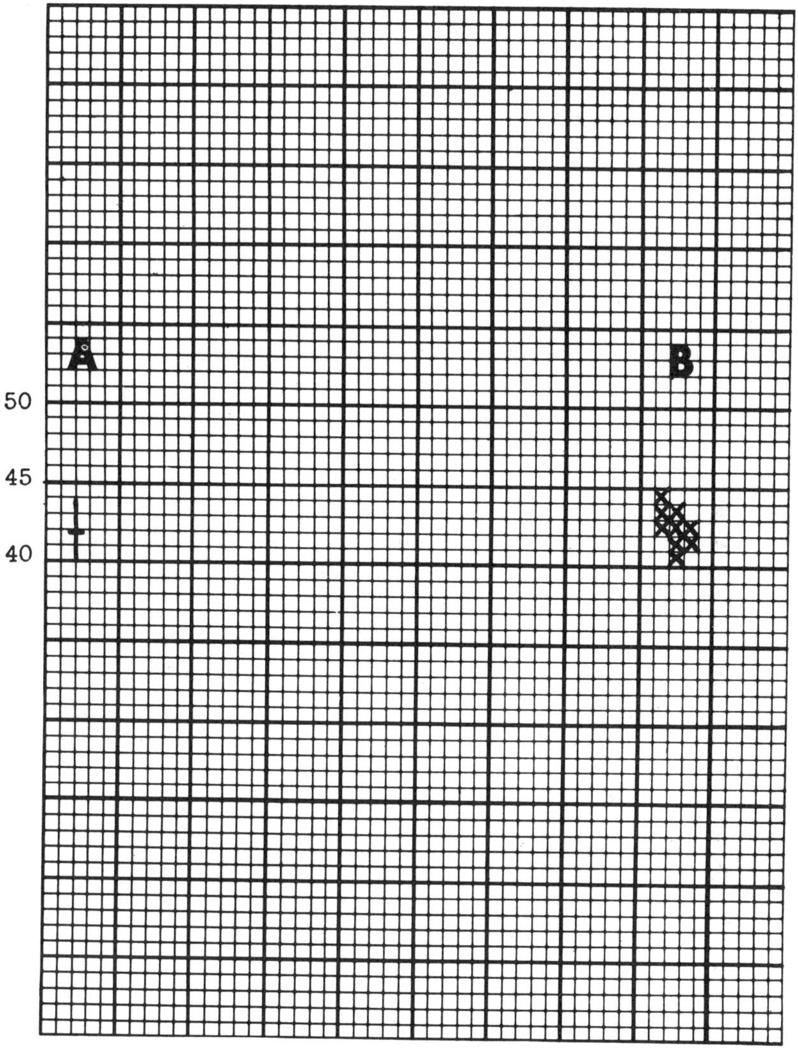

This shows the difference between "bar" and "point and figure" charting. Under A you see a typical day's activity in a stock which opened at 42, climbed to 44, sank to 40, then moved back up to 42 where it closed. The lower end of the bar is the low limit of trading, the upper the high limit, and the crossmark indicates where the stock closed. But on the point and figure chart, each move of a full trading point was indicated by an "X" with the marks going up as the stock climbed, moving to another column when it reversed downward, finally to a third when the reversal to the upside came. Point and figure chart is shown under B.

Point and figure theoreticians believe that the churning in a congestion area eats up the money of the bulls and the stock certificates of the bears. Finally one or the other is exhausted so that a new supply-demand imbalance pushes prices out of the sidewise congestion into an up or down trend. The various columns are used to measure the probable extent of a move out of a congestion area. According to point and figure theory, the volume is there but it is indicated on the chart only at the times when it is most meaningful—when prices change direction. In other words, the volume that produces price movement and reversals is evident (up and down the columns); the volume that goes nowhere is not indicated. Time, in point and figure analysis, seems strangely absent to a chartist who is accustomed to cramming nearly everything into one line. Point and figure theory holds that time is not important; only price movement and the pictures of activity that this movement paints are important.

In the next chapter we are going to look at how buy and sell signals are found on a point and figure chart. Then we will look at that great advantage point and figure people claim for their system—the ability to indicate how far a new trend might be expected to go.

POINTS TO REMEMBER

1. Point and figure charting has a good record for spotting a new trend while it is still new. This charting, in addition, has the advantage of often being able to indicate how many points up or down the chart paper a fresh trend could be expected to carry before it becomes exhausted.

2. Point and figure is not concerned with time. The chart indicates reversals. Out of the churning of price changes, say point and figure experts, comes the eventual exhaustion of either bullish or bearish forces and the beginning of a fresh trend that can lead to profits or warn of a danger to existing holdings.

Chapter 23 : : HOW CHARTS TELL YOU WHEN TO BUY OR SELL

POINT AND figure charting is easier in some ways than bar charting or volume-oriented systems. When there is no price movement of significance, the point and figure man can lean back and watch the tape or go out for a cup of coffee. But in other ways point and figure charting entails more work because the daily open-high–low-close data published in the evening paper is inadequate as a source of information; the point and figure chartist must have tape data.

At this point it might pay to reread the last chapter. Point and figure charting is not like any ordinary chart methods although in many ways and at many times its signals will tend to come at the same times as signals given by bar charts.

Point and figure charts do not take time into account. Instead, they note reversals of direction. (However, they note only reversals of a full point or more. Should our stock, Swingeroo, Inc., swing from 41 to 41⅞, it might as well have stood in bed, to quote an inspired quip from a prizefight manager of long ago. The move would not appear on a point and figure chart until the stock sold at a full, round 42.

Point and figure has an advantage not claimed by *afiiconados* of other charting schools: It gives an idea of how far a move can carry.

The devotees of point and figure charting have a vocabulary of their own. The basic words in this vocabulary are "congestion" and "catapult." The former sounds like symptoms of a disease widely mentioned on television. And the latter brings up pictures of little boys at play with rocks and basic rock-throwing machinery. Both can be immensely important to your eventual investing profits.

To the point and figure man a congestion area is a back-and-forth kind of price action we have met before in discussing market timing charts. It can be called a "trading range," "rectangle," "triangle," or even, as the early Dow Theorists termed such action, a "line."

Whatever you choose to call it, the congestion (which, henceforth, we will call by the point and figure term while we are discussing point and figure charting) denotes an area in which the price reverses back and forth, making no large or permanent gains and taking no sizable or lasting losses.

The catapult is the spring out of a congestion area.

When you get a catapult upward from a point and figure congestion area, you have been put on notice that a new advance is likely to be under way. When you see a catapult downward from the same kind of congestion, you know that a warning has been served that trouble in the form of a new price decline might possibly be in your stock's future. I have been careful to use words such as "might possibly" because you should know that point and figure analysis of a stock's price action is not infallible. But neither is any other kind of dealing in probabilities.

Think back to two important words: "support" and "resistance." If you consider your point and figure chart from the point of view of these two things, you will quickly master the concepts of congestion areas and price catapults.

(You do not have to keep your own point and figure charts if you lack time or inclination. Weekly books of point and figure charts of most stocks on the New York Stock Exchange or the American Stock Exchange are available. Your broker may have such books in his office. Your public library may also have them, or might be persuaded to order a subscription for local investors' use.)

A chart is a visualization of price action. It tells you more of what has gone on and what may be in progress than long, wordy descriptions could possibly say. And so, rather than describe at length the patterns that form on point and figure charts and

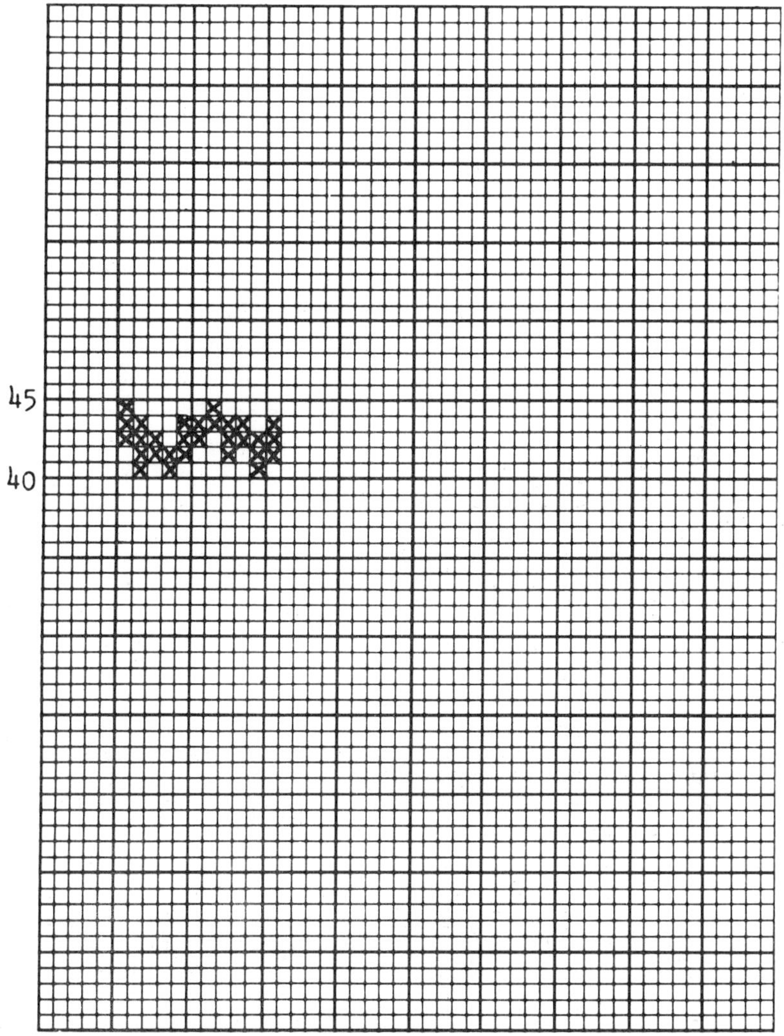

A typical congestion area taking place in the stock of our corporation, Swingeroo, Inc. Note how price reversals come frequently but carry nowhere. Such a congestion area with approximately parallel upper and lower boundaries is termed a fulcrum. The area might have slanting boundaries and still fit the fulcrum pattern. Often, strong new movements catapult out of such congestions.

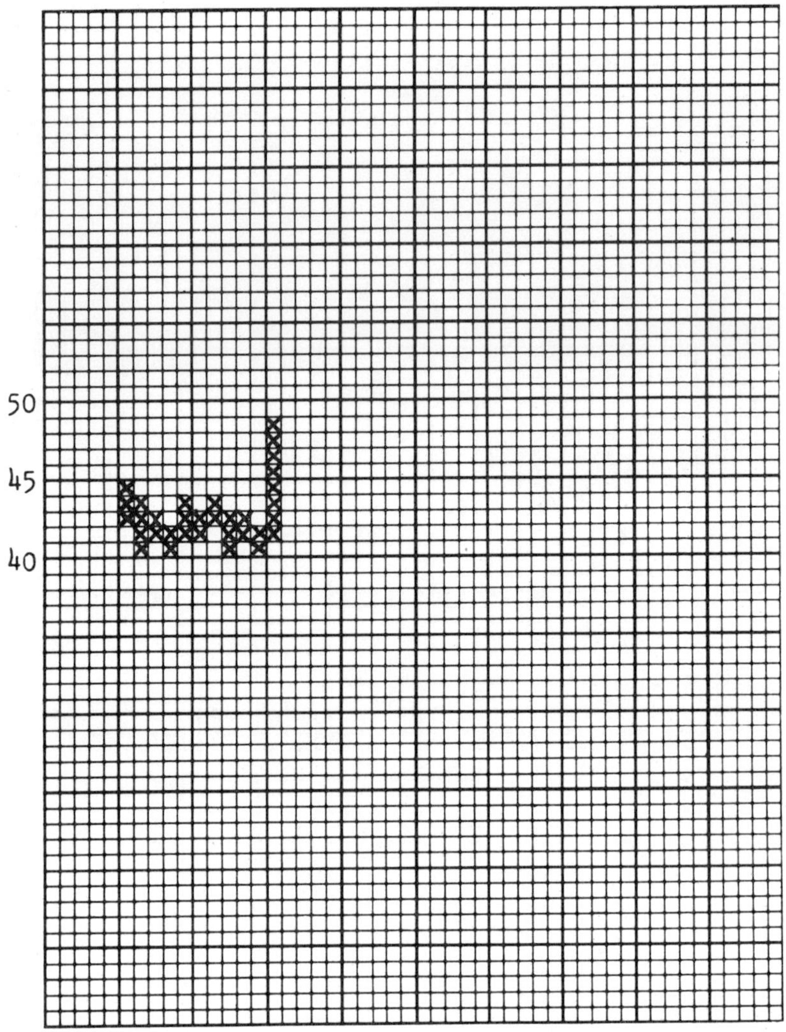

This shows the same fulcrum congestion in Swingeroo, Inc., with an eventual catapult to the upside.

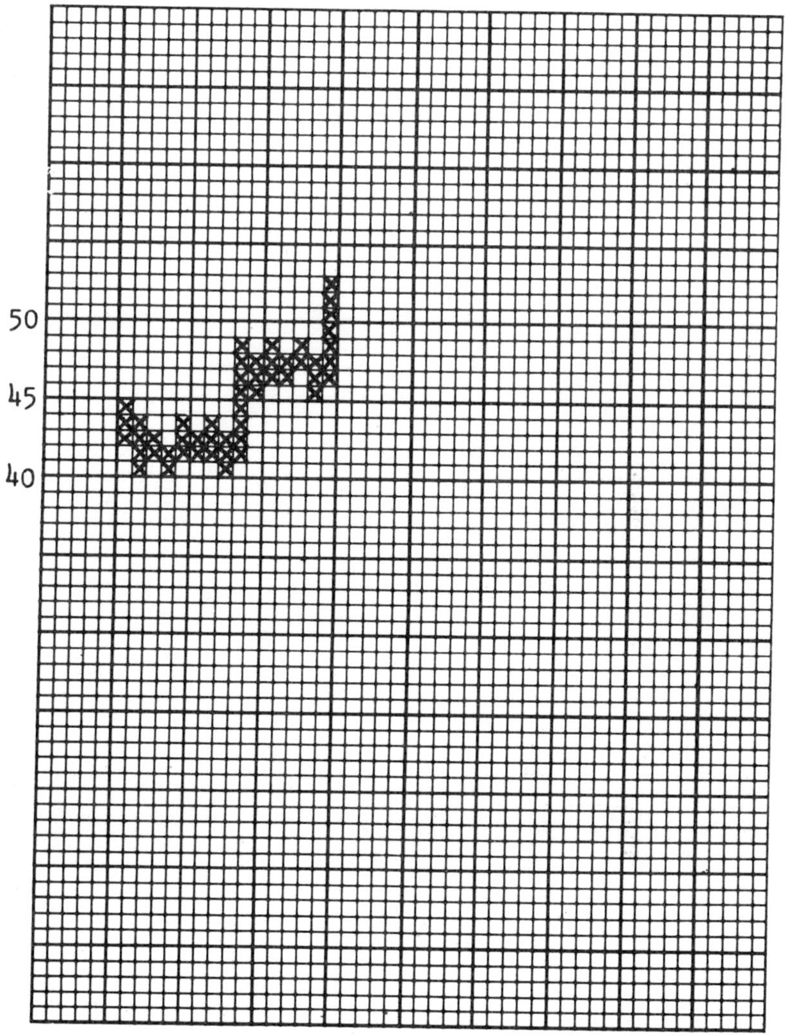

Here is a fulcrum on top of a fulcrum. If you were to see this traced out on the chart of your stock, Swingeroo, Inc., you would treat the whole area as one bigger fulcrum, although you would give it the name, compound fulcrum. The eventual true catapult out of a compound fulcrum should be in the direction of the catapult out of the original simple fulcrum. In this case, you would expect the final movement to be up.

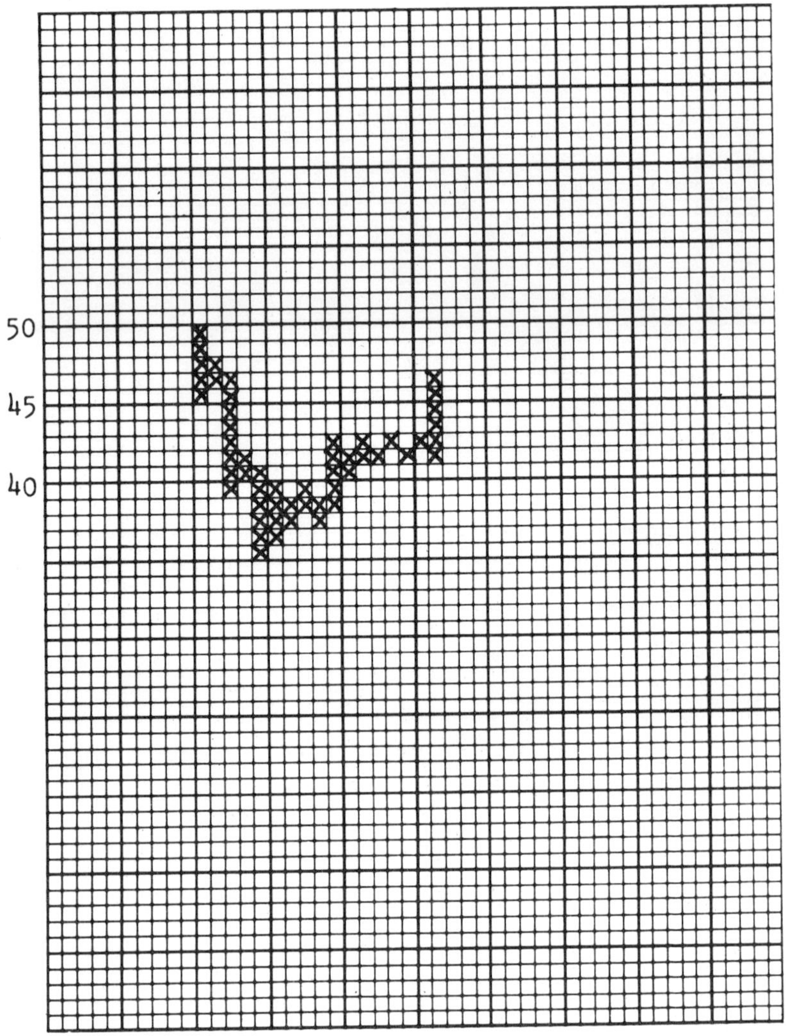

Because at quick glance it looks so much like the familiar kitchen implement, this congestion area in Swingeroo is sometimes referred to as a skillet. Note the bottom area with "handle" on top of it. The important catapult was the move upward from the skillet handle.

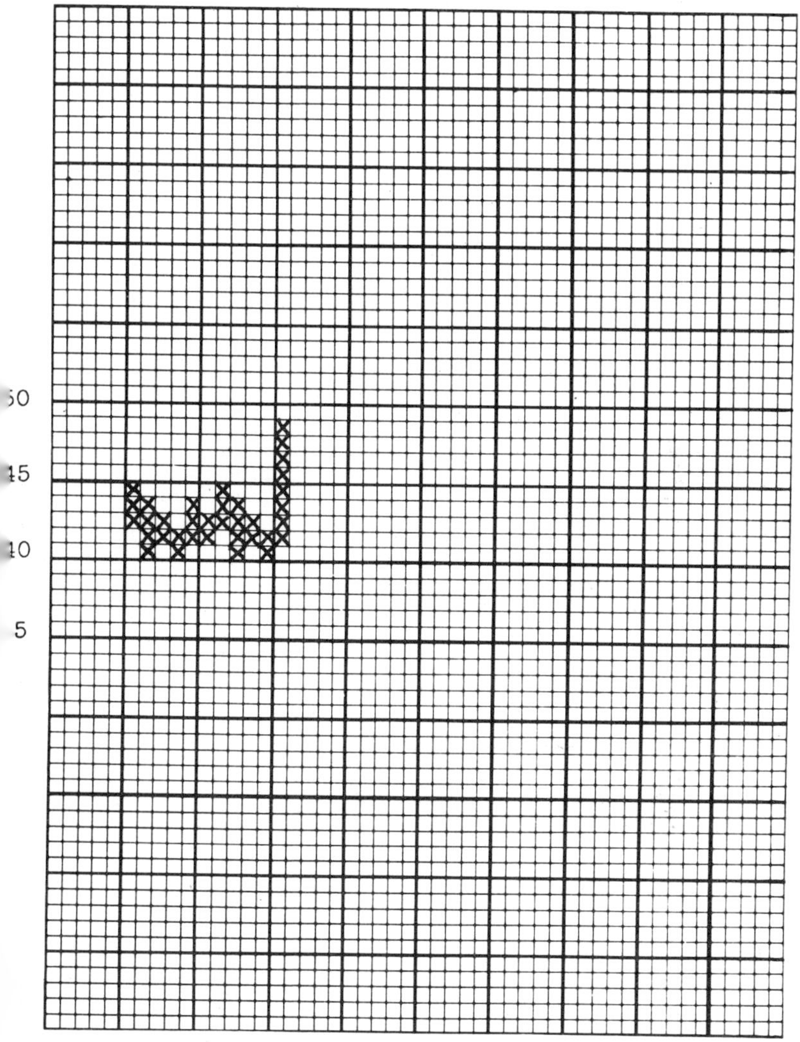

Point and figure theory holds that a move out of a congestion area will probably move about as many points upward or downward (depending upon the direction of the catapult) as the congestion had squares in its width. After this catapult above the 45 level, Swingeroo could thus be expected to move to about 55 (there were ten squares across) before consolidating or reversing direction.

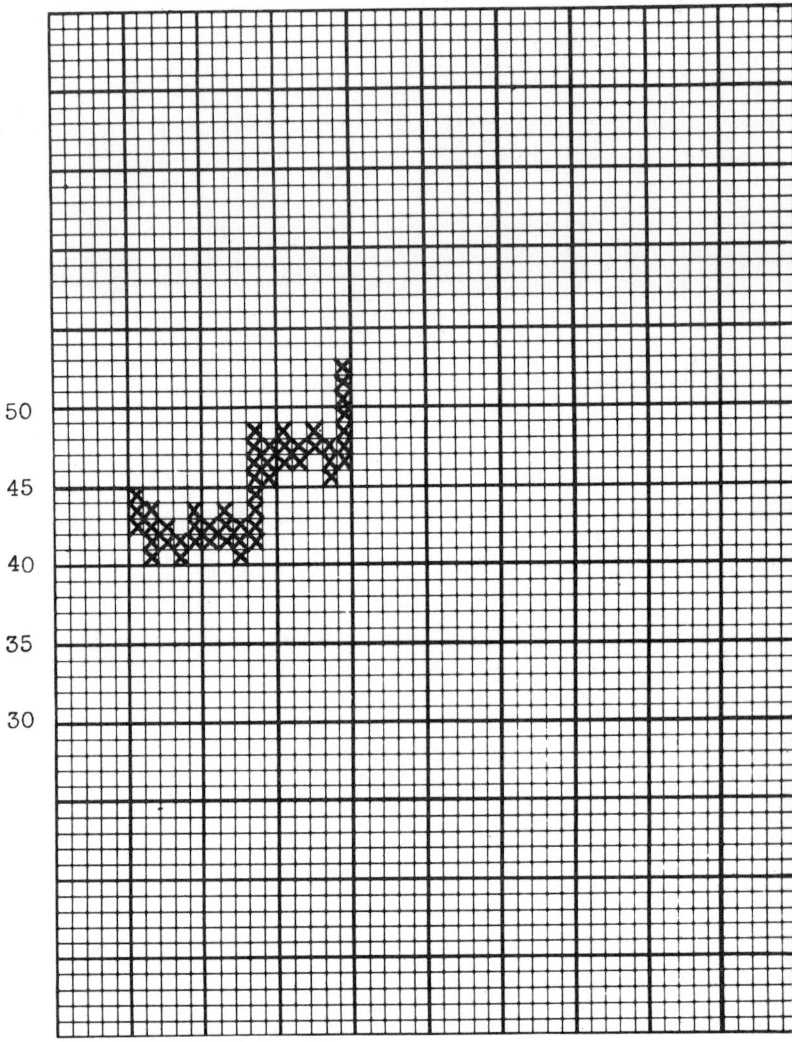

Across any uneven congestion area such as this compound fulcrum, it would be correct to count two things. The first would be squares across the middle. The second would be squares in the line with the greatest number of X marks. Usually, two different figures will result. These can be considered minimum and maximum expectation.

what they denote, I am going to fill the next several pages with charts of our theoretical stock, Swingeroo, Inc.

Congestion areas such as those we have illustrated can come at tops, at bottoms, or in the middle of long up or down movements.

If after a long decline, the price pattern forms a congestion, then the price catapults upward—odds are that the old trend has been turned around and that a new upward trend will follow. It may not come immediately. There may be further backing and filling of the sort that turns a simple fulcrum into a compound fulcrum. But the odds are in favor of an upward move.

However, if the congestion comes after a long up move, and the catapult out of congestion is downward, then a conclusion should be drawn that the bulls have had it and the bears are about to enjoy their day with the stock. If you own Swingeroo and that happens, sell. Fast.

Sometimes a congestion area comes after a long decline or advance and the catapult is in the same direction as the trend that came before the congestion. Say that after an advance in Swingeroo, Inc., the price wobbles back and forth, reversing frequently but going nowhere and the chart next shows an upward catapult. If you own Swingeroo, you can take friends down to the corner bar and stand them a drink, for your stock is probably going to engage in fresh bullish fireworks. The congestion in the middle, followed by a catapult in the original direction, gave notice of resumption of the first trend.

Out of a catapult from congestion, how far might you expect a move to go?

Point and figure charts offer a "count" on how far a beginning price movement could carry.

Pinpoint accuracy is not possible in every case. An approximation of an eventual target price for the newborn movement to reach is quite achievable, however, and the approximation is enough for an investor to tell whether or not the move will be a major one.

The premise behind the point and figure count is that a move that catapults out of a congestion area will be about as long as the congestion area was broad.

But getting the count is not always easy. Point and figure formations being by nature imprecise in boundaries, it is sometimes hard to tell how wide is wide.

Consider the illustration on page 155. This shows a simple fulcrum. Throughout its congestion-consolidation, the illustrated stock traded back and forth in the area of 40 to 45. Catapulting at last out of the fulcrum, it gave clear indication to a point and figure technician that the resulting up move should carry to a level about ten points higher than the breakout since the fulcrum measured ten chart squares across. (It is important to remember that no point and figure indication can be precise. Point and figure, like other forms of technical analysis, deals with the actions, emotions, purchases, and sales of people. People are less predictable, if more interesting, than computers or even simple machines like bicycles.)

No point and figure analyst would attempt to say when such an objective might be accomplished, only that the supply-demand factors in the market for common stock of Swingeroo, Inc., were such that a price objective of X number of dollars would be a likely point for a trend, now beginning, to end.

While there might be a temptation when dealing with a simple fulcrum having precise edges to skip the hedging word "about," an investor has to employ it with other kinds of point and figure congestions. This does not alter the value of point and figure analysis since even an approximation of a move's future extent can be valuable in forming investment strategy.

Illustration on page 156 shows a compound congestion area. In typical compound fashion, it is one fulcrum atop another. On the final catapult from the upper fulcrum, how far should an analyst expect the move to carry before it tires out? Where should he mark the spot to take profits?

If based upon a count at the bottom, this would include only the lower fulcrum.

If calculated across the top, this would give a short count across only a part of the whole congestion.

Knowledgeable point and figure people do neither of these things. They measure any irregular point and figure congestion two ways: First, take a count right across the middle; next, count across the line of horizontal squares where the most X marks are found, indicating that the greatest part of the congestion area's churning took place there (Count all the squares between the outermost X marks, not merely the marks).

Generally, this will yield two different counts and therefore a seeming disagreement on the chart. But only seeming. Here, as in everything concerned with technical analysis, we deal with probabilities rather than certainty. A safe assumption might be that the move to come will carry no more than the higher number and no less than the smaller figure. If you make such an assumption as this, you will bracket the eventual price target in a very large number of cases. And you will know, from a maximum-minimum count, whether the upcoming new trend is going to be big enough to attract your capital.

Should the movement look as if it is running out of steam after achieving the minimum count, an investor would be well advised to take profits there. If the move appears full of energy and zip, he should hang on for the maximum gain. Any irregular congestion can be treated in this way.

A skillet should be measured across the handle where it is widest and then back over the intervening blank area to the portion of the earlier trend that had led into the skillet's bottom. Don't measure only the handle; take all of the skillet.

POINTS TO REMEMBER

1. Catapults out of congestion areas afford the point and figure chart watcher signals on which to get aboard an expected new upward move (if the price catapults up from a congestion area) or to sell his stock and salt away profits (when the catapult, after a congestion, moves downward).

2. Point and figure congestions come in many recognizable patterns. Remember that they must, indeed, be congestion areas and not mere two-column stops along a trend, and that the eventual catapult gives the directional clue.

3. Point and figure charts are available from commercial services and sources. They can often be read in brokers' offices or

libraries. But it is more resultful to maintain your own because doing so compels you to notice new signals you might miss in skimming through a book containing hundreds of charts.

4. The width of the congestion area affords a strong hint as to the probable extent of any new upward or downward trend catapulting out of the congestion.

Chapter 24 : : MEASURE YOUR STOCK'S STRENGTH

When a gambler gets ready to bet on a boxing match he tries to find out which man is probably stronger. Knowledge of which stocks are strongest would give investors just such an edge in their unending battle to get and stay ahead. But how? Compare every stock on the exchanges and over-the-counter to see which appears mightiest? Even those possessed of computer time find this hard. But you can measure, if not every stock, at least those in which you are interested and determine whether each appears to be stronger than the overall market. You can do it in minutes per week.

For decades, analysts have toyed with this idea of measuring relative strength of stocks. They have come up with a variety of methods nearly as great as the number of analysts who have tried their hands at the task. One thing all have found: You can't measure both volatile strength and consistent strength. You have to settle for one or the other, or you have to get some sort of combination.

The simplest relative strength measurement is to divide the price of a stock under study by the price level of the market average (in this as in other market analysis, I prefer the broad, weighted New York Stock Exchange Index).

Computation with a slide rule is easy. But it is confusing to read. First Whistle Missile shoots up from 40 to 45 while the average stands roughly still. Whoosh! Up toward the sky goes the volatile rating of Whistle Missile. Then the next week it has a perfectly normal reaction back to 43, with the market up 5 percent and wham! Down goes the relative strength measurement. Such volatility is hardly usable as an investment timing tool.

Analysts have tried to smooth out a computation of this sort by turning it into a moving average. In figuring a moving average, they average off the volatile relative strength numbers of the last ten weeks (some analysts prefer twenty, others plump for five—everybody has his pet number) then enter the average figure. This average would "move" week by week because each week the last digit would be removed and the latest week's figure added to arrive at a new average.

Moving averages indeed smooth out the volatile up and down hops of a simple relative strength measurement like that we have described. It ceases to look like an electrocardiogram graph and begins to go across a chart page with some dignity. But moving averages have a big fault.

They are slow.

If you make one that is sufficiently long in time to smooth out volatile figures, it becomes a slow indicator that wigwags warnings and signals long after the time for action may be past. Constructed short enough to lessen this drawback, it begins to hip-hop again as when unadjusted.

What matters for an investor's profits is not volatility but the consistent ability to outperform a market. We need a system to emphasize consistency and play volatility down. Let's look at such a system and assume that we are studying the momentum of Whistle Missile common.

A cumulative differential line does not straggle behind as moving averages do, and yet it avoids the jerkiness of an absolute chart and relates the ups and downs of each week to the preceding week.

If our stock goes up from 38 to 39, with the market, measured by the broad NYSE Index, making only an 0.23 percent gain, Whistle Missile has obviously outperformed the market. We are not interested in the degree to which it did so; this measurement's bias is toward consistency. We will therefore advance our cumulative differential line (explained below) by one number.

If the next week finds Whistle Missile unchanged at 39, but the New York Stock Exchange Index up 1.1 percent, Whistle has failed to meet the market's performance and the momentum rating therefore drops by one unit (regardless of the degree to which our stock beats or does not beat the market). On a week when it performs exactly like all other stocks we will give Whistle Missile's momentum rating an even mark by extending it out at the same number as that of the week before.

It might be instructive to see this system's results during a recent period.

In late March, 1968, the consistency momentum rating said "Buy!" for Atlantic Richfield. The signal came at 55⅛ (adjusted for later two-for-one split). Less than four months afterward, the stock had reached 98¼.

Results are not always this spectacular, for few companies make the giant strike that Atlantic Richfield found in Alaska. Beatrice Foods is a slower plodder. Its momentum rating told investors to buy the stock in April, 1968, at 58. A sell signal came later with Beatrice Food's loss of momentum in September, after having reached a price peak of 76 in July. The sell message was flashed at 72¼ for a $1,425 profit (less commission) on a $5,800 investment in five months.

Looking at a third and different industry, the momentum of Joseph Schlitz Brewing in late January, 1968, flashed "Buy!" at 37¼. The stock was trading above 58 by September.

Momentum studies, weighted as these are for consistency, are also useful in determining which industries are in Wall Street's immediate favor. In a policy speech several years ago, the late President John F. Kennedy noted that "a rising tide lifts all the boats." This applies to the stock market where it pays to know those groups with the strongest momentum.

Within an area of fast-moving stocks, all equities generally are lifted by investor interest. If steel stocks outperform the market, the probabilities are that every stock within that group will act well, although some will do much better than others. The fact that stocks do move by industries is demonstrable. In the early years of this decade when investor interest focused upon makers and merchandisers of consumer goods, Procter and Gamble had the most rapid price appreciation of the thirty stocks that make up the Dow-Jones Industrials. Yet only a few years later, Procter and Gamble was last among the D-J Industrials in relative performance. The fickle favor of investors had shifted to other groups.

Similar stories could be repeated almost endlessly. The point is that if an investor can be guided aboard a rapid express train, even the caboose of the train will arrive at the destination of higher capital value.

For such study it is not necessary to compile industry charts of your own. *Barron's* Magazine, Standard & Poor's, and other statistical sources offer industry compilations weekly, and it is a matter of moments to compare appreciation or depreciation of an average with that of the whole market. A momentum index would be constructed exactly as described for individual stocks.

There is another way to build momentum references. A stock or an industry can be compared to itself as well as to the market. These are the steps:

Each week look at the present price of Whistle Missile (or its industry average or even the mighty New York Stock Exchange Index if you wish to measure the whole market).

Relate it to the price thirteen weeks ago. Express this as a ratio by dividing the present price by the three-months-ago figure.

Do the same with the closing price of a week six months ago.

Repeat the process for the price one year ago.

Average the three ratios (short, intermediate, and long-term). When the resulting average ratio remains above 1.0—and preferably above 1.3 or 1.4—the momentum of our stock, our industry, or the market itself is not in danger.

POINTS TO REMEMBER

1. Strength, like so many other things in this world, is comparative. A stock strong by comparison with the whole market often shows worthwhile profits to its buyers.

2. A simple ratio can give you this information. But such a ratio is volatile. It is better to find out the consistent relative strength. This is known as momentum to many investment analysts.

3. Stocks can also be compared to themselves to determine whether their velocity is decreasing or increasing.

Chapter 25 : : PICKING THE MUTUAL FUNDS THAT ARE IN FAVOR

A LEADING bus company has long used the advertising slogan: "Leave the driving to us." Many investors like to leave the driving to someone else, and so they buy the shares of mutual funds. Some aggressive investors have found ways to speculate—with fine results—using mutuals instead of common stocks as vehicles.

Today, a whole range of mutual funds is devoted to what polite people call "aggressive investment," and many old-timers term outright speculation. And a number of more sophisticated investor-speculators tie these funds, in turn, to a buy-them-then-sell-them-out trading strategy of their own.

To do this, some rely on industry study. They look into economic prospects as well as chart patterns of many industries. When it appears that the whistle industry is about to come into favor, because of an expected shortage of whistles for pro football officials, they look for a fund holding a package of whistle stocks, and buy that for participation in the expected rise.

Theirs is a good approach and it has worked well in the past. But there are a limited number of mutual funds devoted to specific industries. Most have a broader-ranging approach to Wall Street.

However, the performance of these funds can vary as much as the performance of a good pro football player differs from that of a high school boy playing his position for the first time. To weed out the probable pro from the inept operator, many fund speculators rely upon relative strength studies of "momentum." Fund investors and speculators often find that the mutual fund outperforming everyone else tends to continue doing so. It will eventually run out of steam, to be sure, but the momentum of its climb has somewhat the same force that the momentum of an object has in the study of physics.

Two questions arise for an analyst whose problem is to devise relative strength momentum studies: (1) Relative to what? (2) Will the studies be weighted for volatility or consistency?

Answers, although not difficult to obtain, are vital to the setting up of an effective plan for measuring the performance momentum of mutual funds. Momentum can be studied as outlined in the previous chapter.

To make the momentum index for Beefsteak Fund easily readable, it can be plotted out across chart paper. When, after weeks of steady rise, this momentum level drops, but not lower than the last level it reached on a drop, you still have positive relative strength and should stay with the fund. When it drops below an earlier drop, however—beware! This may be the time to get out of Beefsteak and into a better-performing fund.

Warning: Don't take every little drop below "support" too seriously. Count it only if the past support level is one at which a decline of three or more earlier weeks was halted.

A study like this tells the trader-investor whether his fund's background portfolio of stocks, on which net asset value per share is figured, is performing well. When a fund stays too long with the wrong stocks, or fails to get aboard promising new moves of other stocks, its management may not be alert to current opportunity. This comment applies, of course, only in the case of gunslinging "go-go" funds, which base their operations on just such quick perceptions.

It's okay for a long-term mutual fund investor to hang on in those circumstances. But a speculator should be on guard to bid old Beefsteak Fund farewell in favor of a romance with newer, possibly more glamorous, funds that appear better tuned to their current surroundings.

In addition to thus moving in and out of funds when their

performance relative to the rest of the market begins to slow down, most of the people who employ funds as trading vehicles for gains rather than the kind of long-term investment that Grandpa used to lock up in his safe, also watch the signals on market movements.

If you become convinced that the clouds are gathering over Wall Street and that pretty soon comes the deluge, you should then get quickly out of your funds, however good each of them may be. The managers of these funds might be—usually they are—smart fellows who are just as able to spot coming trouble as you are. But they cannot do a great deal about it even if they do see a bear market looming up.

The reason is that they sit on pools of capital from tens to hundreds of millions of dollars in size. Sometimes they manage billions. No one can be nimble with such vast amounts. If the fund manager wanted to sell, his own selling would further depress the market, and instead of stashing away gains at a high price, he would defeat his purpose by making those gains vanish. He can (and usually does) sell some of his holdings. But he can't liquidate them all.

However, you can sell your shares in his fund when overall market climate gets stormy.

POINTS TO REMEMBER

1. If you prefer to leave the driving—the picking of individual stocks—to an outside expert, you can often obtain top investing results in mutual funds.

2. You should, however, have criteria for judging when the funds are performing satisfactorily according to the objectives you have set for yourself.

3. If the aim is capital growth performance, then the funds you choose should be able to produce 20 percent per year growth in net asset value.

4. Furthermore, that growth should continue to exceed growth in the prices of average stocks. You can keep a running check

on this by setting up a momentum index for each mutual fund in which you are interested.

5. Successful investor-traders who do their thing with mutuals also watch timing signals in the overall market. When a bear market threatens, they reason that all stocks, including those in the portfolios of mutual funds, stand in danger. They, therefore, sell fund shares.

Chapter 26 : : DO STOCK SPLITS REALLY HELP YOU?

THE VOICE on the telephone was excited. "Good morning, Mr. Doe," it said, "this is George—your broker. I've got good news. One of your stocks is going to split two-for-one!"

To most investors this is welcome news indeed. People like stock splits because they have twice as many shares after a two-for-one split or three times as many after a stock splits three-for-one, and it is nice to feel that you are the owner of more stock. They like splits, too, because these are usually accompanied by a raise in dividend. There is a feeling that when a stock gets too high in price it enjoys a market "narrower" than a medium-priced issue and that, too, is a factor in favor of stock splits.

But most of all, investors like to hear such news because a stock sometimes goes up in price after a split. Or most people believe that it does. To determine whether this is fact or folklore, we have conducted research covering all splits over a three-year period in the stocks that make up the prestigious Dow-Jones Industrial Average. These thirty stocks were chosen because they are, in general, the bluest chips on the Board and because they are found in more portfolios and bigger portfolios than most other securities. What happens after splits in the D-J stocks should have considerable bearing on general market behavior.

"Split," for the purpose of this research, was determined to include any stock dividend of a size sufficient to influence the price of the stock. Such dividends as 5 percent or 3 percent are pleasant to receive, but hardly meaningful in a study of the effects of a split on price action. Split, it was decided, would exclude anything smaller than a five-for-four distribution (a 25 percent stock dividend). Some of these distributions are called splits, others are announced as stock dividends—a two-for-one split and a 100 percent stock dividend, for example, may be different from the company accountant's point of view but not from the investor's.

This study was made in July, 1967. Going back to June, 1964, it was found that in the thirty big Dow-Jones components there were only nine splits or sizable stock dividends, although there were numerous year-end extras of stock. Looking at the price at the time the split occurred, comparison was made with the price one month later and three months later. The average closing price for the month during which the split occurred was substituted for the price on the day the split took effect, because it was felt that this afforded a fairer picture of resulting price action up or down. Average prices were also used for one month and three months later in order to achieve fair comparison.

What happened?

The last of the nine splits occurred in May, 1967, when Anaconda Company distributed a share to every stockholder for every share he already held. May, 1967 was a soggy month in the overall market, with prices tending downward for most stocks. The average closing price of Anaconda during May was 44½.

There was an almost immediate effect on Anaconda. Big A, as some Wall Streeters call it because of the single A ticker symbol, was soon trading at 50. However, since insufficient figures could be had at the time of this research it must be regarded as only partly conclusive.

Many of the D-J corporate planners apparently had bad luck in timing their stock splits because the first on the alphabetical list, Eastman Kodak, split its stock at a time of great market unrest. This was in May, 1965, just before the serious slide of May and June in troubled 1965. And yet the stock prospered.

The average price during April when Eastman split was 78. A month later, in May's selling flurry, it was up to 82¾ and three months later was at 83⅝.

International Harvester, another of the D-J components to

choose April, 1965, for its two-for-one split, sold at an average price of 40 during the month of the split. Unlike Eastman Kodak, Harvester found the going rough during the big sell-off of May, 1965, and was at an average of 38¼ one month later. Three months later it sold for 35¾.

Owens-Illinois also distributed 100 percent in stock in April, 1965. Selling at an average price of 58 at the time of the split, OI held that price one month later and three months after the split it sold at 57½.

Sears Roebuck split early in 1965. Selling at an average price of 66 at the time of the split in March, Sears was at 67¾ a month afterward and averaged 67 three months following the split, despite the drastically worse overall market conditions of June as compared to March.

Swift chose April, 1967, to split its stock two-for-one. Selling at an average price of 24½ then, the meat packer's stock was at 26¼ a month later, and three months after was selling at 26½.

Union Carbide's two-for-one split took place in May, 1965. The price of the stock averaged 67½ during the month of the split, was at 63¾ a month afterward, and three months later had dropped to 61.

When United Aircraft distributed a 50 percent stock dividend (a three-for-two split) to its stockholders in October, 1965, the stock sold at 61½. A month afterward it was trading at 70½ and three months after the split at 84½.

The three-for-one split in Woolworth in June, 1964, found the stock at an average price of 28. The following month it was plodding stolidly at 28¾ and three months later at 28¼.

The average price of these split stocks at the time of distribution was 47. They traded a month later at 48½ on average and three months afterward at 49¼. This represented a gain of 4.6 percent in three months, which, annualized, made a respectable profit—again on average—of 18.4 percent following the stock split.

What causes such gains to happen?

Financial analysts point out that part of the effect of rising prices following a stock split is usually psychological; as noted earlier, the investing public likes to have more shares, even if at a lower price. But part is caused by measurable financial background conditions, because stock splits usually occur at times when a corporation's directors see sunny commercial skies ahead, and thus the effect of increasing earnings (and often dividends) is frequently felt in increased stock prices.

POINTS TO REMEMBER

1. Part of the folklore of Wall Street is that stocks go up after being split.

2. Research into post-split behavior of stocks on the Dow-Jones Industrial Average shows that such a tendency has indeed existed.

3. A split is not a sufficiently strong tool to be used by itself. But public psychology does accept split stocks as having higher value, marketability or whatever, in the mind of investors tends to make two packages of three marbles each seem worth more than one package of six marbles. Therefore, a split, upcoming or recently accomplished, is an added reason for buying if other investment criteria also show the stock in question to be a sound purchase.

SECTION IV :: If You Want To Speculate

Chapter 27 : : MAKE YOUR INVESTMENT CAPITAL DO MORE

HARRY AND Walter are twins. As small boys they dressed alike, went to the same schools, later to the same college. Now they have separate families, but both use the same broker, subscribe to the same market letter, and follow identical suggestions to buy the same stocks, generally at the same time.

Last year, Harry cleared about twelve hundred dollars in capital gains from his investments.

But Walter's portfolio—identical with Harry's—produced a four-thousand-dollar gain.

The difference was leverage.

Long ago, a Greek named Archimedes lived in the city of Syracuse. His thing was math, and he invented some of the basic ideas that mathematicians use today. He was quoted as saying, "Give me a lever long enough and I will move the world."

Everyone knows the kind of lever Archimedes had in mind. When you take an iron bar, balance it atop a rock, and use it to flip another heavier object out of position, you are employing leverage. The bar is the lever, the rock on which it is balanced the fulcrum. Physical leverage of that kind multiplies the power of muscles. Financial leverage multiplies the power of the money you invest in the stock market. Employed wisely, financial leverage can make your money multiply like jackrabbits.

A simple kind of financial leverage is a mortgage. George and Mary want to buy a forty-thousand-dollar house in a neat new suburb. But alas, they have only six thousand dollars saved up. In a cash economy, their situation would be hopeless. Enter leverage in the form of a mortgage—using someone else's money to swing a big deal you can't swing alone—and the seemingly inadequate six-thousand-dollar stake of George and Mary turns out to be quite enough to put them into that forty-thousand-dollar home in a desirable suburb. Buying a home with the help of a mortgage is an unsophisticated, basic kind of leverage. This chapter will examine other kinds of leverage and how they can help you to build a fortune fast in the stock market.

(But be warned! Leverage works two ways. If you press down on that iron bar and don't succeed in moving the obstacle you want to get out of the way, the weight of the obstacle might send you kiting up into the air. Leverage, so wonderful when things go right, can be disastrous when things work out badly.)

Basic Margin: The Federal Reserve sets margin rates. These vary from 50 percent to 100 percent and are presently at 65 percent. This means that if you buy stock you put down 65 percent and can borrow 35 percent of the cost from your broker. It might appear to be only a small potatoes way to increase profits. But consider: Say you have become convinced that Swingeroo, Inc., is going to be one of the big stocks of next year. Its price is currently at 40. You might buy one hundred shares at that price and, if it should go to 60, you would be a two-thousand-dollar winner on a four-thousand-dollar investment (commissions omitted) for a 50 percent profit.

But say you decide to buy on margin (using the 80 percent rate that held for a long time until early 1970 and to which margins might return). Now you can swing 125 shares for your four thousand dollars. If the same 20-point profit accrues, then you would be twenty-five hunrred dollars richer. Your gain on actual investment of four thousand dollars would be 62½ percent.

Buy the Warrant: We discussed warrants in an earlier part of this book. A warrant is an option to buy stock at a set price. Not all companies have warrants outstanding. But many of the newer growth-type companies—the swingers in which so many profit opportunities exist today—do have warrants. If you are interested in leveraging your way to a fast fortune, you should always inquire about a stock that you believe will go up, "Does it have warrants outstanding?"

Consider our theoretical stock, Swingeroo, Inc. In common with many fast-moving newer companies, its capitalization includes an issue of warrants, which entitle warrant owners to buy the stock at 45 if they choose to do so. Swingeroo is now selling at 40. The warrants themselves should, in theory, have no value in this situation since the stock will have to advance 5 points in order for the warrants to be exercisable. But Wall Street is a land of hope and Swingeroo, Inc., a stock of promise. The warrants have a price of 4.

Walter, being a swinger, uses his four thousand dollars to buy one thousand warrants rather than one hundred shares of the stock. He does this aware of the fact that the Swingeroo warrants will bring him no dividends, and that unlike the stock they represent no ownership; they are an option and nothing more.

If the stock, as in our earlier instance, then advances from 40 to 60, probabilities are that the warrant will retain its slight premium. Say that it still sells at a four-dollar premium since speculators are of the opinion the stock has further to go and, therefore, that the warrant has attraction. Exercisable at forty-five dollars, the warrant has a basic value of fifteen dollars now that the stock is at 60. Add the premium of four dollars, and we can get a quote on warrants at 19. Walter's four-thousand-dollar stake has, therefore, advanced to nineteen thousand dollars to give him a whopping profit of fifteen thousand dollars or 375 percent of his original stake. That compares with a simple profit of 50 percent on the stock itself, and of 62½ percent on the stock if margined.

Margin the Warrant: Like stocks, warrants can be margined. Let's look at the arithmetic when Walter buys warrants with his four thousand dollars and then margins the whole shebang:

At the 80 percent margin rate, he would be able to put 1,250 warrants into his portfolio instead of the 1,000 bought on straight purchase.

When Swingeroo, Inc., rose to 60, our friend Walter could cash up his 1,250 warrants at $19 each for $23,750 (out of which, of course, his broker would not forget to subtract commissions). His dollar profit would come to $19,750. His percentage of gain would be an almost unbelievable 492 percent.

In a deal like Walter's, it pays to keep a tight hand on the button you'll push to say "Sell." For if Swingeroo had not performed as expected, but instead had dropped in price, the percentage loss in the warrant might have become much greater than in ownership of the stock itself. And the percentage loss in a doubly leveraged margin position in warrants could become ruinous.

Try Puts and Calls: Also options, these are different from warrants and available on nearly any listed stock. A call entitles its holder to "call for" the stock at a predetermined price, during a period that might be anywhere from thirty days to six months, ten days, and occasionally up to a year. A put allows him to "put it to" the one who sold him the option, during a set period and for a set price.

As a rule of thumb, three- and six-month put and call options might cost from 8 percent to 12 percent of the going market price of a stock. Let's assume that no warrants were available and then apply put and call leverage to Walter's successful play in Swingeroo, Inc., during its move from 40 to 60.

Cost to acquire call on 1,000 shares of Swingeroo at 40, options costing approximately 10 percent of purchase price	$ 4,000.00
Call exercised at 60 by calling for 1,000 shares at 40 and then selling them at 60	$20,000.00
Less cost of calls	4,000.00
Net profit (commissions omitted)	16,000.00
Profit percentage (above original stake)	400 percent

It should be noted that while puts and calls are capable of producing spectacular capital gains, they are also capable of producing total losses. When you buy or sell a stock itself, even on margin, it is not likely that it will drop to absolute zero. A decline that ended above zero would not wipe out your stake. But if a stock fails to advance during the call period, the investor's loss is every cent he spent to purchase his option. Even warrants, leveraged as they are, seldom produce such a loss. Puts and calls are tools to be used with utmost care. Yet it is true that substantial fortunes can be established in fast time through employment of puts and calls.

On the other hand, loss with puts and calls can never be larger than the amount used to buy them, and they can allow a trader or investor to control sizable blocks of stock at moderate cost during the periods of time when he expects the action to take place.

Employ Convertibles: As we saw in a prior part of the book, some bonds, debentures (unsecured IOU instruments of a corporation), and preferred stocks are called convertibles because they can be turned in at the holder's option for common stock. A convertible allows a conservative investor to enjoy the usually higher yield from a senior security, take a lessened risk, and at the same time participate in any growth in the price of the common. That happens because, since the convertible preferred or debenture can be changed at a set figure, its market price must increase if the common increases.

For a swinger like Walter, convertibles have an added advantage. They can be margined at a lower figure than common stocks. During spring, 1970, when this was written, convertibles could be margined at 60 percent.

Walter's play in Swingeroo during its rise from 40 to 60 would not have produced such remarkable results using convertibles as with warrants or with puts and calls. But it would have involved much less risk. And it would have brought in bigger profits than either straight or margined purchase of the stock itself.

Consider: Investigating, Walter discovered that 5 percent debentures of Swingeroo could be converted at a price of 45. With the stock selling at 40, the debenture was available at par of 100. (Debentures are generally issued in one-thousand-dollar denominations but many—like those of Swingeroo, Inc.—come in one-hundred-dollar packages.)

His four-thousand-dollar capital could thus buy 40 convertibles.

When the stock reached 60, the converts naturally tacked on proportionate value. That put the debentures at 150. While the rise in stock price above conversion figure of 45 was not as great as the rise from 40 to 60, there is a tendency with convertible securities, as with warrants, to continue selling at a premium over straight value as long as the underlying common stock still appears attractive to analysts and investors.

Fifty-dollar profit on 40 of these convertibles came to the same two-thousand-dollar profit made on a straight trade of one hundred shares of stock. But—where it was possible for Walter to buy 125 shares of the common stock by employing his 20 percent borrowing power on stock margin—he could swing 66 convertible debentures using 60 percent margin and 40 percent borrowing power. When these were sold at the new price of 150, Walter counted $9,900 in the palm of his hand, out of which he had to pay back $2,600 he had borrowed. What remained was a profit of $3,300 ($7,300 less $4,000 original investment), a return of 82½ percent capital gain.

Leverage by the means above can add a great deal to your stock market profits. But leverage makes it doubly important to select the right securities in the first place, for it is like a two-edged tool that slices through obstacles when used correctly, but slices through its user instead when it is badly applied to the problem.

POINTS TO REMEMBER

1. Leverage in physics allows a greater weight to be moved by muscle power. Leverage in the financial world means applying power to increase the ability of an investor's capital to bring about profitable results. It can make every dollar do the work of $1.20, $1.50, $2.00, even $3.00, $4.00 and as much as $10.00.

2. It becomes important to run quickly from a leveraged investment situation that starts to go wrong lest leverage destroy instead of building up capital.

3. Basic margin, at 65 percent at the time this is written, can add to the ability of an investor to swing more shares using the

same funds. Margin rates are set by the Federal Reserve. They vary, depending upon the Fed's attitude toward inflationary and boom-bust problems. Your broker extends margin credit.

4. Warrants are options to buy stock. They move proportionately faster when the stock goes up. Highly volatile, they are employed as leveraged instruments by many traders and speculators. Some even add margin leverage to the existing leverage of the warrants.

5. Puts and calls can add to the building power of capital. But they have limited life spans. If a stock fails to move during the option period, an investor's loss might be total. On the other hand, loss is limited to the amount spent for the option and does not grow greater should the stock take a plunge.

6. Convertible preferred stocks and convertible debentures are generally available on margin lower than that required for stocks. If a company has convertibles outstanding, it pays a leverage-minded investor to buy these rather than the underlying common stock.

Chapter 28 : : THESE FUNDS BRING BUILT-IN LEVERAGE

THE LAST chapter looked at all kinds and varieties of leverage that you can add to a planned investment to make each of your dollars do the work of several. This chapter describes an investment medium that has in-built leverage of 100 percent for those who seek capital gains.

This leverage is found in a variety of mutual funds called dual purpose funds.

In the spring of 1967, the merchandisers of mutual funds introduced with great fanfare a new breed of fund that, their excited salesmen told investors, would do everything for everybody.

"High income for those who want to make money on their money as they go along," promised the sometimes over-enthusiastic salesmen of these funds. "And if you want capital gains, great potential there, too. Something for everybody in one package. And last: leverage so that everybody has 200 percent of his capital working for him all the time!"

The funds so enthusiastically peddled to doctors, businessmen, housewives, career gals, men-in-the-street, and others interested in investments have been around now for quite a while; sufficient time to have established a track record. To live up to such claims and the kind of apparently far-out performance looked for would have required brilliant performance indeed.

Considered coldly in the light of today's market, which is unenthusiastic for these new funds (at the time this is written in spring, 1970), it can be seen that they have in many ways performed nearly as promised. No one would call the dual funds a nostrum good for any need and guaranteed to cure monetary problems in the way that peddlers' concoctions of a century ago were hawked as miracle cures for every disease of man or horse. But the record of dual funds is impressive. Among them an investor now might find rare investment bargains.

Although they have many features different from orthodox funds, the duals are still mutual funds just as a calf with two heads is still a calf. Remember that mutual funds are poolings of capital. Many people together own a mutual fund. One man might put six hundred dollars into it, another six million dollars. Both own proportionate shares in the fund, and both participate in its triumphs and in its occasional inevitable losses. The fund in its turn hires managers to try to keep the losses small and the gains big. After expenses have been paid, it distributes the dividends and interest it has received and capital gains, if any, to its shareowners. A dual fund is no different from other funds—up to this point.

However, where most mutual funds dedicate themselves to one of two basic financial drives, the dual funds go after both. These alternative aims are to achieve income as high as possible with reasonable safety and to amass capital gains by the bundle. In most cases an investor or fund manager can have one but not both.

The dual funds, however, have two parts and an investor buys either the preferred shares dedicated to income or the capital shares. Preferred shareholders receive all of the income that accrues from both halves of the portfolio. The capital shareowners come eventually into all capital gains from both portions.

A setup like that has obvious leverage. Since both halves of the portfolio are at work for both investors, the leverage is tremendous.

Say that you are interested in growth and you put in one hundred dollars when one of these was first formed in 1967. You might have had to pay an 8 percent front-end load charge, about average for most funds at that time, leaving ninety-two dollars of assets for your one hundred dollars. The investor interested in income buys a like amount, also having ninety-two dollars of assets left. Assume now that the whole fund is invested in stocks that yield, on balance, 3 percent. That allows a 5.52 yield for the income stockholders (less the expenses of running the fund and the fees charged by professional managers who direct the fund's activities). All of the net income goes to your friend who plumped for yield. Thus, he has nearly twice as much capital working for him as the amount he put in.

What about your one-hundred-dollar growth investment?

Let's say that a typical year is good but not extraordinary and that the New York Stock Exchange Index goes up 10 percent. Your fund's managers do about as well. You had $184 of net capital working for you, just as your yield-minded fellow investor had double his investment working for him. Ten percent of $184 amounts to $18.40 in capital gains, an 18.4 percent profit on your investment of $100 even after the deduction of the front-end loading charge.

But there is more to dual fund leverage than this, and alas, the market does not always go up. Nor do managers, even seasoned professionals, always do a superior job.

Let us assume that this is a year in which your favorite dual fund just doesn't bring it off. It goes down 10 percent in asset value. Now, where does the growth-minded investor stand? He is just where you'd expect him to be. The leverage that was such a cause for joy when things went well has doubled his losses when things went badly.

The foregoing was not written to scare any reader off dual funds. But an objective report must point out the two-edged nature of the leverage sword, and make you aware of what its side effects might be—even though those side effects are far from likely to occur.

Happily, an income-oriented investor shouldn't be hurt in a bad year that drops the growth component. His income is semi-guaranteed. Most dual funds assure income investors of a minimum return over the life of the contract. That return might not be earned in certain years. But if unearned it accumulates in arrears. The income portions have maturity dates. Any income that has been guaranteed but not paid will come out of the growth investors' asset values at that time. After the income portions mature, the "capital" shares thereafter own 100 percent of the fund.

Dual funds are "closed-ends"—that is, they do not buy from investors and sell to investors as do the "open-end" mutual funds with which most of us are familiar. Most of them list their own shares on exchanges. Thereby, some added leverage, and a bargain potential, comes into existence. For like many other listed closed-end funds these frequently tend to sell at less than their asset values. When you buy at less than asset value, your one hundred dollars might be purchasing the capital gains potential, not of two hundred dollars, but as much perhaps as two hundred fifty dollars.

At the time this is written one fund that boasts a per share net asset value of $22.16 is selling for $18.75 per share. Another, whose net asset value comes to $13.99, is at $10.25. Discounts from asset value range from 7.3 percent to 23.2 percent.

The income investor has some added leverage going his way, too, over and above the income he receives from a portfolio twice the size of the stake with which he bought into the fund. If he buys below value then he, too, receives a kicker in the form of added percentage yield. Moreover, his income might tend to rise over the years at a pace faster than the erosion of inflation since the portfolios of dual funds are often heavy in growth stocks and it is the tendency of stocks like these to pay out increasing dividends.

Another angle to the leverage of dual funds should not be ignored. These can be purchased on margin. Most are listed on the New York Stock Exchange. They are subject to the same margin rules as other Big Board stocks. This means a further multiplier of your money's force should you buy listed dual fund shares on margin.

However, all dual purpose funds are not equal in performance, any more than the more familiar types of mutuals do as well as each other, or than every doctor, dentist, housewife, or carpenter is exactly as good or as bad as the next doctor, dentist, housewife, or carpenter.

The shares of dual funds lend themselves admirably to trading in tune with market signals. Suppose an investor had bought one of the better performers among this group every time the New York Stock Exchange turn signal (explained fully in Chapter 34) had given a buy signal for the overall market, and then sold his leveraged dual fund on every sell signal. Suppose he did this during the stormy eighteen months from the start of 1968 to the middle of 1969. This period comprised all kinds of markets, swung about by all kinds of war scares, peace hopes, inflation, deflation, and fear of recession.

Our theoretical investor would have done these things:

Bought 12⅛ in April, 1968.

Sold this holding at 13⅜ in July, 1968, for a 1¼ point profit.

Bought at 14¼ in August, 1968.

Sold this holding in January, 1969, for 17¾. Gain 3½.

Bought in the spring, 1969, market rally at 15½.

Sold the holding when the spring rally petered out in June for 16⅝, a 1⅛ point gain.

Total gain would have been 5⅞ points. During this time, he would have been protected from any serious decline in the whole market by selling his holding each time the market appeared in overall danger.

Not everybody likes such a short-term approach. So he might instead have held for the longer pull by using the hi-lo index (explained fully in Chapter 34) as a triggering device for buying and selling. This would have signaled a buy in April, 1968, at around 12⅛ cost figure. It would then have had the investor hold staunchly, not being moved by the shorter-term messages of the NYSE turn signal, until the hi-lo index's sell signal in early March, 1969. At that time, the dual fund used for example was at 15½. The overall number of points achieved by such longer-term holding would have been fewer than by in-and-out trading with the short-range NYSE turn signal. However, commissions would have been smaller.

POINTS TO REMEMBER

1. Certain kinds of mutual funds, known as dual funds, have their own built-in leverage and, therefore, make useful trading vehicles for the investor who wants to make each of his dollars do the work of many.

2. Duals have two parts. Income investors buy one kind of shares and receive all yield on the whole fund. Capital investors buy other shares to which all capital profits accrue. If you are interested in dual funds for their leverage with capital growth in mind, you should seek the capital shares.

3. In each of these parts, an investor has roughly 200 percent of his money at work. Other leverage might be added when a discount from asset value exists. And an investor can apply still more leverage by purchasing on regular margin.

4. Not all dual funds produce equal "go-go" type performance. Criteria discussed in an earlier chapter can be applied for judging performance-history of any dual fund.

5. For the investor who wants to be in stocks during rising periods and out of them altogether or in part when the market goes down, dual funds can make very leveraged vehicles.

Chapter 29 : : SOMETIMES HEDGE FUNDS MULTIPLY INVESTMENT LEVERAGE

STANDARD OPERATING procedure for the investor-trader who wants to make the most in Wall Street is to buy when market trends favor the upside and then to sell out entirely when the longer trend seems to have turned against him. Such a policy makes money sit idle at times. But the money—when big trends are correctly judged—only seems to be idle, since it is increasing in value in terms of stock it can buy at cheaper prices near a market bottom.

There is a sophisticated way to get still more mileage out of money by putting it to work even during down periods. This is called the hedge fund concept.

Hedge funds are the hottest idea currently circulating in Wall Street. A hedge fund, according to numerous thoughtful financial analysts, utilizes at one and the same time the most audacious way and the most conservative way to put money to work. An approach to investing rather than a specific investment, the hedge idea is applicable to a portfolio of almost any size. The dictionary gives a number of definitions for the word hedge, but only one is relevant to the thinking behind these new investment vehicles: to try to avoid or lessen a loss by making counter-balancing bets or investments.

The objectives of the new hedge concept are: to attempt to make money on both sides of the market by holding both long positions and short sales; to depend upon these positions as a hedge against sudden short-range shifts in the market since the counter-trend positions, hopefully, will make profits even if the main positions stand still; to vary the percentage of long and short positions in accordance with the stage of the market so that a typical hedge fund might at one time consist of 80 percent long positions (this means stocks you own) and 20 percent shorts, at another time be 40 percent long and 60 percent short, perhaps at unsettled periods hold 50–50 positions, and at bearish periods be 80 percent short and 20 percent long. A hedge fund, however, always will be both long and short.

This approach is for truly aggressive investors. Yet, its partisans say, it also is tailored for ultraconservatives with its emphasis on avoiding loss.

A parenthetical word on short selling. It is a technique very little understood by the public. But there is nothing either complicated or diabolical to it.

In the ordinary course of investing, you buy a stock first, hoping that it will go up in price, then you sell it later. Short selling is the opposite of that. First you sell the security in the hope it will go down in value. Later you buy it back. If it goes down as you expected it to do, you can buy back at a lower price than you sold and you have a profit. If it confounds your expectations by going up, then you "cover" the short sale at a higher price and instead of a profit you have a loss.

Short sellers seem to be fiends and demons to some unsophisticated investors. But without them, markets would not be nearly as stable as they now are. By furnishing sell orders in a rising market, the short helps to keep prices from running away on the upside. Similarly, by buying in later on a down market, he stabilizes that kind of trend.

Within an overall direction every market has little winds that blow one way or another. In the best of up markets, some stocks decline. During the severest of down markets, it often happens that some stocks stubbornly go up. Within the overriding major market moves are sharp rallies in bear markets, and short but definite declines in bull markets. Recognizing these facts, the hedge fund approach tries not only to guard against possible sudden dangers but actually to take advantage of against-the-current moves.

In general, 1967 was a good year for investors. Whether an analyst used the broad-based New York Stock Exchange Index, the Standard & Poor's weighted averages, or the venerable Dow-Jones Industrials for his yardstick, he was forced to conclude that things had gone well indeed for owners of common stocks.

"Which owners?" ask those who push the hedge fund idea, pointing to the following anomalies produced by crosscurrents during a typical year:

While the overall market moved satisfactorily on the upside, the average of airline stocks showed a decline of about 10½ percent. The apparel stocks, as measured by their average, appreciated 60 percent during the same period. The aluminum stocks average was down for the year. Automobile and auto equipment stocks were up. Brewing stocks moved only in a sidewise trading range that went nowhere, while building material stocks soared, then lost part of their gain. Cement stocks moved sidewise, chemical stocks were down for the year. Coal mining stocks appreciated quite well, but the stocks of communications companies dropped. The conglomerates and cosmetics stocks were up spectacularly, container stocks and discount stores less so, with farm equipment stocks sharply down.

One could go through the alphabet from aircraft to vending stocks and see an equally topsy-turvy picture of gains and losses during a demonstrably good year in the market.

Advocates of the hedge fund concept point to these crosscurrents and counter-trend movements in making their case. These advocates further contend that some financial analysts possess sharp tools for determining market turns, but none has a crystal ball that will spot the exact top or bottom of a trend. An investor hedged at all times is protected from unforeseen twists and turns in the big market at Broad and Wall.

There is a way to follow the hedge fund approach and at the same time maintain extremely high leverage so that a move, for example, of 20 percent to 25 percent in the price of a stock might produce a doubling of invested capital. This involves the use of puts and calls. These options can permit an investor to use only moderate sums for his counter-to-the-main-trend hedges and yet achieve, under optimum conditions, the advantage he could obtain from the holding of regular positions. The loss on a put or call, moreover, is limited to the cost of the option.

Where do you find short sale (or put option) candidates? A rereading of previous charting chapters can help here. You will be seeking the weakest chart patterns instead of the strongest. You will look for downside catapults out of congestion, and using the point and figure count to calculate possible declining moves that might render the best short sale profits.

A mild-mannered, publicity-shy New Yorker named Alfred Winslow Jones generally is believed to be the father of the hedge fund idea. Numerous mutual performance funds have impressive records over past years, but few can bear comparison to the record of quiet Alfred Jones, who manages limited partnership poolings of capital that take the hedge fund approach.

Inspired by Jones' success, others have established hedge funds. Until now most of these funds have been, like Jones' two vehicles, limited partnerships. But the hedge fund idea is taking hold elsewhere. Three mutual funds presently selling shares to the public have taken this approach and other funds currently are in registration.

The most exciting thing about the hedge fund idea, however, is the idea itself—it is an idea every investor can apply to the management of his own portfolio with the objectives of simultaneously minimizing risk and maximizing profit potential while he increases the work potential of his capital.

POINTS TO REMEMBER

1. The hedge fund concept allows you to add to leverage of your capital since short sales are always made on margin, and since the process of going short means that your money will be at work seeking capital growth even during the bear markets when you would ordinarily be holding capital idle.
2. But the hedge fund approach is tricky. It should be handled with care.
3. A hedge fund is always pointed in two directions. Part of

capital always holds stock. Another part is always "hedged" in short sale positions. The idea is to make money both ways under best conditions, risk it less when shifting winds blow since the counter-trend holdings afford protection against unexpected changes.

4. Within every market, there are minor currents moving in different directions. The hedge fund investor attempts to take advantage of these, being long the strongest and short the weakest stocks.

5. Percentages of capital that he keeps long and short vary with the position of the stock market cycle.

Chapter 30 : : WHEN BONDS ARE THE BEST BUYS

INCOME INVESTMENTS with limited gains appeal have become latter day Little Orphan Annies in Wall Street. Annie gets herself periodically in tight, tough spots, both in Wall Street and on the comic pages. Her fans know that Daddy Warbucks eventually appears, however, to rescue the gal from tight situations. Perhaps investors should look periodically for the day when Daddy reappears to bring easier money conditions.

At times "go-go" investing gets overdone.

At such points, goggle-eyed Annie might have more potential glamour than the sexy stocks.

Not long ago, I spoke before a seminar of union-management administrators of pension funds. Before doing so, I examined their portfolios and was surprised to see that, along with some portion dedicated to hoped-for growth, a large portion was "invested"—the word is deliberately in quotes—in areas usually considered the preserve of the little investor socking away a portion of his salary. Some was in savings and loan accounts. Some was in bank certificates of deposit, the rest in similar situations. When I expressed wonder at the funds' passing up all the juicier yield available in high-grade corporate bonds and Treasuries, one of the union men explained.

"You see," he said, "all of those funds are insured by the U.S. government." An insured account, he felt, was somehow safer than the direct debt obligations of that same U.S. government. The point of trying to suggest higher-yield avenues to pension administrators was to show how growth could be had, slow but safe, in the scorned Orphan Annies of Wall Street.

Today, Little Annie can give you such returns as those below, which I jotted down on a Wednesday afternoon in summer, 1969, from figures available to every financial officer and investor:

Selling at 90, Alcoa 6 percent bonds due 1992 yielded a mouth-watering 6.7 percent.

The 4⅜ percent bonds of good Mother Bell, at 75, offered 5.8 percent current income, while Ma Bell's 5⅞'s of 1992, priced at 85½, gave an even better 6.8 percent.

Consolidated Edison's 4⅝'s 1991 were at 68¼ for a 6.9 percent return.

In government bonds, too, yields were high. The 4¼'s of 1987-92 were on the bargain shelf at 75¼ bid. Pension people who picked these up were rewarded with a yield of 5.6 percent.

The above are bonds of impeccable quality. Dipping just a little in a quality scale, yields of 6.8 percent to 8 percent were obtainable, and even higher returns reward the bond investor bold enough to grab for the cat-and-dog sector of the bond market.

The examples above describe current yield. Yield to maturity is even higher. Consider those Treasury 4¼'s of 1987-92 with a current yield of 5.6 percent. To maturity (counting in annualized increment of the capital gain that will be there when bonds are redeemed at face value rather than market price) those Treasuries were yielding 6.23 percent. Similarly higher yields could be figured for the corporate Orphan Annies selling well away from par values.

Daddy Warbucks always comes back. And so does easy, low interest money inevitably succeed tight, costly conditions. It may take time for inevitable to arrive but time is a thing wise investors are willing to spend.

It is argued—with some merit—that the easy money days of the forties and fifties, with prime rates around 3 percent, are not likely to return soon. "We had an abnormally long period of abnormally low interest rates," one shrewd analyst told me not long ago. "Now, I fear, we may be in for an abnormally long period of abnormally high interest rates." He could well be right.

But even if that is so, interest rates will continue to fluctuate. When the Federal Reserve is attempting to choke back a fire of inflation, it will make already high rates higher. (It did this in 1969.) When it wants to ease things a bit, it may return them to a state that would have looked high in the fifties but that in the late sixties or early seventies would be low.

With a return of easier money comes the kicker in the form of a built-in capital gain for bondholders who buy around the peaks of interest rates.

Let's look at a little history:

A comparison of the action of the Dow-Jones 40-Bond Average in 1967 and the action of the Average in 1966 is revealing. When the year 1966 opened the Average stood at around 87.0, a level indicating a money situation neither tight nor easy. The Average, however, did not pause long at that level. Dropping swiftly through the spring and summer months, it reached 80.0 in early September. At this point the Average worked five weeks building a bottom and then rose—but tiredly with no significant volume accompaniment—to 81.2. Only two weeks of rapid decline were required to put the 40-bond Average back again at 80.0, where four weeks of shuttling back and forth established a second bottom. Observers could not be sure, however, that a valid double bottom had been established. Their doubts began to vanish shortly afterward. Three weeks later (late December) when the Average rose swiftly above the intermediate high made following the first bottom, the technicians clearly labeled the movements of fall and early winter as a definite double bottom.

Reflecting the then money-easing activities of the Federal Reserve, the 40-bond Average made a quick advance that carried to 83.5, where it turned over for what appeared to be a normal reaction after so fast an advance. This movement bottomed at 82.9. The Average then went up again to 83 and stopped, then dropped. Going through the 82.9 intermediate level, the 40-bond Average followed its clear double bottom of fall-winter, 1966, with a double top made during spring, 1967.

Now suppose you, as an investor, had bought an "average" bond at 80. We will assume you sold it at the 83.5 level. This was, after all, a very minor little bond move and many moves in response to money easing are much greater.

In approximately half a year you would have made a 3.5

"point" advance on your purchase. Bonds generally come in one-thousand-dollar denominations. This means that 3.5 points equalled thirty-five dollars per bond. Say you purchased ten bonds at $8,000 and realized $350 profit. The bonds at the time you purchased them would probably have returned about 6 percent, so you received that interest amount for the half year you held them. Add $240 to your $350 and your total gain came to $590. (Bond commissions are so infinitesmal that many people wonder how brokers can handle the transactions; we can safely leave commission out of the computation to make it clearer.)

The $590 overall profit on an $8,000 investment comes to 7.4 percent. That is, it would be a 7.4 percent gain if you had held onto the bonds a full year. You owned them for only half of the year, so your annualized gain was 14.8 percent. A nice profit.

But you could have made it even better by using borrowed money. Bonds can be swinging investments indeed, if bought at the right times when a capital gain is logically to be expected.

But even without capital gains kickers, yield investing offers some mouth-watering examples of how income, carefully compounded back into capital, can bring about capital growth. You can't plow it all back, but in an era such as the present one when high-yield investments often go begging you can put back sizable portions.

Recently, I examined figures that indicated the results of applying this plow-back technique to a mutual fund. The fund started out with yield lower than those available now on high-quality bonds. But being largely in common stocks, it had the advantage of gradually rising returns from the increasing corporate dividends of the prosperous years.

These figures showed that in one fund, if an investor had started with $10,000 in fund shares (reduced almost instantly to $9,200 by commissions) and had then plowed back his capital gains distributions but withdrawn $50 every month (using capital itself when ordinary dividends didn't furnish enough for his need) he would have withdrawn $6,000. His original capital would still have increased to $29,682.

That growth was achieved not from go-go investing but from

the oldest technique of all, the search for good income. Multiply ten thousand dollars by whatever multiplier you wish to bring it to the size of your own funds, then consider the fifty dollar monthly withdrawal—multiplied to your payout need—and the resulting growth this example illustrates would not have to hang its head in shame when confronted with results of "go-go" investing.

POINTS TO REMEMBER

1. All of the profits are not made in stocks bought for glamour and gains. There are times when the best action is to be seen in bonds.
2. Such opportunities come seldom, however. They are most in evidence when there is a turn in monetary conditions, with the Federal Reserve loosening the bonds of tight money.
3. Although more expensive interest rates may be around as a semi-permanent condition during current years, there will always be times when the Fed eases money, other times when its aim is to tighten the lid lest an inflationary explosion burst forth. Bond prices respond to money market conditions. Easing of interest rates will usually bring up the prices of depressed bonds.
4. You can play a bond deal straight, going for your expected gain and also pocketing the high interest rates to sweeten the play. Or you can leverage a bond package with a loan and strive to increase the percentage of gain. If you do this, remember that leverage cuts two ways; if you should be wrong, the leverage will increase losses. Therefore, be careful to sell out early should things not go as expected.
5. Even without the effort to buy and sell for capital gains, the purchase of securities with high current incomes can lead to wealth if you carefully plow back income, compounding it into capital.

SECTION V : : Beware the Bear Years!

Chapter 31 : : HOW DO YOU MEASURE THE STOCK MARKET?

WHEN A bell rang to close trading on the floor of the New York Stock Exchange Tuesday, August 20, 1968, the level of the market stood at 888.67, the closing figure on the Dow-Jones Industrial Average. On the same day the market also closed at 320.48, at 107.70, and at 55.54, figures given respectively by the Dow-Jones composite average (of thirty industrial, twenty rail, and fifteen utility stocks), the Standard & Poor's, and the New York Stock Exchange Index.

It is easy to see that measuring the level of the stock market is not a precise business. Qualified statisticians argue the merits of arithmetic averages, weighted averages, geometric averages, and breadth indexes. All of these have validity but you can come up with very differing answers depending upon which kind of yardstick you measure the market against. Such confusion is avoidable, but the diversity of measuring methods should be understood as a first step in mastering the tools we will meet in this section for timing stock purchases and sales.

In late January, 1968, a period of uncertainty about what the new year might bring, two financial analysts were discussing the market. "I'm worried," said one. "It seems the market has already failed to run up at year-end to its high of last summer, and the summer high, in turn, was considerably lower than the high of early 1966. Aren't you concerned about this inability of each major rally to carry as far as the major rise that preceded it?"

"I don't know what you are talking about," said the other analyst. "The market in 1967 carried a lot higher than its top of

1966, and the year-end rally was a beaut. The market went up almost to—although I will admit not through—its earlier rally top of the summer. Now the market appears to be in a steady trading range with two tops and two bottoms. It could break out in either direction from here, but it is not as bad as you seem to see it. Were you, perhaps, watching the stock tape from Mars?"

This conversation might sound as if one man was talking about apples while the other was busily describing oranges. But both had in mind the same stock market at Broad and Wall at the same period in its history. However, the analysts were not measuring that market by the same yardstick.

The first analyst watched the market as described by the gauge of the old, accepted Dow-Jones Industrial Average. The other was watching market action traced by a chart of the newer, broader New York Stock Exchange Index. Different viewpoints are given by different measurements and those viewpoints will color outlook and timing steps.

The Dow-Jones Industrials started 1967 brightly by giving—in conjunction with the D-J Rail Average—a clear Dow theory "buy" signal. The Dow Industrials were at about 785 to start a year marked by the wildest gyrations in postwar market history. From that point the Average climbed steeply until September, 1967, when it established a top at around 942 (closing price). The Dow then retreated to the 845 level where an earlier summer decline had been stopped. It rallied—but not to its September level—and then slowed down. Altogether the D-J put on quite a swinging performance in 1967. From the bottom of the first week in January to the top made in September, the Industrials appreciated 157 points or 20 percent. From the beginning-of-year level to the 887 level (closing price) at which the Dow ended 1967, the oldest and most widely followed of all market measurements went up 102 points or 13 percent.

Did this appreciation of the Dow properly reflect the market? Numerous analysts and statisticians would say "No." They claim the wider New York Stock Exchange Index, embracing every stock listed on the Big Board and "weighted" for size of capitalization, did a more realistic job. While the Dow failed to match its 1966 high at the 1967 top, the NYSE Index was in high ground at its top. Followers of the NYSE Index claim it presented a truer picture of the action of the newer types of companies not included in the composition of the Dow-Jones averages.

Beginning the year at about 44, the NYSE Index ran up to approximately 54¼, making a peak in early October, somewhat later than the D-J Industrials. This rise showed a gain of 26 percent for the market, a 30 percent better showing than that of the old Dow. Then while the Dow Industrials were declining sharply, the NYSE Index put on a decline of its own, bottoming at about 50½ (closing price). It next shot upward. Instead of failing to meet the autumn peak, by year-end the New York Stock Exchange Index rose close to, but not above, the October top and from there declined again after the first weeks of the new year.

From the market bottom that started 1967 to the end of that troubled year, the NYSE Index showed an appreciation of 21½ percent, considerably more than that indicated by the Dow-Jones measuring stick.

The market may be one thing, but the average or index employed to study it can possibly be quite another. What the market does may well depend upon the kind of glasses through which it is observed.

An arithmetic average like the four Dow-Jones indexes (rails, industrials, utilities, composite) begins by adding together the prices of all stocks and then dividing by the number of stocks. But stocks split, pay stock dividends, and occasionally the compilers of an average have to substitute one stock for another because companies merge out of business or cease to represent a worthwhile segment of the economy.

What then?

The Dow averages solve this problem by changing their divisors whenever a split, stock dividend, or substitution occurs. Thus the thirty industrials are divided now by 1.894, the twenty transportation stocks by 4.060, the fifteen utilities by 3.912, and the overall composite by 10.125.

Some analysts scoff at such a method of measuring market movements. They have compiled "weighted" averages that give account to the size of a stock's capitalization so that General Motors and General Whatzit will not appear equal when in fact they are not. The NYSE and Standard & Poor's averages are weighted.

"Haw!" say the Dow followers. "You are back where we are when you weight, because the big stocks still swing your average."

To get around this problem there is a third method of market measurement employing what is called a geometric average. Some analysts believe that a geometric average has advantages over both an arithmetic average and a weighted average. And other analysts urge the use of a breadth index as the best way to measure the market as a whole.

In theory a geometric average duplicates the performance of a fund with exactly equal amounts of capital in each stock used in the average. To avoid the heavy swing of big stocks, analysts who calculate a geometric average multiply the numbers by each other and then take the nth root of the result.

(For example, assume that a twenty-dollar stock and a five-dollar stock are to be geometrically averaged. Multiplying the prices gives a result of 100. The nth root of 100, in this case, the square root, because only two numbers are involved, is 10, which is the geometric average [the arithmetic average would be 12.50]. If an analyst used thirty stocks he would multiply all their prices and take the 30th root of the result.)

Happily, there is a simple method for achieving the same result. An analyst adds the logarithms of the prices and divides the sum of the logs by the number of stocks to arrive at his geometric average.

"Aha!" say the advocates of other systems, "but what about stock splits in calculating a geometric average?" "Simple," say those who work with geometric averages. "When a stock is split two-for-one, the log of its price will drop by the amount of the log of two. So we add this log to the total, and the adjustment has been made."

There is a fourth type of market measurement that has the advantage (according to its advocates) of measuring not thirty, sixty, five hundred or even one thousand stocks, but all of the market. It is called a breadth index. The breadth index is also known as an advance-decline line. This name is descriptive of its computation. A breadth index can be maintained on either a daily or weekly basis. It could also probably be maintained on a monthly basis if an investor did not object to being out of date for a large part of every month. Weekly compilation is usually best.

The breadth index is computed from two figures. Each week a statement is issued of the number of stocks that advanced on the New York Stock Exchange, the number that declined, and the number that were unchanged. If, during the week for which the breadth index is to be computed, there were 880 advances, 480 declines, and 129 stocks that remained unchanged, it would be a plus week and the indicator would move up. The figure on issues unchanged has no bearing on the breadth study. The analyst subtracts the 480 declines from 880 advances to obtain a difference of 400 advances. This figure is added to the cumulative differential for the previous week.

A cumulative differential can begin with any number. Assuming a level of 1,000 for the previous week, the addition of 400 advances to this figure would extend the cumulative differential line to 1,400 on the chart paper. If in the next week there were 425 advances, 790 declines, and 265 unchanged, the difference would be 365 declines, and this difference would be subtracted from the figure of 1,400 for the previous week to move the cumulative differential breadth line down to 1,035.

This cumulative differential line becomes the breadth index.

Sometimes the breadth index diverges from other market measurements; one will go up, while the others point downward. Many analysts find this divergence significant. Unless the various measurements again mesh, they say that the probabilities are that the market average will turn eventually in the direction already taken by the breadth index.

POINTS TO REMEMBER

1. There is no such thing as "the market." You can get a statistical approximation, however, by employing a market average, and if you are to engage in study aimed at avoiding the terrible traps of a bear market, you must do so.
2. However, all market averages are not the same. While they

generally tend to move in the same direction, they do not do so to the same degree and at times even move in divergent directions for short periods.

3. Some are arithmetic averages. Others are "weighted" by allowing for the number of shares outstanding. This is done to avoid having a little company called General Whatzat swing as much weight in computing average price as does a big company called General Motors. A few price averages are geometric.

4. Some yardsticks average as few as thirty stocks. One takes in every stock on the New York Stock Exchange list.

5. An average of all stocks would seem to have greater value than an average of a limited number. Therefore, in the author's opinion, the most representative model of the market you can use is the broad New York Stock Exchange Index.

Chapter 32 : : NEXT YEAR: FOR RICHER OR POORER?

"ECONOMICS," ONE of the practitioners of the profession remarked, "is the dismal art."

I can't agree with him.

Anything that has the potential to tell you whether you will be richer or poorer tomorrow—and, by informing you in advance, help to influence which of the two alternatives will actually come to pass—cannot be dismal. It can help you to come out a winner.

This chapter will not attempt to turn you into a finished economist after a half-hour's reading. It does set out to acquaint you with theories of economic forecasting. The first step toward stock market success is to have some kind of a forecast of what tomorrow will be like. The more accurate it is, the more likely you are to find yourself on the rich end of the stick.

Today the basis for most sophisticated economic study is money. The theories propounded brilliantly by Dr. Milton Friedman of the University of Chicago have largely replaced old notions held by followers of Maynard Keynes, and for an understanding of economic effects, you must look at the monetary causes. Dr. Friedman and those economists who follow him are called the Chicago School. Ideas of the Chicago School are that money is something like food. If you give extra food to a cow, she fattens. If you thin down her diet, she is likely to lose some of that fat, and if you keep her on the thin diet long enough, she may get scrawny or even die.

The Federal Reserve System controls, through many measures, the creation and withdrawal of money from our economy. Before considering the ways you can watch the Fed's feeding or starving of the economic animal, consider what money itself is. It is not just the amount of dollar bills and coins that pass from hand to hand. Recently, the Federal Reserve System's Committee on Education and Publications prepared a study for use by the Joint Council on Economic Education. It was authored by a man knowledgeable about money and very adept at explaining things. He is Thomas O. Waage. In a booklet reprint of Mr. Waage's study issued by the Federal Reserve Bank of New York, he noted:

> Since checks are so important to our economy, we must certainly include checking accounts in our definition of money. Is there anything else that should be included? Savings accounts? Let's leave them out because you cannot pay someone with a withdrawal slip on your thrift account at the bank. You can go to the bank yourself, with your passbook, and withdraw the money, asking the bank to give it to you in the form of cash or a check. But, as you can see, what you have done then is "convert" your savings deposit into money of the kind we have been talking about, just as you originally "converted" your money into a savings account. The same distinction should be made with savings bonds and other securities, shares in a savings and loan association or the cash surrender value of an insurance policy. Our money supply, then, consists of coin, currency, and the checking account balances of people, business firms, state, local and foreign governments.

There is the little gimmick we want to watch: money supply. When the Fed expands that, the chances are that an economic expansion is going to ensue before too long a time has passed. When the money supply is being tightened, and interest rates raised, then a leveling off of the economy—possibly a recession—is likely to be in the offing.

Boom spells better profits for corporations whose stocks you buy and sell.

Leveling off or recession spells an end to the process of increasing profits. Hence, a stagnation of stock prices and, in probability, a decline in the overall market that is likely to carry along with it most stocks, the good with the bad.

Noted Jerry L. Jordan of the Federal Reserve Bank of St. Louis in a study entitled "Money, Interest Rates, Prices and Output," which appeared in the November, 1967, issue of the *Review—Federal Reserve Bank of St. Louis*:

> In financial markets, interest rates are the prices at which quantity supplied and quantity demanded of particular financial assets are equated. The way in which the money stock is related to the demand for any supply of some financial assets is somewhat complex. On the one hand, an increase in the money supply and bank credit adds directly to the supply of lendable funds. An increase in money results in the bidding up of the prices of financial assets, causing interest rates to be lower than they otherwise would be.
>
> On the other hand, some argue that a rise in the money supply and bank credit also has expansionary effects on the total demand for goods and services. If dollar balances and credit are increased rapidly, given existing assets, incomes, prices and interest rates, people will attempt to exchange the "excess money" for goods, services or other financial assets. Any increase in the demand for goods and services will result initially in the running down of inventories and, subsequently, a rise in production and an increase in credit demands. . . . If the rates of increase in money supply, credit and total demand are faster than the rates at which output can be increased, prices will rise. Rising prices will cause increased demands for credit, since more funds are needed to finance a given volume of goods. With expectations of inflation, borrowers are willing to pay higher rates since they expect to repay with cheaper dollars, and lenders charge higher rates in order to net the same real return in the process of allocating limited funds.

Boiled down, the message is this: Increases in money supply generally result in inflation.

Inflation creates, at first the reality, then the shadowy appearance, of greater prosperity.

Prosperity means better stock prices because people turn away from money and want to have their funds in things likely to go up as the dollar goes down.

A steady increase in money supply, therefore, is likely to bring on a more frantic economy, possibly inflation, unless it is handled with great skill. It forms the background against which great bull markets often occur.

A steady decrease in money supply can bring about the opposite result in the form of slower business activity, decreased profits, a possible end to inflation. That is the background against which many bear markets happen.

You can keep your finger on what is happening and get a pretty sound idea of the trend of the Fed's money-making or money-contraction by watching money supply figures.

There is a simple way to observe this swelling or contraction of money supply and all it will cost you is a couple of postage stamps plus a few minutes each week to peruse figures. Affix one of these stamps to a letter of request addressed to the Federal Reserve Bank of St. Louis to put you on its mailing list to receive *U.S. Financial Data.* The St. Louis Fed's research department has done pioneer and valuable work with monetary data. In the *U.S. Financial Data* mailing, you will receive a number of charts and abundant information. For example, here is a paragraph from the issue reporting on the week ended September 10, 1969:

> The monetary restraint which became evident early this year apparently intensified during the summer. The money stock, after increasing 7 percent in 1968, increased at a 3.6 percent rate from last December and has been about unchanged during the last three months.

Use the other postage stamp to write to the Federal Reserve Board, Washington, D.C. for the *Federal Reserve Statistical Release.* Then armed with the two tools, you will be in position to become something of an economic prophet.

At this point you may be getting ready to rise up in your chair and say, "All very well. So something can be done to predict economic conditions that are to come. But I don't want to be an economist. I want to be an investor—a successful one. What have the economic data and the money indicators to do with me?"

The answer is—plenty.

For stocks are not things that exist in a world by themselves. They are the stocks of corporations. Generally, in buying corporate common stocks investors want to be able to secure a piece of some kind of action, preferably action in the form of increasing profits. Should recession hit, all corporate profits are likely to take a licking and in the process all stocks are likely to take a drop in price. If business conditions to come are boomish, then profits tend to go up. Investors bid stock prices up, too. That, and not the down profits–down market kind of atmosphere, is what you need as a background to successful investing.

It is true that stocks do not always move exactly in line with corporate profits. Sometimes profits go up and, sad to say, the prices of common stocks tumble down. This occurs because the stock market, while generally rational and in most cases acting in line with the background business conditions it expects to occur in future, does not always do the things a totally sane organism would do. It discounts prosperity too far, then it gets scared and takes a dip downward. Or it goes down too far in expectation of a recession and then, awed by what it has done, rushes to make up some of the loss it brought about.

Over a long-term period, the stock market does work out in line with whatever expectations it has of coming economic gusts and sunshine. But since it has its irrationalities and does tend to exaggerate moves in either direction as investors' fears or hopes go to extremes, then you must study the tides of the market as well as the bigger tides of economic activity. Next we will take up that important area.

POINTS TO REMEMBER

1. The "dismal art" of economics can help you to at least partly pierce the veil of the future in order to observe what background business conditions might be six months or a year hence.

2. Stock markets move—although imperfectly and sometimes irrationally—in response to these conditions of the overall economy.

3. Classic economic theories of the followers of Maynard Keynes are being increasingly superseded today by the newer economic theories of the "Chicago School," led by Dr. Milton Friedman.

4. The Chicago School theories hold—in simplified essence—that economic activity takes place in response to the plentitude or the scarcity of money.

5. Monetary interest rates are less important, the Chicago economists say, than the availability of money.

6. Against a background of monetary expansion, booms usually occur, often accompanied by inflation. If the money supply faucet is carefully watched, inflation does not get out of hand. A steady increase in standard of living and corporate profits—important to corporate investors—can result.

7. Against a background of declining or level money supply growth, recessions often happen. Preceding price booms level out. Corporate profits cease to grow from quarter to quarter and from year to year. Frequently, bear markets result.

8. Easily obtained statistical data from Federal Reserve sources can help you to spot changes of money supply expansion or contraction and give advance notice of possible major changes in stock price movements.

Chapter 33 : : WILL THE STOCK MARKET GO UP NEXT YEAR?

SOME FINANCIAL observers advise investors that they should forget the movements of the market itself. "We have a market of stocks, not a stock market," they say wisely, nodding their heads to drive the cliché home.

Anyone who sat through the disastrous bear markets of the 1960's armed only with this comforting thought can have drawn scant joy from the fact that his company was indeed doing well although the market went down. For with no more than a handful of exceptions, each time the market took a massive tumble, the "good" stocks along with the bad were swept down the slope. There is an old expression: I'd rather be right than be President. If you want to be self-consciously right, cling to the old shibboleth of there being no stock market but rather a market of stocks. You will be correct most of the time, for the good stocks will always move better than the bad ones in an up market. But when it counts—when the floors under stock prices crack and the quotations day after day drop by quarters, halves, and full points —then your pretty little philosophy will stand you in poor stead. Eventually, in every bear market, nearly all go down.

So you must have some idea of what you believe the stock market itself is going to do. That will be our concern in this chapter.

But the market, as many have sadly noted, does not always do the same kind of thing. Some of its up-and-down movements are ripples lasting only a few days. Some are vast tides.

We will first consider methods of predicting, and of taking

advantage of, those vast, long-sweeping tides known as bull (up) and bear (down) markets. As a general thing you will want to own all the stocks you can get your hands on during the bull tides. During the devastating bear markets you will want to be out of stocks altogether or in part, hoarding your important capital against the day when a new bull movement looks as if it were under way. On such occasions your capital can be employed to best advantage. You may even want to sell stocks short. The next chapter will open the question of short-term movements that are so important to the trader.

When a bull market has been going on for a long time, it gets tired. The participants become cockier. The kind of strong, long-term investor whose holdings and buying made the market go up during its early phases gets scared and often withdraws his money, leaving the frantic, hectic action to those who believe that the trend will never end. Around such a time, you are likely to find:

1. Optimism is rampant and people scoff at the idea that the market could go down. One has only to think back to the months of 1968. The typical boardroom was like a sundial, recording only the sunny hours. Suddenly the skies opened and the bull market was no more.

2. There are practically no bears to be found. A bear is a fellow who believes that things are going down and acts accordingly. He sells his stock and goes short on stocks he considers weak. You can detect his presence or absence around the twentieth of the month when the "short interest" (total shares sold short) figures are released.

Old Wall Street hands have a measure they apply to these figures: When the short interest is greater than an average day's trading, they sigh with relief—the bears are still around and, paradoxically, the bull market still has some distance to go. This yardstick calls for some explanation. How does a short seller help to prop a bull market?

Eventually every short sale has to be "covered" through purchase of the stock sold short. This means that short interest represents a pool of future buy orders. Should the market turn downward, the bears will cover and take their profit, and this buying will help to stem the decline. If the market advances, they will again buy, this time to lighten their losses. Consequently, while the short interest remains above an average day's trading, there are enough bears around to help sustain a bull market. As it dwindles—when short interest falls below an average day's trading and stays there for many months—the smart people in Wall Street glimpse an end of the bull swing.

3. The "public" is rampantly in the market. Back in 1929 you could get market tips from elevator operators and shoeshine boys. This is how stock market mania had possessed the public.

A Wall Streeter might tell you in a frank moment that the public is always wrong. This is something of an exaggeration, but it is true that the public tends to be very wrong at those turning points when being wrong can hurt most. You can rarely interest its members in stocks when the market is down and the smart money buys. But when the professionals are selling at the top, amateurs come into the market with a whoosh.

Just who is the public and who are the pros? Can one tell when the buying is by the uninformed public and the selling by old Wall Street hands?

Take a look at the odd lot statistics in the financial pages of your daily paper (odd lots, for definition, are trades of less than the unit of trading on the exchange floor, usually one hundred shares. An odd lot order is filled through an odd lot dealer who charges a small fraction for his services. Thus statistics are available on the volume of odd lot trading.) It is a fair assumption that most odd lot trading is done by the public, round lots by the Wall Street pros and the richer, and usually better informed, private investors.

Next, it has been established that the odd-lotter buys more than he sells—usually taking on 10 percent more stock than he lets go.

So we look at the odd lot figures. The public is selling more than it is buying. No end to the bull market yet. When it buys as much as it sells or even more, things are still fine unless purchases exceed sales by more than the rule-of-thumb 10 percent.

Actually, financial analysts pay little attention to the day-to-day changes in the relationship of odd lot purchases to sales. It is only when things get out of gear and stay that way for months that they begin to recognize that the public is once again struggling against the incoming tide.

4. The fever for cats and dogs is high. Cats and dogs are low-priced stocks, usually selling for under twenty dollars a share. Feverish speculation in these cheaper stocks is often a sign of the approaching end. Since every financial page carries a record of the day's most active stocks, it is easy to determine when trading in cats and dogs is growing out of proportion. If the fever persists, the bull market may be dying.

5. Nobody cares about values. Many factors contribute to the value of a stock. How well is the dividend protected? How stable are earnings? Is the stock in a field vulnerable to unanticipated assaults? Does the price bear a reasonable relationship to earnings and dividends?

At market tops people cease to care about such mundane things. (And, interestingly, at market bottoms no amount of extra value seems to tempt anyone except hardheaded pros.) The price-earnings ratio (price divided by earnings per share) rises to astronomical levels when the market is close to a top—and then it goes higher yet, because the public heeds the cry of the siren to buy, buy, buy, buy.

Beyond these reasonably observable danger signals, there is an important test applied to markets by the professionals. When the whole market starts to decline while the averages continue to rise, a crash may be on the horizon.

To discern such a state of affairs, analysts contrast the number of issues that advance in a day with the number of declines.

A consistent pattern of more declines than advances at a time when the Dow-Jones Industrial Average is climbing into new high territory spells danger. In the late summer and through the fall of 1961, for example, there was a marked divergence—predominating declines and a climbing D-J Average. Suddenly, in January, the average joined the rest of the market. What happened thereafter is painful history to the people who were caught.

Usually, danger signals continue flashing for quite a while. Some may presage a crash by as much as a year, though I would not count on it because every crash makes its own rules. Play safe. Lighten your holdings at the first suggestion of an ill wind. Lighten them still more as the signals persist. If you are careful about your decisions and actions, you will probably find yourself out of the market by the time it goes to pot and your less astute friends start to moan and beat their breasts.

But suppose you get out and the market still goes up?

One grand old man of Wall Street who had made a very large amount of money in the Street, starting from scratch, delighted in saying, "I made it all by selling my stocks too soon."

If you get out, stay out until there are definite signs of a reversal upward. The tale is told of an investor who, seeing the signs of oncoming disaster, sold out in 1928. But he got bull fever again in '29 and bought back just in time to ride the crashing market down.

The tests I have discussed are as applicable to detecting when the tide is turning toward a bull market as they are for determining when a bear market is about to get under way. For undue optimism, read *extreme pessimism.* For lack of bears, read *no bulls to be found.* For extreme, unbridled public participation, read *public apathy toward stocks.* For cat-and-dog fever, read *no interest in speculative, low-priced stocks.* One sign remains the same at both a top and a bottom—few investors, other than professionals, care about value.

Thus far we have considered fundamental signs found in the stock market at times when it is about to turn upward or when it is about to slide over and spill down. As financial analysts use the term, "fundamental" refers to factors in the economy itself and to the observable signs other than those discernible on chart paper. There is another kind of investment analysis, equally important, that is called "technical."

Technical analysis deals with the internal action of the market itself. If General Motors were to have an increase in earnings for the third quarter of the year, you would call that a fundamental fact. If its stock, with or without the increased earnings news, were to drop two points in the market, on heightened volume of trading, that would be a technical fact that happened internally in the market.

In general, technical study attempts to assess—not always correctly and never infallibly, but in the main rightly—the forces of supply of stocks for sale and demand of investors' dollars seeking to buy stocks and the balances of force between these two.

In the following chapter, we will consider some of the things that relate to the technical action of the stock market and out of which you can help to build an informed opinion that stocks are either safe or unsafe, that an upturn is shortly going to turn down or a dreary down market might be expected suddenly to perk up its ears and begin to head for the land of higher prices.

POINTS TO REMEMBER

1. Even though stock markets and investors who buy in them are more sophisticated than in earlier years, it remains a fact that bull markets and bear markets occur and that they succeed each other. During a bull (up) market, the prices of most stocks are likely to move together toward higher levels. During a bear (down) market, prices all tend to tumble together; and if they do not all move downward on the same days, over the course of a bear market nearly all will eventually find lower levels.

2. A noted show business figure was once quoted as saying, "I've been rich. I've been poor. Rich is better." And so is an upward bull market better for investors who own stocks. During bear periods it is advisable to sell stocks out and to wait for a more propitious time when the same capital might swing more shares. Some adventurous investors also sell short during bear markets.

3. Market movements come in two varieties, short-term and

long-term. Most investors prefer to buy for the longer term, although fortunes have been made by short-swing traders.

4. Certain fundamental signs are found around bull market tops, when danger of loss grows great and when wiser stockholders think more of safeguarding already achieved profits than of trying for new gains. These include rampant optimism; a lack of bearish, fearful opinion; wide participation by the general public; a virulent fever for the kind of lower-priced stocks old-hand Wall Streeters term cats and dogs; and widespread shrugging of shoulders when the topic of basic stock value is mentioned. These signals, in reverse, fly from the market's masthead during the slough of a bear market when the greatest investing values and opportunities are generally to be found.

Chapter 34 : : BULL OR BEAR MARKET? THE TECHNICAL TESTS

At Delphi in ancient Greece a priestess would sit balanced over a crevice. From this fumes arose. As they numbed her brain, she gave out predictions on which the fates of cities, states, and kingdoms often rested. Her predictions were usually so hedged that anything could be read into them and the record over the years was not spectacular. Mankind has tried other ways to foretell the future. Augurs have read the entrails of sheep, astrologers the stars, other experts the flights of birds and the fall of knucklebones. None of these systems has an unblemished success record, and as the centuries passed man's interest in foretelling his future has waned. Except in one direction.

The stock market.

Even there, only the unwary and unsophisticated believe that the future can be unerringly foretold. However, trends can be determined. The assumption is that a trend continues up or down until new evidence shows otherwise. This chapter presents tools, not for foretelling a future that no one can read with certainty, but for reading public psychology and market follow-through with the object of determining when changes in these are likely to bring about, as effects, a turn in the stock market's overall direction.

Oldest, easiest, and one of the most reliable of the technical tests is the "staircase." Whether you consider an average of stocks or some individual stocks, you will observe that even in the strongest of up movements, prices never move in a straight line, each transaction higher than the transaction before. Nor during

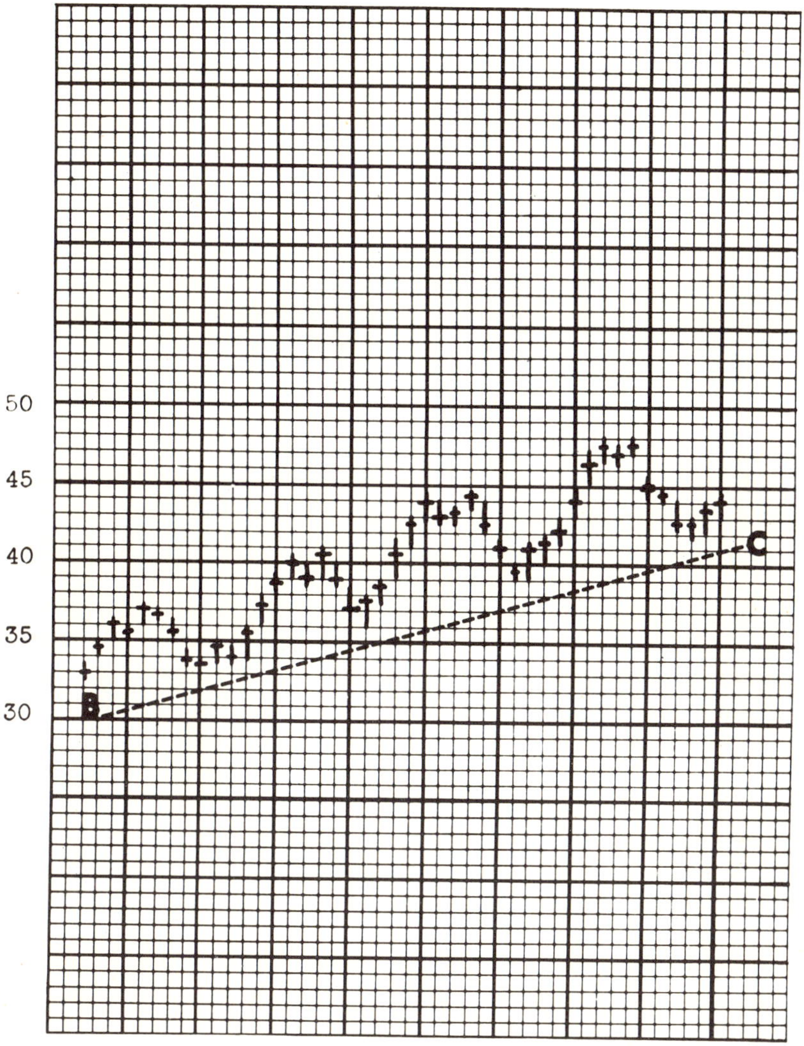

The "staircase" shown here is typical of an advancing pattern in a stock or a market average such as the D-J Industrials, Standard & Poor's, or New York Stock Exchange Index. A first hint of breaking of the staircase to profits might come on penetration of a "trend line." Line B–C is such a trend line. During an advancing staircase pattern, the trend line is drawn to connect the bottoms of reactions. During a declining staircase, a trend line would be drawn to connect tops of the rallies (upward moves).

a down movement do they move in such a straight line. In both cases, prices tend to form a staircase.

That is to say, they will move upward for a time. Then somebody—or a series of somebodies—decides to take profits, and enough new stock comes out for sale to halt the rise for a time. Prices level off, then generally start downward. When they have gone down a bit, buyers often come in to pick up stock at a slight bargain, and as the demand (buyers' bids) begins to overbalance the supply (sellers' stock certificates offered for sale), the stock's price trend starts upward again. If the phase happens to be a rising one, the demand will probably push prices up above the previous temporary top where selling came in to turn things temporarily around. Then the process starts once more.

There are books of charts in every broker's office and in many libraries. Look at one of these and you will see, as it delineates stock movements, how a bull trend tends to take the form of a staircase going upward. A declining trend usually takes the form of a staircase, too, this time heading downward as it progresses across the chart page.

So you can make a rule: While an average of stock prices continues to make an *up*ward staircase, then the trend is up. That is, each small rising movement should carry to a level above that of the movement that came before it. Each little decline should reach a bottom that is higher than the bottom of the decline before it.

While an average of stock prices makes a *down*ward staircase, with all of the signs above holding true, but in reverse, then you can say that it is a bear market.

When the staircase that was previously going down levels off, and then the rallies (upward movements) begin to reach levels higher than before, and the dips (downward movements) bottom out at levels above earlier dips, you're pretty safe in saying that the market has turned from bear to bull.

And, consequently, the time has arrived to commit capital fully to stocks.

Occasionally, your price pattern will go neither up nor down.

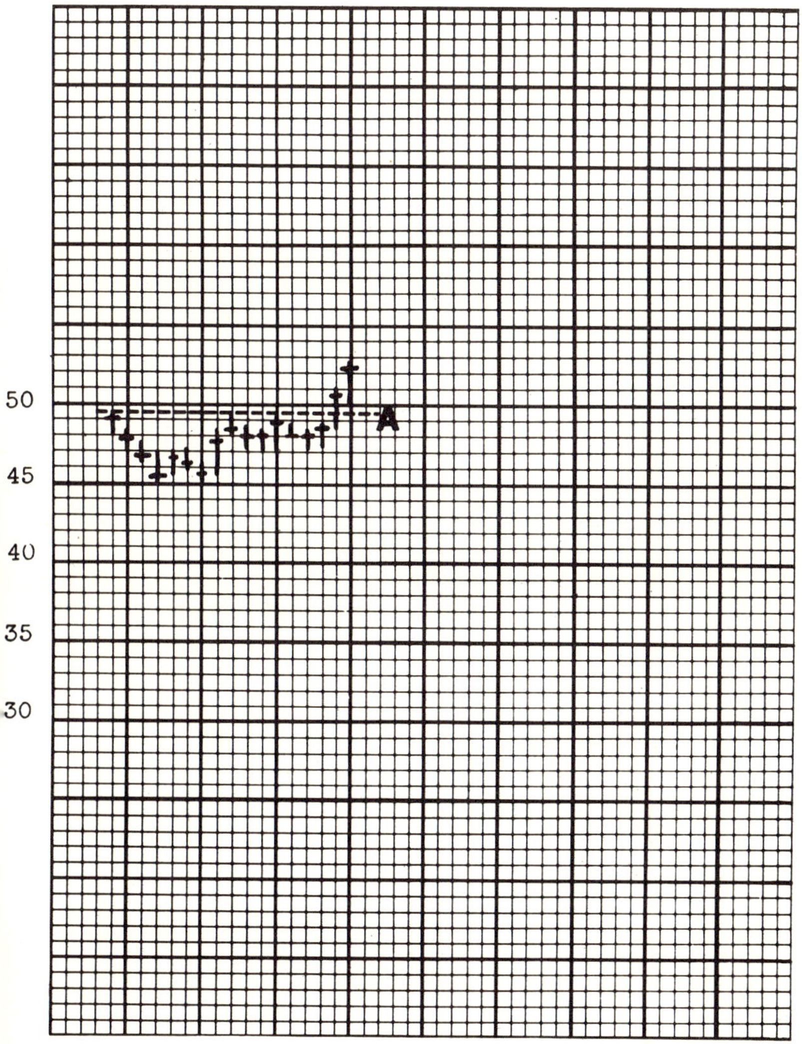

A "resistance" level is any old high where enough selling has come out to stop an advance. A "support" level is one at which enough buying was engendered to halt a decline. When such a tested support or resistance area is finally penetrated—as here when line A was broken by advancing prices—the presumption is that a worthwhile move in the direction of the break will ensue.

It will wobble back and forth, making approximately the same tops, and bottoming several times at approximately the same levels. When that happens, technically minded financial analysts say that the market is in a trading range. Sometimes they refer to such tired, go-nowhere action as a rectangle or a line. Its name matters less than its significance. For when prices eventually burst out of the trading range in either direction, a strong indication has been given that a new trend in market direction is under way and that it will in all likelihood be a long one and a strong one.

Your average of stock prices can be the old, trusted, popular Dow-Jones Industrial Average. Or it might be the Standard & Poor's average that so many analysts prefer to watch. My favorite is the newest yardstick, the New York Stock Exchange Index, which is calculated as an average of all stocks on the Big Board, weighted for capitalization so that the smaller, less important little companies' equities will not swing an out-of-proportion effect upon the index movements. All of these averages are published in financial papers and on the finance pages of most bigger-community dailies.

The staircase study is the oldest technical analysis known to market students. It is nevertheless basic to all study of market direction. But some newer tools have been devised:

The NYSE Turn Signal: This is a shorter-term indicator of market direction. In July, 1969, the New York Stock Exchange Index stood at approximately the same level it had a year earlier. During the intervening twelve months, the Index—and the market it measures—had gyrated sharply up, and sagged right back down again under the impact of Administration and Federal Reserve movements to restrict credit and tighten money as an inflationary fire-fighting device.

During that time, if an investor had bought an "average" stock, he should theoretically have been even.

But instead of the no-gain-no-loss performance the NYSE Index gave, our investor would have been considerably ahead if he had

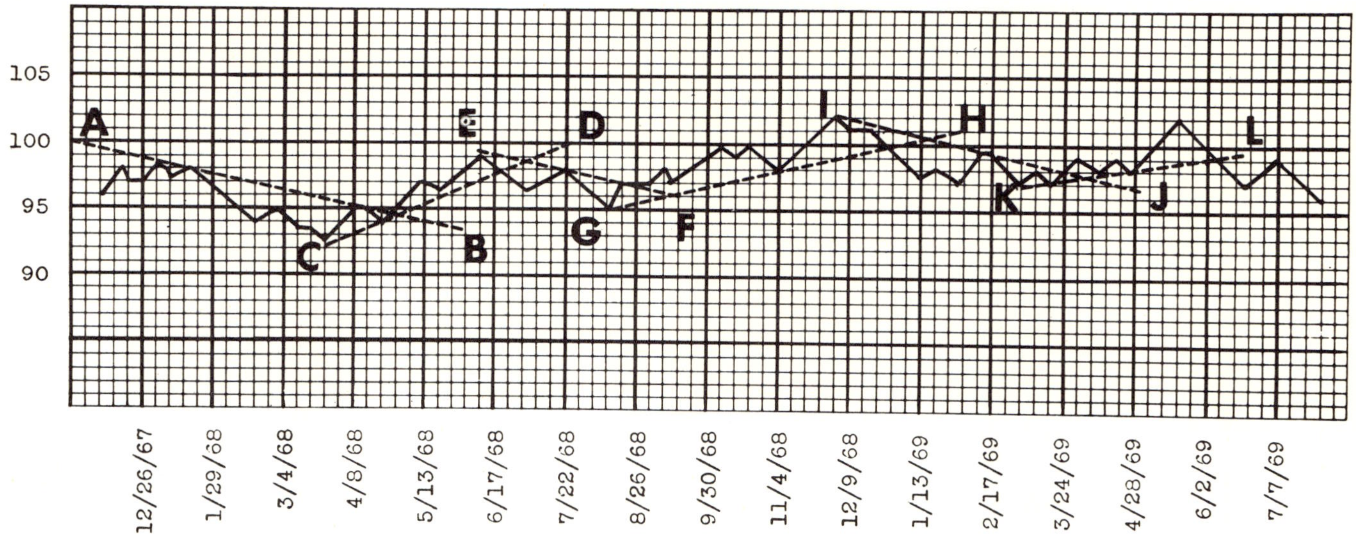

This is the short-term indicator called the NYSE Turn Signal. It compiled a remarkable record during the troubled period of 1968 and 1969 when so many investors incurred staggering losses. Breaking the trend line marked A—B in April, 1968, it flashed a buy signal for the overall market with the broad New York Stock Exchange Index at 52. A sell signal that warned the short-term was running out occurred in June with breaking of trend line C—D; the index then stood at 56¼. A new buy signal foretelling the upmoving 1968 autumn tide was given when trend line E—F was penetrated in August with the Index at 55¼. Then a sell flash was given in January at 60 on the Index. Later, the short-lived spring, 1969, rally was called on fracturing of the I—J trend line in March with the Index showing 56. But the spring rally became a summer decline and the Turn Signal noted a sell warning after K—L trend line was broken with the Index at 57½.

followed indications of an entirely new short-term market indicator. This indicator would have had him buy stocks in August, 1968, when the NYSE Index was at 55¼. It would have had him unload them in January, 1969, when the Index was at 60. Following its signals, he would have participated in the brief spring rally of 1969 by purchasing when the Index had dropped to 56. Before the worst of the summer sag, he would have again sold out in May—again at a profit—when the Index showed 57½.

Here is how we compute the new index:

1. Each week, notation is made whether the NYSE Index advanced or declined.

2. Without regard to the extent of decline or advance, a plus notation is made for every week in which the market advanced, a minus for each week during which it declined.

3. Out of these successive plus and minus indications, a cumulative index is computed. The index was started at a level of 100. Each plus added one number to that level. Each minus subtracted one number. Thus if the NYSE Index were to go up for three weeks, down for two weeks, up for three more, then down for one, the cumulative index would read in this manner:

100
101
102
103
102
101
102
103
104
103

The resulting numbers can be used as an index, with a change-of-trend message considered as having been given every time the Turn Signal declines to a lower level than it made on an earlier decline, provided the earlier declines were not a mere one-week drop. A buy signal would be given after a lengthy decline in the index if the reverse of such action were to occur; that is if the index level were to rise above the top of a preceding rise that was of more than a one-week duration.

Or (and this method I prefer) the Turn Signal can be computed across a page of chart paper. A buy signal would then be considered as given by a trend line break provided that trend line were of at least intermediate proportions. A sell signal is given on the breaking of an up trend line of intermediate proportions meeting the same kind of test.

(A word about trend lines. During an upward staircase pattern, a trend line [line designed to delineate the trend] would be drawn to connect the *bottoms* of the dips along the zigzag staircase. During a downward staircase pattern, the trend line connects the *tops* of the rallies. A break in a trend line is generally taken as evidence, not final but probable, that the trend may have ended. In the case of the NYSE Turn Signal, the trend line would be drawn as indicated, connecting tops of the little peaks along an upward trend, and bottoms of the downward reactions during a bear trend.)

This indicator is not infallible. But it is hard for an observer not to be impressed when its results are traced back over a four-year period. Here is the NYSE Turn Signal's record for that time:

The indicator gave a sell signal very close to the top preceding the long 1966 slide in stock prices. It shouted "Sell!" on February 7, 1966. Then it gave a signal to buy stocks once more on January 24, 1967, with the New York Stock Exchange Index at 47. As 1967's turbulent market proceeded, it indicated a sell signal on August 26 with the NYSE Index at 52½. Next the indicator said "Buy" on September 19 when the NYSE Index stood at 53¾. It indicated the danger of the whipsawing market of the early 1968 months when it gave a sell signal January 22, 1968, when the NYSE Index stood at 54¾. A signal that sunny skies had returned to Wall Street was sounded April 8, 1968, following the then President Lyndon Johnson's speech indicating his intention to seek peace negotiations with the North Vietnamese. The NYSE Index was at 52.

After the spirited rise that followed that speech, there came a summer doldrum. The new index noted this with a sell signal around 56¾.

Then the fall months saw a worthwhile rise in overall stock prices. The new indicator gave notice of this with a buy signal on August 26 when the New York Stock Exchange Index was at 55¼. A sell signal was given January 7, 1969, with the Index at the 60 level.

The spring, 1969, rise was signaled in March with a buy message at the 56 level on the New York Stock Exchange Index and a sell message at 57½.

The Hi-Lo Index: The late months of 1967 and early months of 1968 were confusing times, even for the experienced analysts of stock market direction.

"The market is going up!" shouted some.

"The market is going down!" insisted the followers of other indexes.

And, as events turned out, during those topsy-turvy months that preceded the then President Johnson's dramatic message in late March, both groups of investors and analysts were correct.

The indicators they followed were also correct, despite their contrary indications. The market went up and down, and it did so more than once, whipsawing investors' positions and making many potentially profitable investments end up in the loss column. But throughout this period, one indicator unswervingly refused to give a sell signal for the overall market. Although it was in a sidewise pattern during much of the up-again-down-again period of seesawing prices, at no point did it indicate an imminent down movement. Then prices rose dramatically in April.

The indicator that produced this result is worth examining.

A strong market must be able to generate continual new highs in many stocks. If it cannot do this over any extended period, the leadership of the market is obviously narrow, and the market is not to be trusted. Another example was provided in 1966. Following the February-March decline of that year, the market turned around in April and seemed headed back for new highs.

But it only seemed that way. The leadership was extremely narrow.

The Hi-Lo Index went on making new lows at that time instead of confirming the upward direction the averages had shakily taken, and before many weeks had passed, all that had appeared to have been gained in the April rise had been lost, and the market was sliding ominously down nearly every day. An analyst familiar with the Hi-Lo Index could not have been fooled into more than token participation in that short-lived little April upswing.

The indicator is obviously a good thing to add to your kit of market-timing tools. It can help you avoid being fooled by moves that have strength only on the surface.

As its name implies, the Hi-Lo Index is an indicator of new highs versus new lows. Like so many timing tools, it can be kept weekly or daily. I favor weekly charting.

Taking figures from a financial page or a market weekly, the analyst subtracts the smaller number from the larger, and puts the resulting minus or plus figure into a cumulative differential.

For the sake of review, a cumulative differential, which we met in computing the NYSE Turn Signal, works this way: You begin with any number, for you are studying the movement of your line, not the numbers by which you define it. Say that 133 stocks made new highs the first week, with 29 chalking new low prices. The difference between these two figures is a plus 104 (133 minus 29).

That number is added to the previous week's line. If last week the cumulative differential were 1,108, with the addition of 104 it would now be 1,212, and the chart line would be extended that far. A minus differential—greater number of new lows than new highs—would carry the line downward. Each week, in other words, our chart cumulates the differential.

As is the case with other indexes charted this way, the Hi-Lo Index is studied with the aid of points where old highs and lows were made (old highs are called resistance levels, old lows support areas), plus the chart's trend lines. Any move of the price action staircase not confirmed within a few weeks of its start by a change in direction of this important Hi-Lo Index should be regarded as shaky. The odds in such a case are that the whole market movement could be a temporary one.

The Stock Group Index: Like the Hi-Lo Index, this has for rationale the idea that unless there is follow-through on a broad front, the movement of a price average during a bull market is suspect. Conversely, broadening of advancing trends indicates growing bullishness even at a bear market bottom, and frequently indicates that the worst of the financial storm has been seen and that the sun of rising prices can be expected to start shining again soon.

The Hi-Lo Index tells what is going on in individual stocks. The Stock Group Index shows what is going on in a number of group averages.

One such industry average would be an average of automotive stocks, another an average of banking stocks, a third an average of oil stocks. You can obtain these averages from many statistical sources and services. Or you can use the averages found in financial magazines.

Each week, the number of averages that advanced is compared to the number that declined with the resulting difference—plus or minus—being added to or subtracted from a cumulative differential.

The Stock Group Index is plotted on chart paper and whenever a trend line is broken by new upside or downside movement, an appropriate signal of market change has been delivered.

The Market Fuel Indicator: Like the gasoline gauge on an automobile, this indicator measures the availability of fuel for firing an engine—in this case the stock market engine. Automobiles run on gasoline, but stock prices are determined by money. The Indicator measures money, the availability of which can keep the market going, but the lack of which can cause the market to stall.

Two averages sensitive to money market conditions are employed in tandem to compute the Indicator. They are the Dow-Jones 40-Bond Average and the Dow-Jones Utility Average. The

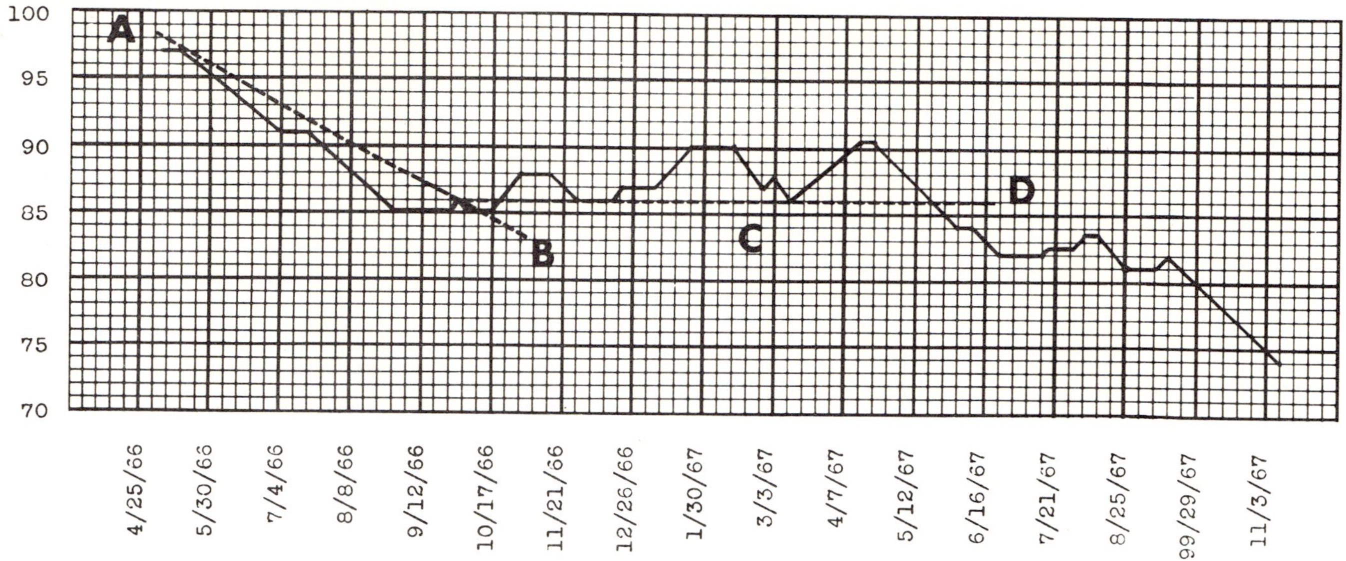

During the 1966 bear market, the Market Fuel Indicator gave an early signal to begin buying stocks, almost at absolute bottom, when it broke down trend line A–B. The signal that the market was deteriorating inwardly came far in advance of the 1967 top, which slid over in early 1968 to become a bad decline. Note penetration of support line C–D.

Bond Average directly measures money availability and cost. When money rates rise, the Average drops, reflecting the effect that new, high rates on fresh bond issues have upon older bond issues. (A 3 percent bond would sell at par if debt instruments of its class returned, on average, 3 percent. If similar corporate debentures were paying 5 percent, the 3 percent bond would have to sell at close to 60 to be comparable. Thus older bond issues that make up the Dow-Jones Bond Average fluctuate in value, and the Average reflects this movement as money rental rates change.)

The second sensitive-to-money indicator is the Dow-Jones Utility Average. Profit prospects for utilities are closely affected by what these companies must pay for the constant infusions of new financing required to pay for expansion. Because of the regulatory lag, months and sometimes years elapse before rate commissions allow a raise in the profit rate for a utility. When money costs more, investors tend to sell utility stocks down because they know that the profit margins for the utilities are subject to a potential squeeze.

Each week, the closing price of the Dow-Jones Utility Average is compared to the close for the Average a week earlier. Has the Utility Average risen or declined? If the Average is up, the utility indicator is rated plus; if the Average is down, the utility indicator is rated minus. A similar computation takes place with the Dow-Jones 40-Bond Average. The pluses and minuses from these two computations are put together to form the Market Fuel Indicator. As with other technical computations, this becomes a cumulative differential. If both averages are minus during any given week, the analyst will subtract two from the previous total. If the averages are both plus, he will add two to the earlier figure. If the averages balance with one up and one down, the analyst carries out the line unchanged.

The Market Fuel Indicator need not be put onto chart paper, but reading its signals is simpler if the Indicator can be observed graphically. When a tested support level has been broken downside, the probabilities are that market fuel has been running thin. If, after a decline, a trend line has been broken and a tested resistance point has been penetrated, the Indicator points toward a more ready supply of money once more.

Signals of the Market Fuel Indicator seldom have a fast confirmation. This lead time is an advantage. You have time to let existing positions ripen fully. When this indicator does say "Sell," however, it is well to be aware that the stock market engine is apt to start sputtering soon and any sputter might be the last gasp before the market turns down.

Breadth-Momentum: Cool investors for a long time have watched what many call a "breadth index." This is a comparison of advances with declines, usually plotted into a cumulative differential line. It shows hidden strength in a down market, should such exist and be masked by a decline in a price average. Or it warns of hidden weakness when a market gets toppy.

Breadth-Momentum is a sophisticated refinement on a plain breadth index.

Its aim is to determine whether the old-fashioned breadth index has greater or less "momentum" than the price average. Momentum is a Wall Street word that indicates pretty much the same thing it does in an auto race—the ability to move fast. If the breadth index is moving at a faster clip than the price average, a French-speaking investor would shout "Bon!", a Spanish-speaking investor "Bueno!", or a fellow acquainted only with English would call out "Good!" For the indication is that all stocks have a lot of strength, not just a price average where weakness of two-thirds of the list might be masked by extreme price strength of the remaining third.

Breadth-Momentum tends to pinpoint a spot where performance of the broad market is picking up faster (or dropping to a slower pace) than the price index. Such an indication is often a good sign of an important, long-term turn in stock tides.

The Breadth-Momentum Index is computed this way:

Each week, the percentage of advance (or decline) of the breadth index is computed and compared with a similar percentage for the New York Stock Exchange Index. Percentage advance or decline is considered to be a percentage of the cumulative

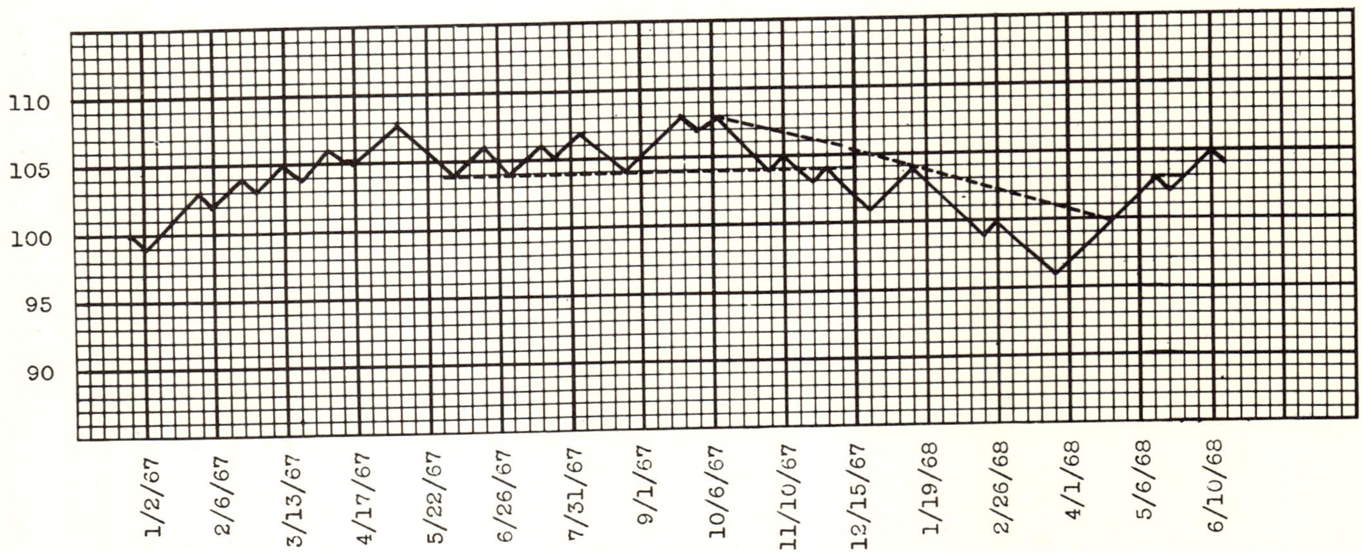

Breadth-Momentum warned of impending market trouble that actually came at year-end when, in November, 1967, it dropped below a well-defined "support" level. Following the then President Johnson's peace speech, Breadth-Momentum began a new rise.

differential line's level. Thus if there were a differential of fifty stocks advancing over declining, and the cumulative level the previous week were 1,000, the percentage advance from 1,000 to 1,050 would be 5 percent.

If the breadth index has momentum superior to that of the market average by going up more in a bullish week or down less in a bearish period, the Breadth-Momentum Index advances one unit. A performance worse than the market average is rated minus and carries the cumulative differential line down. A change-of-direction signal would be given on the breaking of a tested support level (for a downside signal) or, after a market decline, when an important resistance level previously tested was penetrated upside.

POINTS TO REMEMBER

1. There are no infallible ways to spot a stock market turn, but certain technical indicators have compiled records that make them worth following. These do not foretell the future. They do, however, frequently spot changes in trend direction out of which profitable vast new trend movements can grow.
2. It is well to choose one market yardstick and employ it consistently. Many investors prefer the older Dow-Jones Industrial Average. Others use the Standard & Poor's, some the newest, broadest average, the New York Stock Exchange Index.
3. Old but still worth following is the study of "staircase" patterns. While the upward-pointing staircase remains intact, with no step reaching lower than the one that preceded it, a bull trend is considered to be intact and investments safe. Frequently, bear market bottoms are signaled by the reversal of a down staircase to an upward one presaging a new surge in stock prices.
4. The NYSE Turn Signal is compiled from advances and declines in the price of a single market average. It is a short-term trend indicator.
5. The Hi-Lo Index shows longer-term movement trends in the market. Its components are the number of new high prices made each week, and the number of stocks reaching fresh low prices.

6. The Stock Group Index attempts to measure follow-through of industry averages.

7. Stock markets run on money as an automobile runs on gasoline. The Market Fuel Indicator measures this supply of money, and its cost, through measurement of two indexes sensitive to the monetary action.

8. A refinement on the older tool of advance-decline or "breadth" measurement is Breadth-Momentum, whose purpose is to pinpoint the spot at which most stocks begin acting differently from an average of stock prices. Like the Market Fuel Indicator, Hi-Lo Index and Stock Group Index, this indicator tends to signal longer-term price movements and to ignore the short-term moves.

9. An investor's strategy with these tools should be to buy stocks with all of his capital when a new upturn is indicated after a protracted bear market. He should sell all of his holdings when the long-term tools (Breadth-Momentum, Market Fuel Indicator, Hi-Lo Index, and Stock Group Index) signal beginning of a bear market.

10. The NYSE Turn Signal can be used by an investor interested in trading for the quicker turns, and in being all or partly out of the market during short-range down movements even though these occur in a basically bullish market.

Chapter 35 : : DOW THEORY – AN OLD FORECASTER THAT STILL WORKS

IN THE late spring of 1966 the Dow Theory rang out a warning, the first time it had done so in four years. "Bear market!" it said. "Sell out." Many investors, including some professionals, took the warning with a mountain of salt.

"We've heard that before," one investor said. "Some Dow Theorists called a bear market just a year ago in the summer 1965 drop, and that drop was quickly succeeded by one of the fastest rises on record."

Was the Dow Theory calling a bear market signal in 1965? Or did some of its more eager devotees jump the gun? Does the Theory really work, and, if so, what about its 1966 warning?

Dow Theory is the oldest of the technical analytical tools. It was first informally propounded by Charles A. Dow around the turn of the century. Later, William P. Hamilton and Robert Rhea refined and defined it. Today it is possibly the best known and least understood tool of the investment technician. Basic to the Dow Theory is the idea that the stock market is a barometer. The market, Dow and his followers believed, collectively knows more than anyone in it. It learns this not by what investors and institutions are saying, but by their buying and selling actions.

Two averages comprise the yardsticks of individual and collective measurements that give Dow Theory signals. The first is the Dow-Jones Industrial Average. This average of thirty blue chip corporate stocks has been denounced as being a statistical monstrosity and as being too narrow to measure the market. Its components, however, are a cross section of the great industrial might of America. Similarly, the Dow-Jones Rail Average (now called the Transportation Average) does as well as any existing average in furnishing a transportation yardstick.

When the national economy is prosperous, both transportation and manufacturing companies must participate, since manufactured goods not carried to market are hardly in a position to sell, say Dow Theorists. A beginning upturn touches both; a beginning downturn must affect them equally.

Theorists note that market movements come in three sizes, which they liken to movements of the sea. There are the vast, all-engulfing tides; there are the waves, which refer to intermediate movements lasting anywhere from a few weeks to many months; lastly there are the ripples, the small daily movements. The small daily movements are meaningless to Dow Theory except insofar as they make up intermediate waves, and these intermediates, in turn, count because they make up the big bullish and bearish tidal movements.

Any trend, state Dow Theory experts, must be considered intact until a full-fledged reversal signal has been given. Such a signal starts when one of the two averages—assuming the trend has been upward—makes a top, followed by an intermediate reaction and then a new intermediate up movement. The new movement, however, is tired; prices reach wearily for that previous high but they cannot attain it, much less exceed it.

Now prices round over and drop into the next intermediate reaction. The reaction speeds up and, to the alarm of watching Dow Theorists, slices through the support of the preceding intermediate bottom. Half of a change-of-direction warning has been given.

It means nothing, however, unless the same thing happens in the other average to "confirm" this signal. Such confirmation need not come on the same day as the signal from the first average, although sometimes it does. It might come weeks, even months, later. Reverse this description of price action when a market turns over from its long-term top and you have the classic Dow Theory signal that alerts investors to the ending of a major down movement.

Sometimes price action does not take place in exactly the way we have described here. Instead of reversing the existing staircase pattern of prices, one average or both might move back and forth in a narrow trading range. Dow Theorists call this a "line" and a breakout in a new direction from a line has the same technical significance as the classic type of price action.

Dow Theorists pay attention only to closing prices and, unless an average closes in signal territory, they ignore what happens intra-day. Any penetration is enough to give a signal once the correct conditions exist; a penetration of only one cent counts. None of this action is important—this is what the shouters of bear market in 1965 forgot—unless it takes place in a "third phase" market.

Both bull and bear markets, the Dow Theorists say, have three phases. Generally, serious rallies or reactions against the major trend separate these phases, and each phase has its own atmosphere.

A bear market, for example, begins in the heady enthusiasm of a bull market top, and it takes a long time for investors and their advisers to realize that what is happening is not just another little reaction. By the time they soberly see that a real decline is under way, the market is in a second phase, when prices slide remorselessly downward. The third bear phase is a time of deep gloom.

A bull market starts out of that deep gloom and its first phase shows caution. Investors' caution vanishes by the time the second phase arrives amid a mood of steady optimism. In the third phase, common sense is often thrown to the winds. In such a phase, it is the cats and dogs and the pie-in-the-sky high-fliers that rule, and blue chips are neglected.

Much confusion about the workings of the Theory and its effectiveness dates from the 1965 "signal" that proved false. While some vociferous Dow Theorists made a great deal of noise about the message they believed they had seen, there were other technicians who, at the time, quietly labeled the "signal" as a mistake. Two facts made many doubt the validity of that 1965 warning.

First, no atmosphere of a Dow Theory third phase existed, and it is an axiom of the Theory that no signal can be valid except in a bull or bear market third phase.

Second, the too-eager analysts who saw a bear signal had actually seen only half of the necessary action. The Industrial Average had indeed made a lower bottom than the intermediate bottom that came before, but it had not preceded this with a top lower than the existing market high.

Third phase atmosphere was demonstrably absent in the summer of 1965, but it was present when the signal loudly clanged in 1966.

The Dow Theory is not infallible—no analytical tool is—but it works, and you ignore its signals at a peril to your pocketbook.

POINTS TO REMEMBER

1. The Dow Theory is the oldest technical tool for attempting to tell turns in the market. It was first employed in a rough way about the turn of the century.

2. It is a clumsy tool, say some analysts, since it gives its signals far from market tops and bottoms. Yet it has usually worked in the past when properly applied and, therefore, retains value today.

3. It can be used best in conjunction with newer, more sophisticated methods described in the preceding chapter.

Chapter 36 : : WHAT TO DO IN A BEAR MARKET

In the first half of 1962 the stock market—which a new generation of investors had come to believe knew only one direction, up—slid sickeningly. From December 15 to June 15, the market, measured by the popular averages, lost over 25 percent of its value. And this was small compared to losses in some popular stocks such as Litton, Polaroid, and IBM.

What should a smart investor have done in such a down market?

Ride it out?

Sell all his holdings indiscriminately? If so, how should he know when to sell? Or when to buy back?

Hold on to some of his stocks? If that course, which stocks should have been held and which sold?

Such questions are far from academic to people who watched carefully and sometimes painfully accumulated capital evaporate in the drop of early 1962. Another and equal blood bath was taken by investors in the 1966 and 1969–70 bear frolics.

The first thing is to determine that you are truly in a serious bear market and not in a normal intermediate market reaction, the kind that does not go too far down and is followed by a new rise to higher levels. It is sometimes possible to tell in advance that a decline is coming. Its extent, however, must wait for later evidence, and an investor often has to miss the top 5 percent to 10 percent of a market in order to insure against being whipsawed through selling too soon in what turns out to be an intermediate decline rather than a full bear market.

Earlier chapters have discussed some of the tools used to tell when a market may be about to turn and confirmatory indicators such as the old but still workable Dow Theory. Our concern here is what to do about the bear market that you're convinced may be about to descend or that your tests indicate is already in its early stages.

It is often better to pursue a policy of selling stocks only as each appears to be weakening rather than to dump everything overboard or blindly cling to a belief that all will "come back."

For even where stocks do come back after a relatively mild decline, it is not always the same stocks that lead the next advance. Therein lies the weakness of a policy of riding out each decline. In a deep or disastrous drop nearly all stocks go down. By selling only on signs of individual weakness, an investor will find that in most cases his watch-them-individually policy has cleared out his whole market position. While if a decline is somewhat mild, he has sold only the stocks that are unlikely to participate in the next advance.

A bear market is not a thing to fear. In fact, a bear market offers opportunity to the investor who sold near the old bull market top and now sits with hard cash to snap up stock bargains near the bottom, while other investors are either too broke or too discouraged to buy. But it is important to determine by technical and fundamental tests that a bottom has indeed been reached and that it is not a mere intermediate low to be succeeded by a later, still lower bottom.

Buying of bonds in a bear market was for a long time a classic financial move. Bonds could often be bought at a time when stocks turned from bull to a bear trend and later sold at higher levels. Bonds generally moved in the opposite direction from the stock market at crucial times. But now things may be different. It is to be doubted that the classic bond gambit will always work. The outflow of gold from the U.S. has brought a new factor into the picture. The government cannot introduce easy money policies (which would boost the bond market) without inviting trouble in the form of an increased outflow of gold. During the

1966 donnybrook, holders of bonds fared as badly as stockholders when tightening money conditions drove up interest rates, forcing down bond prices as they did so. This happened again in 1969–70.

If you want to sit passively and wait for a turn, earning something on your capital the while, then Treasury bills are the thing. Issued each Monday morning at a weekly auction, bills are due in ninety days. (There are longer maturities but those do not fit into a down market investment strategy.) If you expect a drawn-out movement, put one-third of available capital into ninety-day bills the first Monday, another third a month later, the last third two months later. Then each month you will have a third of capital in maturing bills and can decide whether to cash up or "roll them over" for another ninety days.

For the aggressively inclined, two courses are open. The first involves gold. Here is what I wrote at a time when such a down phase was expected:

> A ploy that usually works during market downturns is to buy gold mining stocks. Mankind's faith has been pinned to the yellow metal throughout most of his recorded days on this earth, and gold has never failed him in the way that paper money, beads, promises, and prospects have had a way of doing over the centuries. Frightened that a down market may be forecasting a recession or even depression, many investors turn to gold at such times and the result, often, is a rise in the price of gold stocks while the overall market declines.
>
> Is the buying of gold stocks a good idea now?
>
> Possibly. But let's consider things first.
>
> All speculation in gold shares hinges on whether gold's price will eventually be raised. If it comes, this move, so long anticipated in vain, could result in fantastic profits from the stocks of gold mining companies.
>
> If by "eventually" we mean in the far, uncertain future, then the price of gold will almost certainly be raised—some day. But I am afraid this won't happen in the immediate future, barring something unexpected, and if the increase comes it will do so against the wishes of the economic planners of this and most other Western nations. All the efforts of the International Mone-

tary Fund's leaders seem bent on making the new "paper gold" plan workable (as it well might become) and because of this a rise from gold's present price appears unlikely for now.

However, the prices of gold stocks reflect wishes as well as facts and if a sizable number of well-heeled investors believe gold will go up in price, their buying will make the gold stocks rise. It has been so in every post-World War II market drop.

The other bear market tactic for aggressive investors is to sell short. This is a tricky business and some people feel uneasy about it. They wonder whether short selling isn't somehow un-American and akin to being for sin or against American motherhood.

Looked at realistically, short selling is nothing of the kind.

In fact, from the realist's viewpoint, buying stocks is the same as selling money short. Consider it this way: When an investor buys—and who is against that?—he hopes to sell the stock for more money than he paid. From a relative standpoint, he expects money to cheapen in relation to the value of the stock.

Similarly, when he sells a stock short he expects dollars to go up in relation to the stock.

A short sale must be made at an "up-tick," which means at a price at least one-eighth higher than the last sale. An exception to this rule is when the previous sale was itself an up-tick; then it is permitted to sell short at the same price. The up-tick rule poses a problem for every short-seller in this way:

Say you want to sell XYZ short at 45. It might drop steadily from 45 to 42 and only at the lower figure turn around and provide the needed up-tick for establishing a short position. Whether you are long or short a stock, it is seldom wise to chase its price. Therefore, it behooves a short-seller to put in his orders at a limit price.

POINTS TO REMEMBER

1. It is folly to ride out a bear market if you possess methods to tell when disastrous slides are under way. Money conserved by timely sale close to the top of a bull market can buy more shares

of the same stocks (if the same stocks should again look like good buys) close to the market bottom.

2. Earlier, bonds proved good hedges during bear markets for stocks. In recent bear markets, however, bonds have been as dangerous as stocks and that classic bear gambit needs to be looked at with caution.

3. Classically, gold stocks often rise during the first half of a bear market, but frequently drop back in the second part. Gold stocks can thus prove profitable buys during declining markets for other stocks. It will be wise to apply the timing tests learned earlier before purchasing any gold stock.

4. Some aggressive investors and speculators sell short.

Chapter 37 : : HOW A CASH RESERVE CAN HELP YOU

"CASH RESERVE? Whaddya mean, cash reserve? Does that mean holding some of my money in cash instead of investing it? If that is what you mean, I won't do it. My money has to work all the time." The investor stood there, steamy and beginning to grow angry at a suggestion that part of his portfolio might—for that moment, at any rate—be kept in reserve, which means holding cash or things such as Treasury bills equivalent to cash.

At quick glance, his objections looked reasonable as well as real. Why should anybody work hard to accumulate an investment stake and then do nothing with part of it part of the time?

Cash reserve is just what its name implies; a reserve amount of cold cash (or equivalent) in a brokerage or bank account that is not at the moment "working"—to employ the phrase of those who cannot see such a use for capital—but is being held in liquid form awaiting a more advantageous time for investing.

In all of the literature of Wall Street, constant references are made to "cash reserve." Yet the number of investors who actually maintain a cash reserve is probably small. What percentage exists is composed almost wholly of professionals.

Yet a cash reserve at certain periods is a useful thing to have; on a few occasions it is the only safe thing to hold.

This is a hard concept to sell to investors. One man I know grows restless when there is loose cash in his brokerage account. If this cash is not reinvested promptly, it is likely to end up in the form of a new automobile or a vacation trip—things useful and pleasant, but hardly legitimate ways to employ investment capital.

This attitude hurts him in two ways: by removing capital in dribs and drabs that soon add up to worthwhile amounts and by tying the hands of his investment counselor, forcing the professional adviser to choose reinvestment vehicles at a time when in his judgement the market or individual stock conditions work against sound stock choice.

The advantages of keeping a cash reserve are:

1. Good investment opportunities are not always available at every moment and phase of the stock market.

The Duke of Wellington was famous for his refusal to offer battle except on ground of his own choosing. A professional investor, like the great Wellington, will not commit capital except at times and prices that offer him the greatest advantage. And like Wellington in war, such a pro in Wall Street wins more often than he loses because he has all possible factors working in his favor.

2. Cash reserve is contrary to the "fully invested" school of thought.

A determined effort to be "fully invested" every minute of every market day has probably cost stockholders untold millions. There is nothing wrong with being fully invested; frequently my own account is totally committed. The folly arises when an investor takes what is a good idea in a rising market and attempts to apply it in every phase of every market. By gearing your thought to the wisdom—and even the necessity—of frequently holding a cash reserve, you can free yourself from this expensive frame of mind.

3. Capital is ready when opportunities open.

Every investor has seen times when a bright potential seems to exist in a stock but he has no money to take advantage of it. The investor who has held reserve cash after selling a former commitment, instead of unwisely reinvesting it quickly merely to have it "at work," is usually the fellow to whom such an opening is profitable.

Market history provides many examples of how cash reserve is generated and its uses. I remember the late summer of 1961 when the averages were still making new highs and it was apparent that the internal structure of the market was weakening. Breadth studies of advances and declines gave particular evidence of weakness. As some individual stocks appeared "toppy" and were sold, the proceeds were therefore held in cash reserve waiting for a cheaper market. Labor Day was an expected turning point; the actual turning point came two days later.

During the early December rise, the same warnings of a heavy market were seen. And once again, as "toppy" stocks were sold, proceeds were held in reserve for later reemployment at better prices. This time the high was targeted for the first ten days of January; it came instead around mid-December.

(It should be said that on neither of these occasions were all stock that were held in accounts sold; the ones that appeared weak were weeded out as they would have been in any phase of the market. Proceeds, however, instead of being reinvested were placed in reserve.)

The last full-fledged bear market was the whopper of 1969 which, as I write this in early 1970, seems still in progress. Cash held through the grueling down months of that lengthy time looks as if it will buy a great deal more stock when the market bottoms.

What are the components of cash reserve? Usually it is cash—cold, hard dollars. If a longer time is expected before the money will be wanted for reinvestment, or if an unusually large reserve has built up, Treasury bills due in ninety days or six months can be bought to earn a small interest. Or sometimes when a longer wait is envisioned, as in early days of a developing bear market, short- and medium-term government bonds can be used, provided they are bought at attractive prices.

Things that should not be components of an investment cash reserve are commercial bank savings accounts, and savings and loan association accounts or certificates. These have the disadvantage (in most cases) of not paying interest on funds withdrawn before semiannual or quarterly interest dates. A temptation therefore exists to let the reserve stay until its interest is paid—during which time an inviting investment opportunity might slip away.

Maintaining a cash reserve in the investor's brokerage rather than in his bank account has the advantage of not letting capital become mingled with current funds.

POINTS TO REMEMBER

1. The idea of "reserving" cash that is not invested is repugnant to many investors. But the professionals do it when they see no opportunities strong enough to justify commitment of capital or when they judge the trend of the overall market to be bearish.

2. Shorter-term interest-bearing instruments such as Treasury bills make ideal places for putting reserve cash. It can also be kept in a bank or a brokerage account where it is easily and instantly available for opportunities that might offer themselves.

APPENDIX

The Author Answers Questions

Q. What is the safest kind of investment?

A. Unfortunately, you can't be sure. A family has to weigh comparative risks. Cash and things such as savings bonds, bank accounts, and other fixed-value investments offer the long-range risk of loss of purchasing power from inflation. Against this, stocks can go up in value—but they can also go down. Real estate has the same risk and, in addition, ties up capital in an investment not readily bought or sold. No investment is guaranteed safe. A workable answer is to hold both: volatile things, which go up and down in terms of dollars, and some fixed dollars for hedge.

Q. How much income can I expect to receive from an investment in stocks?

A. Common stocks on average pay 3 percent to 3½ percent today. Lower-grade equities return over 5 percent. But some stocks pay no dividends at all. A few pay out 50 percent and more of their profits. Growing companies typically tend to pay dividends that are low in comparison to the prices of the stocks. These firms are generally plowing money back into the company in the hope of obtaining further growth tomorrow.

Q. I can't save at all. My first problem in investing is to get the capital. Have you any ideas?

A. You might set aside one source of income, maybe what you receive from overtime or your wife's salary from a part-time job.

Another way is to borrow. If you are young and on the way up and feel you'll be ahead in earning power five years from now, you should consider the possibility that money you borrow now might be easy to repay then. And if inflation continues, you'd repay in dollars of lower purchasing power.

Q. We have had a whole generation of inflation. Are conventional savings accounts worth having any longer?

A. It is true that money has eroded steadily in value since the end of World War II. But it was not always so, and there is no guarantee that one day the inflation that seems inevitable now will not end. Any family should have at least part of its nest egg in conventional accounts, say many monetary counselors.

People confronted with sudden emergency do not need to be sold this idea. To one family an emergency became a nightmare when in 1966 their eldest child broke a leg. Bills piled up faster than insurance reimbursements could be received.

"We had carefully accumulated an investment capital of over six thousand dollars," the husband said afterward. "In 1966 the stock market was sinking and I had to sell all our stocks to meet emergency costs right at the bottom of the decline. The same stocks have tripled since. Some money in conventional accounts would have served us well."

Q. Where can I get good investment advice?

A. There are financial counselors whose whole work is to guide their clients' investments. But this takes time in each individual case; so advisers' minimum fees tend, generally, to be high. Many people rely on investment letters. There are literally hundreds, published by the week or month and sometimes by the day, for fees ranging from fifty dollars to five hundred dollars a year and even higher in a few instances. You can purchase trial subscriptions to most of these and many people find it a good idea to study several letters this inexpensive way before deciding on one that fits their needs.

Other people turn to a broker for advice. It is well to be aware that brokers are primarily salesmen, not analysts, and cannot give continuing individual attention to every holding of every client. But they try, and many are backed up by full-time research staffs.

Finally, there are a number of good financial magazines, which, with the daily *Wall Street Journal* and the financial section of your own daily newspaper, are fine sources of information. Books —this one in particular—can also help you to acquire investing knowledge. I recommend especially other books of mine: *How to Chart Your Way to Stock Market Profits, Practical Ways to Build a Fortune in the Stock Market,* and *How to Make Money With Mutual Funds.*

Q. Which is better—land or stocks?

A. Both have advantages and drawbacks. Real estate costs more to buy or sell; against a normal commission of 1½ percent on stocks, there are usually 6 percent commissions applied to real estate. However, houses and land are not quoted in the daily paper and thus there is less emotional risk of being nudged into an unwise decision because of temporary price fluctuations. For the average family, most advisers lean to stocks since small amounts of these may be easily accumulated when funds become available and because the liquidity of the stock market offers machinery for turning them readily into cash at need.

Q. Are stocks good for saving for our children's education?

A. The widely followed Dow-Jones Industrial Average stood below 200 twenty years ago. Several times in recent years it has almost touched 1,000. There is no guarantee, of course, that stocks may not experience a drop in value in the next twenty years. But people who have used stocks to save for university costs have generally fared better than the families that depended upon fixed value investments.

Q. What is a growth stock?

A. Most Wall Streeters look for the following in judging growth stocks: a corporation where sales are increasing along with profits and dividends. As a result of this corporate growth, price growth for the stock is likely. But mere profit growth is not as important as growth in per share earnings. This is the amount of profit applicable to each share of stock (a figure routinely computed for you by statistical services). Dividend growth is not a definite yardstick, since some growth companies prefer to plow profits back into more growth rather than pay it out in dividends.

Q. Somebody told me to stick to stocks listed on big exchanges. Is this a good idea?

A. It certainly is not a bad one. Listed stocks, particularly those on the New York and American Stock Exchanges, enjoy wide markets and fluctuate little in price from transaction to transaction. But it is not true that all over-the-counter unlisted stocks should be avoided. Some of the country's soundest corporations prefer to have their stocks traded off an exchange (and in many cases unlisted stocks enjoy a highly liquid market).

Q. I hear that mortgages pay big returns. What is the best way to invest in them?

A. You can talk to local companies listed under "Investments—Mortgages" in your telephone directory. Frequently they are willing to sell some of their inventory of mortgages. Then, too, there are brokers who deal in these. Your bank should be able to help you to find them.

A new way to invest in mortgages is to let the professionals do it for you. An increasing number of mutual funds are being formed to buy and hold mortgages. They offer an investor who is unwilling to concern himself with the details of checking out credit and, if necessary, foreclosing to protect his capital, a chance to let the pros run the show for him. Just as in mutual funds devoted to investments in stocks, these funds offer diversification so that risks are spread out, and it is to be expected that the experts who run them will be likely to produce better results for you than you could do by venturing into a field whose expertise is not your own.

Q. Please let me know if oil drilling programs are reasonably safe as a means of receiving tax benefits when you are in the 50 percent-plus income tax bracket.

A. No oil drilling investment is safe by comparison with conservative methods of handling money. That does not mean that participation in oil programs is bad. Some people have grown wealthy through them. They can be attractive to the investor whose income is high enough for him to afford the risk and whose capital will not be seriously chipped away if the venture should go sour.

One way to do the oil investment bit is through mutual funds, a new breed of investment company allowing all investors participation with professional management of (hoped-for) skill. Your broker can furnish prospectuses of some of these.

Q. In college, a professor told us that there are three objectives for investment: safety of principal, hope for growth, or high immediate income. Which should a young family follow?

A. The answer to that question depends in part upon personal factors. Investors who would be nervous with the volatile fluctuations of growth-type securities should avoid them. But in general most analysts and advisers think that it makes little sense for anyone having excess income to invest for still more current income that will be taxed away at ordinary rates. A try for capital growth would be preferable.

On the other hand, a widow having to live on income from investments her husband left should certainly obtain the highest yield she can without having to take risks. Principal safety, regardless of income or growth prospects, would be the proper policy for a minor's inheritance.

Q. A market letter I received suggested buying bonds. Haven't people who owned bonds fared badly in recent years?

A. Yes, they have. That is not to say the same condition will always apply.

For a very long time in the U.S., we had subnormally low interest rates. People considered a prime rate of 3½ percent in New York as normal and were astounded when it recently got to be more than double the easy money rate of the Truman and Eisenhower times.

The result was that bonds issued in those easy money days have gone down in price so their yields will be competitive with newer bonds issued at realistic current interest rates. And so bond investment looks bad to many people.

Just as the bond market was subnormally high a decade and more ago, it is now around an abnormally low level. The result might be some easing in interest rates. In such an event, bondholders could add capital gains to their high yields. Thus bond investing might well be a happier experience in years ahead than it was in the years that lie behind us.

Q. During the hesitant early months of 1969, some advisers were telling people to keep as much as 50 percent of their money in cash. Why would anyone want to see his money not working?

A. If an employee of yours worked all of the time—twenty-four hours a day, seven days a week—you would not expect much performance from him. You can't expect money to work all of the time either.

Cash reserve is a nice thing to have at certain times. One such recent time was the serious stock market decline during 1969. The market afforded little chance for gain except in a few stocks, and a good chance to lose money in many stocks. If you had heeded the advice of this counselor and kept your cash resting, as you expect your employees to get physical and mental rest during periods when they cannot do anything productive, you would have avoided loss in your weaker stocks, and had funds ready to participate in inviting opportunities when the market climate appeared more propitious for investing profits.

Q. Should an investor keep his reserve in cash at such times? Or perhaps try for some income while the capital sits around?

A. Cash is a sound way to keep it—that is, in a bank or a brokerage account, not in big bills in a dresser drawer. It is sometimes hazardous to try for income on cash reserve in such familiar avenues as savings and loan accounts or bank savings accounts. These frequently pay interest only if money is maintained in the account over a period of time ranging from three months to a full year. When better investment opportunities for your reserve pop up, there you are—stuck in a good old 5 percent savings account and afraid to withdraw the money lest you lose the interest. Better to do things the way investment pros do them.

In such situations, these people generally buy Treasury bills, which are short-term (as short as ninety-day) obligations of the U.S. government, auctioned on Mondays of every week. They come in ten-thousand-dollar units. To buy, you tell your broker or your bank to obtain x-number bills for you at the next sale. Then if you want to take your money out, there is a liquid market for bills. They can be sold, generally with accrued interest, at any time before maturity.

(These comments above apply to cash reserve—not a savings program.)

Q. Is it smart to plunge everything in one stock? Or should I diversify?

A. Wall Street once considered diversification a shibboleth for success. But no longer. Many analysts and other pros are having second thoughts. "Better to get a good one and put a lot of money into it," said the manager of one successful mutual fund. "There just aren't enough good ones at any given time to diversify too widely."

A sound compromise for the average investor might be two or three stocks rather than an old-fashioned package of twenty or twenty-five.

Q. Can we buy stocks a little each month?

A. Through member firms, the New York Stock Exchange makes available a Monthly Investment Plan allowing families to buy as little as forty dollars worth of a stock every three months. Some invest sizable amounts through the MIP because they like the discipline of regular monthly payments. An MIP investor can withdraw at any time without penalty. Mutual funds usually have similar accumulative plans for periodic investment.

Q. How does one sell short? Can anyone do it?

A. First you open a margin account. Then you instruct your broker to sell short whatever number of shares of Swingeroo, Inc., you have decided upon (the sale must be labeled a short sale). He will call upon you for margin. Currently margins are set at 65 percent. You put up the money and you are a short-seller.

That, of course, is a simplified explanation, but there are no other steps you will have to worry about—except for watching your short position carefully once you have established it. No investor who cannot give daily attention to finance should be short. Remember, this is not investing. It is speculation.

Q. Doesn't the person who buys a stock I sell short want to receive his purchase?

A. He does. Since you do not own the stock you sold, you have to borrow it to deliver to the buyer. Or, rather, it has to be borrowed for you. Your broker takes care of that chore; you neither know nor care from whom he borrows it. In practice, such borrowed stock usually comes from the margined positions of his other customers (who have signed an agreement when they opened a margin account permitting him to lend their securities).

Q. Who gets the dividends? It seems that two people own the same stock—the one to whom I sold and the one from whom I borrowed. Which one gets the money?

A. They both do. As the company has understandable objections to paying double dividends on the same stock, you have to pay. The company's dividend will go to the one in whose name the stock is registered. Your account will be debited the amount of the dividend in order to pay the other party who has a right to receive dividends. It is a little cost you put out for the privilege of borrowing someone else's stock.

Q. What does the expression "shorting against the box" mean?

A. Sometimes an investor shorts stock that he actually owns. It might come about in this: Suppose he had two hundred shares of Swingeroo, Inc., bought at 20. The stock had risen to 40. He wished to nail down a profit but was not quite sure he wanted to get out of the long position in case there was a further rise.

He thereupon sold short the stock. If it continued to rise, he simply covered his short position in the normal way. If at 43 he decided there was some life in the old firm yet, and covered, he would have lost three points, but would have made three points appreciation. By covering at 43 he had insurance against a drop and still possessed the stock that was continuing to rise.

But if it went down instead of up, our hypothetical investor again was even—a profit on the short position balancing the depreciation on the shares he held—and would deliver his own stock against the short position instead of buying in stock to deliver.

This is shorting against the box, or against stock you already hold.

Q. What is the "up-tick rule"?

A. In the past, bear raiding was a splendid way of driving markets down unrealistically. Now the Securities and Exchange Commission has instituted a simple rule that makes a real bear raid impossible. It requires that a short sale must be at a higher price than the previous transaction—that is, on an up-tick.

Q. Describe the difference between open-end and closed-end mutual funds.

A. A closed-end fund is like any other corporation. It has a set number of shares. Once these have been sold to the public, investors buy them from each other and sell them to each other exactly as you'd buy or sell Woolworth or Swingeroo, Inc. Closed-ends are generally traded on the exchanges.

An open-end fund will buy shares investors want to cash up, thus shrinking capitalization. And it will sell shares investors want to buy, adding to capitalization. Usually, you act through an investment dealer as agent for the company.

Q. What about load and no-load mutual funds?

A. Both kinds are open-ends and both begin with a figure called "net asset value per share" as a basis for pricing. The net asset value per share is the total value of the fund's portfolio, less debt if any, divided by the number of shares outstanding to determine how much asset value applies to each share.

Most mutuals are load outfits. A load fund applies a sales commission to the asset value when it sells shares to the public. This commission usually begins at 8¾ percent in sales of less than twenty-five thousand dollars and it gets smaller on bigger purchases. Say asset value on the ABC Fund is ten dollars per share. You would pay $108.75 to buy ten shares of the fund. The commission is split among distributor, dealer, and the dealer-salesman who services you with advice and help.

If you sell, the fund usually cashes up at net asset value. A no-load fund does not tack on this front-end commission when it sells shares. It buys or sells at asset value. Investors have to purchase no-load funds directly from the company since local dealers, deprived of commission, are often understandably reluctant to handle no-load funds.

Q. Isn't a no-load better than a load fund?

A. The answer is—not necessarily: A fund is or isn't "good" depending upon how well it meets its buyers' objectives, and the existence of a basically small charge should not be the deciding factor in choice of a mutual investment.

Q. What are "contractual" accumulative plans for mutual funds?

A. Some mutual fund plans call for semi-compulsory contributions to the kitty at fixed intervals. Many people feel that, unless pressured into making payments, they might use the money to buy something less important but more immediately pleasant. Contractual plans have some very good features. They also have drawbacks because they penalize investors who change their minds early in the ten-year game. Most make the penalty a fairly stiff one.

Q. I am interested in setting up a program for three children's college education. I am forty-four and the oldest is fourteen. Therefore, I believe that I should invest in a highly speculative fund. Also, I want to invest for my retirement. How? At my age, I am going to have to make some wise investments to retire at sixty to sixty-five.

A. Your questions, I believe, boil down to this: What is a good speculative "go-go" mutual fund? Your plans for both educational and retirement investing appear to revolve around such a fund.

One thing you must remember about "go-go" speculative funds is that the hot performer of one year is not always even in the list of the first ten performers next year. My suggestion is that you buy a package of two or three of these swinging funds rather than plunk all in one fund. And that you watch performance of each, as measured by growth in net asset value, and be ready to switch quickly should performance slow down.

Q. Sometimes calls come from an out-of-town broker offering to sell me stocks at a few cents a share. He guarantees these will go up. Is a guarantee like that any good?

A. You are on the sucker list of something called in Wall Street a "boiler room" because the salesmanship is so high pressure. Penny stocks are seldom worthwhile investments. They are usually pretty poor speculations, too. Although there are exceptions to this rule, you won't find the exceptions peddled by phone from another city.

Next time he offers you a guarantee, ask this salesman to put it in writing. Or get his address and ask your state securities commission or the U.S. Securities and Exchange Commission in Washington, D.C., about his claims.

Q. Under the Keogh Plan, I can deduct up to twenty-five hundred dollars and invest it tax free for the time, provided I include all employees in the plan. Am I allowed to invest these retirement funds in anything I like?

A. The answer for practical purposes is No. The Keogh Plan permits investment in mutual funds or insurance policies. Special permission can be obtained for a self-managed investment package, but the Treasury doesn't give its okay easily.

Q. I am seven years away from the age when I plan to retire. I have about twenty thousand dollars now. When I retire I will want income. But I don't need very much now. How should I invest the twenty thousand dollars?

A. Conservatively.

It is easy to say, "Let's 'go-go' for growth now and we will turn the twenty thousand dollars into a million on which we can have a lot of income at retirement time."

The fact is that you can't afford to lose the stake you have. My suggestion would be conservative investment. Invest for growth —certainly. But in slower-growth type stocks, or perhaps in growth-oriented mutual funds but not those that trade wildly and often to get short-swing profits. Such funds are fine for somebody else. Conservative growth investing might, if the economy prospers and we see a good market in Wall Street over the next seven years, increase your stake by 50 percent in that time, perhaps more. Wild speculation might increase it to a greater degree. But it might wipe you out.

After retirement, you should switch from moderate growth stocks into better-yielding securities. It is impossible from this far away to say what will be the big income bets by then. When you are ready for the switch, reappraise things based upon conditions of the time.

Q. How much growth should I expect from a growth stock? I'm in my thirties and want to invest to build an estate rather than to get current income.

A. First, are you talking about growth of the corporation's earnings or growth in the price of the stock?

Ideally, if earnings go up steadily and to a worthwhile degree, then the price of the stock should also go up. Although this doesn't work out 100 percent of the time, it is a sufficiently reliable thing to count on. So in a growth company the rate of company growth underlies the increase in stock price.

Earnings growth at a steady, year in and year out, rate of 15 percent annually or better is excellent. Sometimes you can find a company with a much more rapid growth rate. But such feverish increase cannot always be sustained. I recall the president of one big growth firm telling me, "People expect us to continue growing at the same rate now that we are big as we grew when the company was small. I wonder how many of them realize that if such a rate went on for three more years, our company would be bigger than the whole Gross National Product?"

Expecting youthful growth to continue on during corporate maturity is something like expecting an adult to shoot up in height at the rate he grew during his first few years.

So growth is not a forever thing. But as long as it can be sustained at a 15 percent to 20 percent per year rate, you're in a growth stock.

How much the price will increase might depend upon the ratio at which investors multiply earnings to arrive at a reasonable price. Generally, higher price-earnings ratios are accorded to fast-moving companies. Beware a situation with a PER above 25 or 30, however, for it may be discounting growth too far ahead.

Q. I am interested in transferring E bonds into bearer bonds at present attractive rates. I am seventy-four, and am interested in a fairly assured safe income. Would bearer tax-exempts be more advisable than corporate or utility bonds?

A. Before answering your several questions there, let's comment on bearer bonds. Once, all corporate, government, and other debt instruments were bearer bonds. There was no name on them and consequently no transfer problem. Unfortunately there was no safety feature either, as the bond was like cash—it belonged to anyone who found it in the street. To collect interest you had to clip coupons and present them to your bank for collection. Now most bonds can be obtained in registered form like common stock, with your name filled in, a notation on the transfer agent's books, and interest checks mailed to you semiannually. Many are available in either form.

If I were you, I would make the change. You will obtain higher interest. If you hold bonds to maturity there is almost no risk, and certainly not more than in E savings bonds.

Whether you should own corporates, governments, or municipals will depend in large part upon your tax bracket. Discuss this with your income tax adviser. If you are in a sufficiently high bracket, the purchase of tax-exempt securities would definitely be to your advantage. In lower brackets the advantage becomes smaller when stacked against the fact that tax free bonds by nature pay lower percentage yields than those on whose interest taxes have to be paid.

Q. I bought six thousand shares of a small oil corporation based in the Philippines at a very low price per share. Can you tell me if this is a good investment? What do you think of its possibilities of hitting oil in the near future?

A. Are the dice at Las Vegas a good investment? When you win with them—yes.

I say this because everyone should understand that, when he buys a little speculative oil play like this, he is, in a sense, shooting dice. There is nothing wrong with shooting dice. Just don't confuse doing so with investing.

You may have a good speculation there. The trouble with these little oil plays is that nobody knows, even the executives don't know for sure, whether a well will come up with oil or dust. A big oil company puts down hundreds of holes every year, knowing that some will be dry dusters, some will be productive. It can shrug off the loss on the dusters because it is big and the amount it loses in any dry hole is not an important part of its working capital.

Should this little oil company hit, you will be in big. The question becomes twofold: whether it will find oil soon, and how long it can keep drilling if the bit brings up only dust the first few times.

Index